Jesus lived in India

by Holger Kersten

with 57 illustrations
(partially coloured)

Element Book Ltd.

Longmead, Shaftesbury, Dorset SP7 8PL
England
Telephone Shaftesbury (0747) 5 13 39

JESUS LIVED IN INDIA

by Holger Kersten

Supervision of translation:
Teresa Woods-Czisch, M.A.

ELEMENT BOOKS Ltd. Longmead, Shaftesbury, Dorset

ISBN 0-906540-90-9

Holger Kersten was born 1951 in Magdeburg (German Democratic Republic). In 1962 his family emigrated to the Federal Republic of Germany. In the years 1973/74 he went on his first journeys to the Orient. He travelled to Turkey, Iran and Afghanistan. From 1974 to 1979 he studied to become a teacher of religion in a college of the protestant church in Freiburg (Black Forest). Thereafter he stayed several months in India to do his scientific investigations. Up to 1982 he was a teacher of religious education at a vocational school near Freiburg. Since than he has been working as a freelance author and a free-lance contributor to different New Age newspapers. He does a lot of travelling, mostly towards the East. The author's offical place of residence is Freiburg.

The Author

Contents

Foreword

It was purely by a fortuitous coincidence that in 1973 I heard the theory that Jesus was supposed to have lived in India. Very sceptical, but somewhat unsettled in my views about the matter, I attempted to retrace the steps of Jesus' actual life. I soon ran up against the obstacle of there being no sources that could stand up to scholarly scrutiny and be adequate for establishing the historicity of Jesus. Who was this man really? Where was he from? Where did he go? Why was it that he appeared so strange and mysterious to his contemporaries? What did he really want?

In the course of my investigations I finally arrived in India, where I became acquainted with those people who had dealt with the subject of *Jesus in India* in the greatest depth. I received a wealth of astonishing information from them, together with much encouragement and valuable support.

As far as the form of this publication is concerned, I have refrained from writing in a highly academic style, so that comprehension of the simple and logical contents of the book might not be impeded, and so that the details may not pass unnoticed. Many statements may seem bold and others even improbable. This book will open up a broad field of research in many related disciplines. The task of research is too great for one person alone. It means a challenge to the established Churches to investigate all the claims in this book ad absurdum if they can, and to prove the contrary. It will be of great interest to see how the Churches will respond to this challenge!

It is neither my goal nor my intention to undermine the Christian outlook or to leave the reader before a pile of potsherds of a shattered faith. It is simply of vital importance to find again the path to the sources, to the eternal and central truth of Christ's Message, which has been shaken almost beyond recognition by the profane ambitions

7

of more or less secular institutions arrogating to themselves a religious authority. Therefore this book is not the annunciation of a new belief; it is merely an attempt to open a way to a new future, firmly founded on the true spiritual and religious sources of the past.

> Imagine not that I am spinning yarns,
> Get up and prove the contrary!
> The entire ecclesiastical history
> is a mish-mash of error and of power.
>
> Johann Wolfgang von Goethe

Holger Kersten, Freiburg im Breisgau, March 1983

To accomplish the English version of "Jesus lived in India" it took more than two years. Up to this moment in Germany seven reprints of the book have appeared. This translation has been revised and updated several times to the current standard of knowledge. I was told that my personal style of writing might sometimes sound a bit harsh to the British reader. I tried to preserve this uncommon directness deliberately in order to support the clarity of my statements, and to keep from extenuating the facts. I am convinced that in Britain I will find a predominantly tolerant and open-minded audience. At any rate it is possible in this country that a bishop (Rt Rev David Jenkins, Bishop of Durham) is courageous enough to preach in his Easter message about his personal doubts concerning the traditional Christian view of Christ's physical resurrection. (Daily Telegraph, March 30, 1985)

H.K. September 1986

Introduction

The ascendancy of science and technology was accompanied by a rapid secularization of our world and the recession of religion. The glorification of rationalism and the endeavour to explain away every aspect of human existence, led inexorably to heavy losses in mystical, religious and emotional life, even in "humanity". Not least among the causes of the widening gulf between religion and science, between belief and knowledge, was the behaviour of the established Churches. For fear of losing their influence in secular spheres, they asserted their authority where they had absolutely none in the field of empirical knowledge. This merely deepened the need for greater differentiation in the spheres of authority. The resulting schism between scientific thinking and religious belief hurled modern man into a dichotomy that appeared insurmountable. Spiritual sentiments became increasingly hemmed in, as the ranks of those doubting the truth of Christ's message grew in number, and as Christian doctrine increasingly became a matter of debate. Even central tenets anchored in ecclesiastical tradition, such as God, Christ, Church and Revelation, became objects of vehement debate among theologians and laymen alike.

When the most central and fundamental teachings of a Church are no longer accepted as the pure truth even among that Church's own elite and administrators, the end of traditional Christianity is undeniably at hand. The message of the empty pews is quite clear. According to a statistical survey made in 1979, only one in three citizens of the Federal Republic of Germany subscribes to the teachings of the established Christian Churches while 77 percent answer in the affirmative to the question of whether one can be a Christian without belonging to a Church. Regardless of what sectors of the population were approached, nowhere did the majority believe that Christ was the "divine emissary" sent by God. For the established and official Churches have fearfully neglected to inform their parishes about progress in the field of Christianity and have failed to instruct their congregations in a historical and critical approach to religion. Because the established churches have continued to insist on literal interpretations of biblical accounts and a strict adherence to the letter of

9

accepted dogma, they have, in fact, promoted the decline of ecclesiastical Christianity, even among those who are not at all anti-religious or anti-Christian in their leanings.

What we call Christianity today has very little indeed to do with the teachings of Jesus and the ideas that he wished to spread. It is really something quite different, and could rather be designated "Paulinism". Many tenets of the dogma are essentially alien to Christ's message. They are, in fact, primarily the legacy of Paul, who totally differed in his way of thinking. So-called Christianity as we know it developed when Paulinism became accepted as the state religion. The Protestant theologian Manfred Mezger quotes Emil Brunner on the subject: "Emil Brunner has called the Church a misunderstanding. From an appeal, a doctrine was constructed; from free communion, a legal body; from free association, a hierarchical machine. One might say that it became, in all of its elements and as a whole, the exact opposite of what had been intended." Surely it is permissible to investigate the justification for and legitimacy of existing institutions! How is it that a Church-going Christian finds it almost impossible to stand back critically from the proliferation of obscure articles of faith, duties and obligations in which he is ensnared? Without having known anything else and having grown up under the sole influence of the establishment, we are led to assume that because things have so long been as they are, they must consequently be correct.

A person appeared on the bleak horizon, bringing a message full of hope, a message of love and goodness, and what did humanity do with it? Turned it into paper, verbiage, power and business! Did Jesus desire all the acts that were to be committed in his name? Two millenia have passed since the bold young Jesus first tried to extricate humanity from the hold of official Churches, with their ecclesiastical bureaucracy, their laws and their figureheads, their inflexibility, their strife in matters of exegesis, their hierarchy and claims to unique authority, and their cult, idolatry and sectarianism. Jesus wanted the direct communication between God and Mankind, and did not intend to foster any ambitious ecclesiastical careers.

But Jesus' voice no longer reaches us in its natural directness. Access to it can only be gained by privileged experts and through the arbitration of a professional corps. Jesus has been managed, marketed, codified and "booked". Wherever true and living faith has disappeared, being replaced by narrow-minded, ungenerous beliefs based on priestly rationalism, Jesus' commands of love of one's neighbour and tolerance have also disappeared, and dogmatism and fanaticism have replaced them. The struggle for supremacy of an exclusive "true faith" has left misfortune, violence and bloodshed on the paths of the Churches. This struggle has been continued from the days of the apostles up until our own times, and continues to act as the largest obstacle to a reconciliation between the various Christian confessions. The Protestant theologian Heinz Zahrnt has written, "I have suffered a profound trauma in my career as a theologian. I feel abased, humiliated, insulted, dishonoured, but not by atheists, those who deny God, mockers or doubters, who, although godless, are often very humane, no, by dogmatists; by those and the shepherds of those who merely follow the letter of the teachings and believe that that is the only way to reach God. I have been wounded at a most central point, the point that has kept me alive despite a deep melancholy, my belief in God . . ."

Confidence in the value of religious experience tends to diminish in proportion to the development of intellectual capacities. Belief in the power of the rational and provable has taken the place of deep and self-luminous faith as a means of dealing with reality. The process of "growing up" in modern society subordinates religious feeling to the category of the irrational, where it is regarded as unprovable and hence unreal. Logical thought and action alone appear to determine reality. As the level of education increases, the qualities of the transcendental decrease and cease to be things of living experience. The principal cause of this is a misinterpretation of the concept of God. The Divine is not at some Utopian distance, but in each of us; and it inspires us to lead our lives in harmony with the Infinite, and to recognize our short existence as a part of the eternal whole.

For centuries, Western man has learned to view himself as a being separate from God; and in the "enlightened" twentieth century, Western man seems less certain than ever about possible answers to the most ancient human questions about God and the meaning of life. All over the world, new spiritual centres have sprung up, attempting to give answers to those questions which a rigid Church officialdom cannot answer. A kind of syncretic world religion of the future is in ascendance. It is moving towards full self-realisation, to the search for religious enlightenment, to a mystical all inclusive vision of the

11

cosmic context of one's individual existence, and this by means of contemplation, self-knowledge and meditation.

The decisive impetus to such an internalization of religion has always come, and continues to come, from the East, primarily India. Mankind must now *reorient* itself in the most literal sense of the word to turn towards the East. The Orient is the origin and source of our innermost experiences.

We need neither expect the final demise of belief in God, nor fear spiritual and moral decay. Indeed, we can hope for a germination of the seed of the Spirit, a coming to life of the transcendental inner world which has until now only been promised to us in the afterlife. One need not reckon with a general downfall of religion, but on the contrary, a blossoming of mystical consciousness is secretly upon us; and this not just for the elite or the "chosen", but in the all embracing ecumenical context of a world religion. This religion will not set its goals in the superficial and transient world, nor place excessive value on appearances, but centre wholly on the grand spiritual awakening, a turning to transcendental values. Such is the true way of "Deliverance from evil".

Through Knowledge of Truth
All evils are destroyed.
The true Enlightened One stands firm,
Scattering the clouds of deceit
Like the sun shining in a cloudless sky.

Buddha

Chapter one

The Unknown Life of Jesus
Nicolai Notovitch's discovery

In the autumn of 1887, the Russian historian and itinerant scholar, Nicolai Notovitch[1] (born 1858) reached Kashmir in northern India on one of his numerous journeys to the Orient. He planned to lead an expedition from Srinagar, the capital of Kashmir, through the Himalayas to Ladakh. He had enough funds at his disposal to equip himself adequately, and to hire an interpreter and ten bearers in addition to his servant. After an adventurous trek, having successfully braved many trials and difficulties, the caravan finally reached the Zoji-la pass, 3500 metres in altitude, on the natural border between the "happy valley" of Kashmir and the arid "moon landscape" of Ladakh.

Even today, the Zoji-la is the only route of access from Kashmir to that strange and remote country. Notovitch wrote in his diary: "What a bleak contrast I experienced, coming from the smiling nature and the beautiful people of Kashmir into the forbidding, barren mountains of Ladakh and to its beardless, rugged inhabitants!" The plain Ladakhis soon proved to be a friendly lot and "extremely sincere"; thus Notovitch finally arrived in a Buddhist monastery, where he was granted a much warmer reception than e.g. a Muslim might have expected. He asked a lama why he should be favoured over believers of the Islamic faith, and received this reply:

"The Moslems have nothing in common with our religion; indeed, not long ago they forcibly converted a number of Buddhists to Islam after a victorious campaign. It has caused us the greatest difficulty to lead these Moslems who have diverged from the path of Buddhism back to the right path to the true God. The Europeans are altogether different from the Moslems. They not only acknowledge the essential principle of monotheism; they also honour Buddha and are thus very near to the lamas of Tibet. The only difference between the Christians and ourselves is that, having accepted Buddha's exalted teachings, the Christians have parted from him completely and adopted their own

13

Dalai Lama. Our Dalai Lama alone retained the divine gift, the majesty of Buddha, his transcendent vision, and the power to serve as an intermediary between Earth and Heaven."

"Who is this Christian Dalai Lama you are talking about?" Notovitch asked in reply "We have a 'Son of God', to whom we direct our most impassioned prayers, in whom we seek refuge, and who might plea to our one and only God on our behalf."

"We do not mean him, Sahib! We, too, honour the one you worship as the Son of God. But we do not see an actual son in him, but the foremost being among the chosen. In fact Buddha, as a purely spiritual being, was incarnated in the holy person of Issa, who spread our exalted and true religion throughout the world without resorting to fire or the sword. I should like to speak about your earthly Dalai Lama, whom you have given the title, 'Father of the Universal Church'. That was a great sin; and may those sheep who have taken the false path be forgiven!" Thus replied the lama, while once again starting to turn his prayer wheel.

Having recognized the lama's allusion to the Pope, Notovitch probed further. "You tell me that a son of Buddha, Issa, who was chosen above all, spread your faith throughout the world. Who was he?"

The lama's eyes widened greatly at this question, and he looked at his visitor in astonishment, uttering a few words that puzzled Notovitch. Barely comprehensible, he murmured, "Issa is a great prophet, one of the first to come after the exalted Buddhas; he is far greater than any one of the Dalai Lamas, for he forms part of the spiritual essence of our Lord. He instructed you, and led transgressing souls back to the heart of God; he made you worthy of the graces of the Creator, and made it possible for every being to recognize good and evil. His name and his deeds are registered in our holy books."

At this point, Notovitch had become quite baffled by the lama's words, for the prophet Issa, his teaching, his martyrdom, and the reference to a Christian Dalai Lama were increasingly reminiscent of Jesus Christ.

He bade his interpreter not to omit a single word that the lama had uttered. "Where are these scriptures and who wrote them?" he finally asked the monk.

"The most important scriptures, drafted at various times in India and Nepal, depending on the account of events, are to be found in their thousands in Lhasa. There are copies in a few large monasteries. They were made during various epochs by the lamas during their stays at Lhasa, and donated to the monastery as a memento of the time they spent with our supreme master, the Dalai Lama."

"Do you not have any originals yourselves which concern the prophet Issa?"

"No, we have none. Our monastery is of little significance, and since its founding the line of our lamas have not managed to come into possession of more than a few hundred scriptures. The large monasteries have thousands of them. But these are holy things, which no one will show you anywhere."

Notovitch resolved to try to examine these scriptures in the further course of his travels. He thus arrived at Leh, the capital of Ladakh, and finally at Hemis, "one of the most distinguished monasteries in the country." Here he witnessed one of the traditional religious festivals that take place several times each year, and as the head lama's guest of honour, he had the opportunity of gaining a wealth of knowledge about the customs and habits of the lamaist monks. Finally the traveller succeeded in diverting the conversation to his chief interest, and he learned that in the monastery there were indeed scriptures about the mysterious prophet Issa, containing stories that had astounding similarities to the stories of Jesus of Nazareth.

But the guest was obliged to postpone the pursuit of his investigation, for to find those books among the many thousands would have been no small task.

After returning to Leh, Notovitch sent the head of the monastery precious gifts in the hope of being allowed to return in the near future, to be able to inspect the manuscripts finally. While riding near Hemis, he suffered such an unfortunate fall that he broke his right leg and had to remain in the care of the monks. At his ardent request, two thick books with loose, yellowed leaves were finally brought to his bedside. During the following two days, the revered abbot read aloud from the extraordinary document, which had been drafted in verses, and often lacked continuity. Notovitch took notes of his interpreter's rendering. Later, after completing his journey, he arranged all the verses in their chronological order and succeeded in rounding off many of the separate texts so as to give a complete narrative.

The following is a summary of this text, based on the French translation.

Nicolas Notovitch

After a short introduction, the early history of the people of Israel and the life of Moses is briefly related. An account follows of how the eternal Spirit resolved to take on a human form "so that he might show by his example how one can attain moral purity, and free the soul from its coarse shell, in order to attain the perfection needed to enter into the kingdom of heaven, which is unchanging and ruled by eternal happiness."

A divine infant is born in far-away Israel, and is given the name Issa[2]. At some time during the first fourteen years of his life, the lad arrives in the region of the Sindh (the Indus) in the company of merchants, "And he settled among the Aryans, in the land loved by God, with the intention of perfecting himself and of learning from the laws of the great Buddha." The young Issa travels through the land of five rivers (the Punjab)[3], stays briefly with the "deluded Jains", and then proceeds to Jagannath "where the white priests of Brahma honour him with a joyous reception". There Issa/Jesus learns to read and interpret the Veda, and finally he instructs the lower castes of the Sudras. He thus incurs the displeasure of the Brahmans, who feel their position and power threatened. After spending six years in Jagannath (Puri), Rajagriha (Rajgir), Benares (Varanasi) and other holy cities, he is compelled to flee the fury of the Brahmans, who had become enraged by his teaching that the differences in human value among people of different castes was not divinely ordained.

One is suprised by the extraordinary correlation between the accounts in the texts found by Notovitch and those of the Gospels, shedding light on Jesus' personality. Issa of the Notovitch texts opposes the abuses of the caste system, which rob the lower castes of their basic human rights, justifying himself with the words, "God our Father makes no difference between any of his children, all of whom he loves equally." And he expresses reservations about the rigid and inhumane literal interpretation of the law, pointing out that "the law was made for man to show him the way." He consoles the weak: "The eternal judge, the eternal Spirit, who forms the sole and indivisible world-soul, will proceed sternly against those who arrogate privileges to themselves." When the priests challenge Issa to produce miracles, to prove the omnipotence of his God, he retorts, "The miracles of our God were performed on the first day when the universe was created; they take place every day and at every moment; those who cannot perceive them are robbed of one of the most

17

beautiful gifts of life." While questioning the authority of the priests, he justifies himself in the following manner: "As long as the people had no priests, they were ruled by natural law and they retained the purity of their souls. Their souls were found in the Presence of God, and to commune with Him they did not need to resort to the mediation of an idol or a beast, nor to fire, as you do here. You say that the sun must be worshipped, as must the spirits of good and those of evil. I tell you, your teaching is abominable, for the sun has no effect on its own, but solely through the will of the invisible Creator, to whom it owes its existence, and who designed the star that it might light up the day and warm the work and seed of man."

Issa goes up into the Himalayas to Nepal, where he remains for six years and dedicates himself to the study of Buddhist scriptures. The teachings that he spreads there are simple and clear, but above all just towards the oppressed and the weak, to whom he reveals the falsity and perfidy of the priest caste. He finally moves on towards the West, passing through various countries in the role of an itinerant preacher, ever preceded by his glorious reputation. He also quarrels with the priests of Persia, who expel him one evening in the hope that he would soon become the prey of wild animals. But Providence allows the holy Issa to reach Palestine safely, where the wise men inquire of him: "Who are you, and what is the country of your origin? We have as yet not heard of you and know not even your name."

"I am an Israelite", Issa replies, "and on the day of my birth I saw the walls of Jerusalem and heard the sobs of my enslaved brothers and the wails of my sisters condemned to live among the heathens. And my soul grieved sorely when I heard that my brothers had forgotten the true God. As a child, I left my parents' home to live among other peoples. But after hearing of the great sorrows that my brothers were suffering, I returned to the land where my parents lived in order to bring my brothers back to the faith of our ancestors, a faith which enjoins us to be patient on Earth so that we might achieve the consummate and highest happiness in the beyond."

This corresponds to and in a way corroborates all the significant pronouncements of the biblical gospels.

The two manuscripts which the lama from the monastery of Hemis read aloud to Notovitch, selecting all the passages dealing with Jesus, were anthologies of various Tibetan writings. The originals had been compiled in the old Indian language of Pali as early as in the first two centuries A.D. and preserved in a monastery near Lhasa' (lha–sa = place of the gods). The monastery was affiliated to the Potala Palace of the Dalai Lama.

Having returned to Europe, Notovitch attempted to contact several highly-placed dignitaries of the Church, in order to make known his incredible discovery. The metropolitan of Kiev urgently advised him not to publicise his discovery, but refused to give his reasons for this. In Paris, Cardinal Rotelli explained that publication of the texts would give fuel to the camp of blasphemers, mockers and Protestants, and insisted that publication of the texts would be premature at that point in time. At the Vatican, a close confidant of the Pope proffered his opinion: "Why should it be published? No one will regard it as being of any great significance, and you will make a lot of enemies. But you are still young! If it is a question of money, I could arrange a payment for your notes to remunerate you for the tasks you performed and the time you spent." Notovitch rejected the offer.

It was only the church historian, critic and Orientalist, Ernest Renan who showed a lively interest in the notes. It soon became clear to Notovitch, however, that Renan was only interested in using the material for his own purposes, as a member of the Academie Francaise, and so he did not follow up his proposals.

Finally the manuscript was published, but without causing much response. The power, influence and authority of the Christian Churches are so strong that the authenticity of canonical teachings simply cannot be put in doubt. Critics and sceptics are damned as godless heretics, and muzzled or simply ostracised. Notovitch was in no position to gather sufficient scientific support for the testimony that he had found, and because of this it was not taken seriously.

Today, however, it has finally become possible to assert that it is not possible to *dis*prove Jesus' stay in India in view of the body of knowledge which current research on Jesus provides. No historically reliable source, nor any accounts in the Gospels, comment on the period of his life in question (between his twelfth and thirtieth years, approximately). It almost seems as though Jesus' life only began after he had turned thirty, and after he was baptized by John. In Luke alone can one read the terse sentence, "And Jesus increased in wisdom and stature, and in favour with God and man." (Luke 2,52).

The scriptures that Notovitch discovered are not the only documents recording Jesus' stay in India. In 1908, a solitary work appeared in America, ominously entitled "The Aquarian Gospel of Jesus Christ". The author was mysteriously given only as "Levi". This gospel contains accounts of Jesus' years in India that correspond amazingly to the accounts in the "Life of the Holy Issa".

The Aquarian Gospel

In 1844, Levi H. Dowling was born in Belleville, Ohio. He was the son of a minister of Scottish and Welsh descent, and had begun at a very early age to contemplate the more profound aspects of life. He began to preach when he was sixteen years old, became the pastor of a small church at the age of eighteen, and a chaplain in the American army at twenty. Later he studied medicine and served as a general practitioner for a few years, before dedicating himself wholly to the study of spiritual works.

When he was young, he had a vision in which he was commanded to build a "White City". The symbol of the "White City" signified the chronicling of the Life of Jesus. Levi Dowling prepared himself for this task in forty years of meditation and prayer.

In Levi's only work, the Aquarian Gospel, one can find information about the twelfth to twenty-ninth years of Jesus' life. Levi's notes were called the Aquarian Gospel because they originated shortly before the beginning of the astrological Age of Aquarius, and thus seem to be meant for wide promulgation in this "New Age". Elihu, who headed a school of prophecy some two thousand years ago in Zoan (Egypt), said of the coming times: "This epoch will understand but little of the works of purity and love; yet not a single word, no significant thought and no deed will be lost, for all will be preserved in God's chronicle."[5] Tuning into this chronicle, the so called *Akashic Records*[6], Levi received the revelation of a new and more complete gospel in a condition of deep inner contemplation in the quiet morning hours between two and six o'clock. *Akasha* holds the universal memory discussed by metaphysicists. When the spirit of man is in full harmony with the cosmic Spirit, it achieves a conscious attunement with the Akashic Records. The Hebraic masters called the Akasha "The Book of God's Memories".

In the sixth and seventh parts of the Aquarian Gospel, Levi gives an account of Jesus' stay in India. According to the account, the Indian

20

royal prince Ravanna of Orissa[7] meets the twelve-year-old boy in the temple, where he hears him debate; and he then brings him to India in order to grant him the opportunity of deepening his studies. Jesus is accepted as a student in the temple of Jagannath[8], and zealously studies the laws of Manu and the Veda. As in the accounts of Nicolai Notovitch, Jesus astonishes his teachers with his clever and profound answers, and incurs the anger of the Brahmans by his open criticism. He philosophises about the concepts of truth, wisdom, power, understanding, faith and man. Jesus exhorts us not to cling to the word of others at second-hand, or to what has been written, for one can never become wise through trivial traditions and laws that have been passed down. All the wisdom that is expressed in these texts is in allegorical form, typical for Jesus, and it is as powerful and universal a statement as the Gospel words of Jesus known to us.

The seventh part of the Aquarian Gospel contains a description of Jesus' journey through the vast Himalayas to Tibet, where he studies the ancient manuscripts of the masters in the temple at Lhasa. After this, he returns to the region of the Sindh via Lahore, and from there he finally comes back to the Near East.

Of course, modern and "rational" people are hardly likely to be impressed by a text like the Aquarian Gospel, conveyed as it was in an occult fashion to a religious person acting as a medium. The prophetic pronouncements of the canonical writings in the Bible are, however, generally accepted wholesale. Perhaps this is partly due to reverence for old age, which accords the biblical pronouncements a special status. It is nonetheless of interest that the Aquarian Gospel corresponds more or less to the texts found by Notovitch.

If Jesus was indeed in India, we shall have to revise our image of him completely. After two thousand years of ecclesiastical history and theological research, one might be led to presume that there were not likely to be any new developments in the field. Knowledge of and about Jesus seems have been exhausted, and so one can relegate the life of "Jesus in India" to the realm of fantastic speculation. What has been accepted as unassailable for two thousand years cannot just be turned over with a mere sweep of the hand!

At this point it is of vital importance to survey the contributions of modern scholarship to the subject of the historicity of Jesus. Only then can one determine what can be regarded as established fact.

21

The Secular Sources

No other topic in the world has had such overt impact and been the subject of so many books and such passionate discussion than the personality of Jesus of Nazareth. Yet the personality of the historic figure of Jesus has ever remained veiled from scholarly scrutiny. Not until the end of the eighteenth and in the nineteenth century did a few bold thinkers begin to investigate the life of Christ systematically. German Protestant theology has the credit of having advanced the furthest in the historical, objective and critical study of religion. One of the greatest researchers, the physician and theologian Albert Schweitzer, called research on the life of Christ the most powerful and daring development in independent religious awareness. Today it is hard for us to grasp how extreme were the labour pains in which the current picture of the life of Christ was born. It was actually dissatisfaction and indeed hate, according to Schweitzer, that most fostered a scientific approach. "Research into the life of Jesus represents a schooling in truthfulness for the Church; and it has been a more painful and belligerent struggle for the truth than has ever before been witnessed." Today a good 100,000 monographs exist on the subject of Jesus, yet the results of all the research on the historical figure of Jesus can only be described as disappointing. The sources at one's disposal tend to assume that Jesus is irrefutably the Messiah and the son of God, and serve almost exclusively as a document of faith. Truly objective testimonies are hardly available, even among the secular accounts! Thus theologians are still incapable of giving the exact year of Jesus' birth. Possible years are from the seventh to the fourth year before our current reckoning: Christ was certainly born during the regime of Herod, who died four years before our "Christian era" (4 B.C.). Jesus' childhood and adolescence were almost entirely ignored in the known Gospels, even though the early periods of life are of such major significance in the formation of a person's character. Even in the dubious accounts about the short period of his public life, only a few hours and days of trials are depicted. Contemporary historians seem to have never even heard of Jesus or at least regard him as not worthy of mention. How is it possible that historians took no notice of all the fantastic miracles and extraordinary occurrences described in the gospels?

Tacitus (ca. 55–120 A.D.)[9] mentions a man referred to as Christ who had been crucified by Pontius Pilate during the reign of the Emperor Tiberius. The account, which was primarily based on stories current in the second century, was written by the great Roman historian around 117 A.D., about ninety years after the crucifixion. *Sueton* (65 to 135 A.D.)[10] and *Pliny the Younger* (c. 61 to 114 A.D.)[11] mention the sect of Christians but does not spare a single word on the person Jesus Christ. The Jewish historian, *Josephus Flavius*, published an imposing work in about the year 93 A.D. entitled "Jewish Antiquities". It is a kind of world survey from the time of creation until the reign of Nero, in which he relates everything that he considers significant. He describes John the Baptist, Herod and Pilate, and gives a very detailed account of politics and society, but omits any mention of Jesus. Not until the third century did a work appear, written by a Christian, entitled *Testimonium Flavianum*[12], in which the Jewish historian *Josephus* suddenly reports on and confirms the miracles and resurrection of Christ. The Church Fathers, Justinius, Tertullian and Cyprian, still knew nothing of such a "Christianity", and Origen[13] repeatedly reminds us that Josephus did not believe in Christ. The Jewish writer Justus of Tiberias, a contemporary of Christ, lived in Tiberias, near Capernaum where Jesus was supposed to have stayed often. He wrote an extensive chronicle, starting with Moses and continuing on up to his own times, but never once did he mention Jesus. The surviving legacy of another Jewish contemporary of Jesus, the great scholar Philo of Alexandria, comprises five texts. Philo proved to be a specialist on biblical writings and Jewish sects, but he too does not devote a single line to Jesus[14]. It is only through the embittered anti-Christian, Celsus, that we learn a few historical facts, though he is hardly flattering to the "idealised" Jesus. Celsus' belligerent writings offer some information that will be examined in greater detail later. The sole possible source of historical research would thus appear to be the collection of scriptures of the New Testament.

The Gospels

The Greek term for gospel is *evangelion,* which means "good and joyous tidings". The concept had existed for a long time before Christianity applied it to the message of Jesus. The Emperor Augustus for example was called the "Saviour of the world", and his birthday was referred to as "The day of the evangelion".

The New Testament contains four gospels, which have been named after Mark, Matthew, Luke and John. They are an arbitrary selection from among a great number of gospels that were in use in the various communities and sects of early Christianity. The rejected texts were called apocryphal, and many were destroyed, but some of those that have survived shed a strange and mysterious light on the personality of Jesus of Nazareth. The multiplicity of sectarian opinions threatened to split early Christian communities into countless factions and to cause an internal war within Christendom. The Roman, Ammianus Marcelinus, described the situation in the following manner: "Not even wild animals yearning for blood could rage against each other the way many Christians rage against their brothers in faith."[15] Even the Teacher of the Church, Clement of Alexandria, saw in this fierce strife about the various tenets of faith the greatest hindrance in spreading the faith[16]. And Celsus, an open critic of Christianity, wrote in the second century that the only element that the various groups held in common was the word "Christian".[17] With such an abundance of fundamentally differing writings on Christ's life, deeds and words, a few leaders of the early Church saw only one way out of the chaos, a chaos that would inevitably lead to the complete destruction of the conflicting communities. A unification was only possible through the collation of a group of selected texts that had been made to agree. Papias, a Church Father, made such an attempt in about 140 A.D., but he failed due to the resistance of the separate communities. Not until the end of the second century did Irenaeus, using the threat of divine wrath, succeed in "canonizing" the four gospels that are today considered to have a unique validity. He justified his claim of authenticity for the four gospels by asserting that they had been composed by disciples of Jesus himself. This was, of course, not so easy. It is still not possible to determine

24

precisely when and how these gospels came into existence, because neither the original text, nor any early indication that there had ever been such originals, exists. Even an approximate dating cannot be ventured with any degree of certainty. The results of latest research date the text of the gospel according to Mark at shortly before 70 A.D.; the gospel according to Matthew at shortly after 70 A.D.; and the gospel according to Luke at somewhere between 75 and 80 A.D.. Other gospels originated at about 100 A.D. And it appears that the gospel according to John was not written until the first decades of the second century. If Jesus was crucified in c. 30 A.D., the first writings on his existence did not at any rate originate until after two or three generations (with the exception of the epistles of Paul, which deserve special attention).

The source for the contents of the gospels named after Matthew and Luke seems for the most part to have been the gospel according to Mark. The gospel according to Mark must therefore have existed before the gospels of Matthew and Luke. The canonical gospel named after Mark contains a few accounts, however, that are not to be found in the gospels of Matthew or Luke; and here they substitute other stories which are often inconsistent with, or at least phrased very differently from the accounts in the gospel according to Mark. One might suspect that the two later gospels used an earlier draft of the gospel according to Saint Mark as a primary source. A number of theologians have hypothesized that a primary text might indeed have existed; although the theologian Gunther Bornkamm believes that "the attempt to reconstruct an original draft of the gospel according to Saint Mark is a hopeless undertaking."

The gospel according to Mark very clearly indicates a secret about Jesus as the Messiah. Jesus does not announce that he is the Messiah, and in fact even forbids his disciples to declare this (Mark 8,30).

In the gospel according to Matthew, however, Jesus is portrayed as the fulfilment of the religion of Moses, and as the Messiah announced by the prophets. It has long been accepted by theologians that the gospel simply depicts Jesus as the incarnate Revelation. The writer of the gospel according to Matthew was evidently neither a historian nor a very exact biographer of Jesus.

Although the writer of the gospel according to Luke mingles historical events with those in the life of Jesus, no cohesive biography emerges. Here, as in the other gospels, a chronological, historical foundation is missing because of the lack of biographical information, since the early Christian communities had at a very early stage lost all data on Christ's life. The historical figure of Jesus had already been pushed back into the background and his religious image favoured. The gospel according to Luke would seem to owe less to the Judaic tradition than to the Roman and Hellenistic traditions, for Jesus is no longer depicted as a national Messiah, but as a Messiah for the entire world.

At one point, the gospel according to Luke actually contradicts the gospels of Mark and Matthew: they make no mention of Jesus enjoining his disciples to remain in Jerusalem, but in the 24th chapter of Luke, the disciples are told to "tarry . . . in the city of Jerusalem, until ye be endowed with power from on high" (Luke 24,49).

Even in Acts, attributed to Luke, there is conspicuous mention of the presence of the disciples in Jerusalem . The writer is clearly attempting to show that Christendom had Jerusalem as its point of origin, although it has been proved that Christian communities were already in existence at that time in other places. The writer thus dwells on the miracle of Whitsun to explain the existence of Christian sects beyond Palestine. A miracle suddenly bestowed the gift of speaking in foreign tongues upon the disciples which easily settled the question about the problem of language barriers.

The so-called gospel according to John is without doubt the last of the four canonical accounts of the life of Jesus to have been written. Early Christian writings mention the existence of the gospel for the first time in the middle of the second century. A few lines of a papyrus record written in ancient Greek, discovered by the English historian Grenfell, indicate that the gospel could not have been written before the beginning of the second century. It is more a philosophical work constructed on the basis of and complementary to the first three gospels. The Church Father Irenaeus does claim that John, the favourite of Jesus, authored the gospel, though this claim can certainly be questioned because the simple fisherman from Galilee could hardly have been educated extensively enough in theology, philosophy or Greek epistolary style to have written the work unaided.

The writer of the gospel according to John presents all the accounts of Jesus' life in the light of a religious philosophy based on the teachings of Christ. Because of this and the time lapse of at least eighty years between the crucifixion and the writing down of the gospel

,research on the life of the historical person Jesus cannot rely on the gospel of John as a definitive record.

More recently, the so-called "Book of Sayings" has assumed an immense importance in the entire Gospel literature (and Lutheran Church). Rudolf Bultmann believes that the Sayings originated in the first Palestinian communities, and that they belong to the oldest Christian tradition. But Bultmann adds, "There is no certainty that the words of that oldest period of oral tradition were ever uttered verbatim by Jesus. Perhaps this oldest period itself has its own complicated historical background." He continues, "Tradition collects the words of the Lord, alters their emphasis and develops them with additions. Furthermore other sayings are adjoined, and thus many of the words attributed to Jesus in the Book of Sayings will have been placed there by others."

Today, historians are able to retrace the life of a Pontius Pilate or a Herod in great detail; and these are characters who are only of interest because of their relation to Jesus Christ. Information on other contemporaries and earlier figures of prominence can be found in abundance. Yet only a few meagre and scanty lines with little commentary exist about the life of Jesus until his thirtieth year, and even these are too frail to serve as documentation. A specialist on the New Testament in Tübingen, Ernst Käsemann, summarized the results of research on the life of Christ in the following manner, "One is overwhelmed by how little" of the accounts about Jesus in the New Testament "can be called authentic . . . The historical figure of Jesus is only traceable in a few words of the Sermon on the Mount, the conflict with Pharisaism, a number of parables and some further narratives."[18]

Biblical experts are still able to disagree among themselves about what "quotes" can in fact be attributed to Jesus. In his book, The Unknown Words of Jesus *(Unbekannte Jesus-Worte)*, the church-historian Joachim Jeremias narrows the choice down to a mere twenty-one quotations which were definitely uttered by Jesus[19]. And the critical theologian Bultmann maintains: "The character of Jesus, the clear picture of his personaliy and life, have faded beyond recognition."[20]

The Witness Paul

The earliest documents concerning Jesus are the writings of Paul. He came from a strict Jewish family but was able to acquire Roman citizenship, for which his father paid a high price. This permitted him to change his original Jewish name Saul to Paulus. He belonged to the upper class and was raised in the strict Pharisian tradition. He received an extensive and profound education, mastered the Greek language and was widely-read in Greek poetry and philosophy. At some point between the ages of eighteen and twenty (after Jesus' crucifixion), he went to Jerusalem and dedicated himself intensively to the study of theology as a student of Gamaliel I. He was then a fanatical zealot, narrow-minded, straightlaced, an adherent of the law and a vehement opponent of the early Christian sects who posed a hindrance to his career as a Pharisee. Paul went so far as to appeal to the high priest for special permission to persecute the followers of Christ even beyond the bounds of Jerusalem. He regarded his extraordinary zeal in carrying out this task as a means of impressing the priests. While near Damascus, he was seized by the fascination which emanated from Jesus and his teachings; he was suddenly overwhelmed by the realisation of the possibilities which his position presented. He became intoxicated by the image of himself in the role of the spiritual leader of a gigantic movement of the future.

As with Jesus and the other apostles, there is hardly a single historical text about Paul himself. Everything we know about him comes almost exclusively from epistles attributed to him and the Acts of the Apostles, and these tend to be rather biased with the human element, counterfeit in part or in whole, or compiled from various textual fragments. The epistles to Timothy, to Titus, and the epistle to the Hebrews are questionable throughout. The authenticity of the epistles to the Ephesians and the Colossians, and the second epistle to the Thessalonians is a matter of heated debate.

What we refer to as Christianity today is largely an artificial doctrine of rules and precepts, created by Paul and more worthy of the designation "Paulinism". The church historian Wilhelm Nestle expressed the issue in the following manner, "Christianity is the religion founded by Paul; it replaced Christ's gospel with a gospel about Christ."[21]

Paulinism in this sense means a misinterpretation and indeed counterfeiting of Christ's actual teachings, as arranged and initiated by Paul. It has long been a truism for modern theologians as well as researchers on ecclesiastical history that the Christianity of the organised Church, with its central tenet of salvation through the death and suffering of Jesus, has been based on a misinterpretation. "All the good in Christianity can be traced to Jesus, all the bad to Paul," wrote the theologian Overbeck[22]. By building on the belief of salvation through the expiatory death of God's first-born, Paul regressed to the primitive Semitic religions of earlier times, in which parents were commanded to give up their first-born in a bloody sacrifice. Paul also prepared the path for the later ecclesiastical teachings on original sin and the trinity. As long ago as the eighteenth century, the English philosopher Lord Bolingbroke (1678–1751) could make out two completely different religions in the New Testament, that of Jesus and that of Paul[23]. Kant, Lessing, Fichte and Schelling also sharply distinguish the teachings of Jesus from those of the "disciples". A great number of reputable modern theologians support and defend these observations.

Paul, the impatient zealot, decidedly different from the original apostles, called a "classicist of intolerance" by the theologian Deissmann[24], has opened up gulfs between believers and non-believers. Paul disregarded many teachings of Jesus; instead, he placed Jesus upon a pedestal and turned him into the Christ figure that Jesus never intended to be. If it is ever possible to discover any profound knowledge or truth in the heart of Christianity, it will only be by rejecting obvious counterfeits that have been considered so sacrosanct as to be untouchable, and by turning to the true, pure teachings of Jesus and the real essence of Religion. Still, it is easy to forgive all of Paul's human interpretations of Christ's teachings if one considers that without Paul and other dogmatists, probably no-one would know any details about Jesus today.

The theologian Grimm has sized up the situation thus, "However deeply these teachings may have become ingrained in Christian thought, they still have absolutely nothing to do with the real Jesus."[25]

Conclusions

It remains to be seen whether and to what degree known sources can be used for establishing the historicity of Jesus. Sources such as the scriptures discovered by Nicolai Notovitch in Ladakh can definitely fill an important and otherwise unexplored and unexplained gap in the life of Christ. Nonetheless, if unsupported and propounded under the wrong circumstances, a discovery of such magnitude would be bound to seem fantastic, as it would suddenly shine light into the darkness surrounding the origins of the Christian religion. A true-to-life human picture of Jesus can only be attained by an objective, extensive historical investigation, free of the dogmatism of Churches, using all the best resources of modern genius.

In my work as a teacher of Christian religion, I have seen how more and more enlightened theologians are having a hard time finding "myths" forced upon them, the immaculate conception or the death on the cross followed by an extraordinary resurrection with the assumption of the body of Christ, particularly after learning something about the actual history of biblical texts (only at university!). They are forced in an almost schizophrenic manner to keep such knowledge to themselves, and to continue to relate the naïve Bible accounts to their congregations as though announcing God's own words. As recently as November 18th, 1965, the Roman Catholic Church declared in its most solemn and highly authoritative document, its revised dogmatic constitution (Vatican II), that God himself "authored" the Bible, which is thus made holy and canonical in all its parts and in its entirety, as it was written through the inspiration of the Holy Ghost. "Everything written by the inspired authors is to be regarded as having been written by the Holy Ghost." The Bible, according to the Church, is a reliable, faithful and infallible teacher. Millions of Catholics are taught this, and as is well known, "faith" is compulsory in the Catholic Church (discussion on such matters being out of the question). This is particularly hard on those who are responsible for passing on Church dogma and who are well enough informed to know how matters stand; inner crises and human tragedy are almost invariably the consequences of such conflicts.

To ascribe "divine" authority to writings containing countless contradictions, mistakes, omissions, logical errors, false conclusions, oversights, deficiencies, distortions, misunderstandings, confusions, false statements and obvious lies, as does the priestly Church administration, borders on blasphemy.

The Anglican bishop, John A. T. Robinson, has officially challenged the entire Church to finally state the facts of its position, particularly with regard to the Bible. A full examination of the foundations of the Christian religion could result in a reform of dogmatism. But the Church still seems to shun every form of enlightenment, and continues to treat courageous progressives such as the theologian of Tübingen, Küng, in a medieval manner. Does the Christian Church not demand uprighteousness, openness, honesty and love of truth from its followers? And is this fraud or not? But what can the Church be afraid of? Are they honestly concerned about the welfare of the souls of men that can only be saved if the dogma of salvation is kept intact, or is it simply worried about losing its administrative status and power? The Church has tended to use every means to ensure that the mysteries behind Jesus remain unclear and that every attempt to investigate rationally the phenomenon of Christ is bound to fail.

The truth about Jesus and what he actually wanted is a thousand times more fascinating than all the stories that have been invented about him. He certainly did not want an institutionalized, official church, full of self-righteous neo-Pharisees with claims of infallibility. He also surely did not want to force anyone to convert to his faith under threat of death or eternal damnation. He never instructed or authorized anyone to fulfill great divine functions on earth. He never used to refer to himself as the incarnation of God on earth. He never forgave sins, nor did he grant anyone the authority to forgive sins; and he never promised the coming and constancy of a Holy Ghost apart from him. And finally, he did not order a gospel to be written (otherwise he could have written it himself). What Jesus really desired, we can only surmise, looking at the traditional image we have received of him as a figure of great moral integrity and deep humane and spiritual sentiments.

What Albert Schweitzer said in 1913 is more valid today than ever: "Modern Christianity has to face the possibility that the historicity of Jesus could be revealed at any time."[26] And Rudolf Bultmann said: "It would't shock me in the slightest, if the bones of Jesus were found today!"[27]

It is an act of Providence that the "gaps" of such hallowed age in Church records, could be filled by a journey eastwards, to the deep Orient which has proved so crucial for an understanding of present spiritual movements in the world. The Moslems had always preserved the story, and the 20th century accumulation of documents and its accelerating expansion of research finds soon led to its rediscovery. Jesus linked his soul with the Spirit pervading the very atmosphere of old India. We are led now to discover Jesus the Oriental, the figure of *Ex Oriente Lux,* of Eastern light and promise.

My Travels in the Himalayas

In 1973, a report appeared in a major German weekly[28] about a professor who claimed in all seriousness to have found the tomb of Jesus Christ. The article was even accompanied by photographs of the supposed tomb of Christ. The professor stated publicly that Jesus not only spent his youth in India, but survived the crucifixion and returned to that unique country, where he lived as an itinerant teacher or guru until his death at an old age, and apparent burial in the Kashmirian capital, Srinagar.

This truly was a tremendous claim, and the journal that dared to publish it was swamped with thousands of letters full of invective and virulent protests. Some letters, however, bore interested inquiries from open-minded people who had always turned the eye of reason on those pious fairy tales, the immaculate conception, resurrection and assumption of Jesus.

Inquiries about the report, which continue to arrive at the journal's office more than a decade later, could not be satisfactorily answered, because the proposition that Jesus might have resided in India has not been treated in hardly any of the many thousands of books about Jesus. It seems incredible that none of the sceptics ever pursued the question of where Jesus could have in fact been buried; because although the miracles Jesus was said to have performed can somehow be explained, it is really mysterious that the body of Jesus simply dissolved into thin air, as the Bible says, "being taken up into the heavens."

32

After receiving dissatisfying and evasive answers to the question of the historic figure of Jesus from professors during my studies, I decided to go to India myself, to do my own research after completing my studies as a teacher of religion. In the spring of 1979 I flew via Egypt to India, landing in Bombay. I went on by train and bus to the foot of the Himalayas at Dharmsala, where the Dalai Lama has resided since his flight from Tibet in 1959. I requested a letter of recommendation for the abbot at the monastery of Hemis in order to be granted permission to study the scriptures that Notovitch wrote about almost one hundred years ago. I had to wait four days for an audience, but finally I received the desired document with the signature of His Holiness, the fourteenth Dalai Lama. I went on by road to Kashmir where I heard that in a few days the famous mystery plays were to take place that had so delighted Notovitch. The festival, called *Cham* or *Setchu*, honours the Buddhist saint and prophet Padmasambhava and takes place from the ninth to eleventh day of the fifth Tibetan month.

The Hemis monastery is situated at a height of nearly 4000 m in the Himalayas, 34 km from Ladakh's capital Leh.

Today one can reach Leh, the capital of Ladakh, in relative comfort by a two-day bus trip over the western outliers of the Himalaya. When I finally arrived at Hemis, the festival was already underway. There were countless people, and although the country had been opened to foreigners just five years before, one could see crowds of Western tourists. I had no desire to announce the intention of my visit in that hubbub, so I went back to Leh and did not return to Hemis until three weeks later. Hemis is the largest, richest and most important abbey in Ladakh. The name is derived from the Indian word, *Hem* or *Hen* (from the Sanskrit *Hima* = snow, cool), which allows one to conclude that there had already been a settlement here before the present Tibetan culture.

Patience and perseverence are important virtues that foreigners are obliged to evidence, so at first I was given little attention. I merely joined the monks in the kitchen, which looked like the laboratory of a medieval alchemist, where I waited and drank the salted butter tea. As evening approached, a monk, gesturing silently, showed me a small room in which I could sleep. During the next days, I was mostly left to myself, and I roamed through the dim passageways of the monastery, went for long walks in the country, and only rejoined my friends in the kitchen when I felt the pangs of hunger. On the morning of the fourth day of my stay in the monastery, a young monk appeared in my cell and indicated that I should follow him. I followed him through dark corridors and up steep wooden steps into the upper regions of the monastery, which I had not entered till then. Finally we reached the roof of the grand temple. On the large terrace, under the shelter of the portal at the entrance to the topmost room of the complex, I found a huge table around which an assembly of monks was seated. A dignified, middle-aged monk sat behind the table and addressed me in almost impeccable English. It was Nawang-Tsering, the secretary and interpreter of the abbot, who explained that His Holiness, the Dungsey Rimpoche, had heard of my interest and wished to speak with me.

While waiting for my audience, I learned an interesting story from Nawang-Tsering concerning the former abbot of Hemis, who had at the same time served as the head of the Dukpa Kargyupa sect in Tibet. He had been missing since the invasion of the Red Chinese. The abbot, who at the time had been engaged in higher studies in his homeland of Tibet, was not granted permission to leave the country

34

because he insisted on taking his parents with him rather than abandon them to an uncertain fate. After a while, the communist government forbade him all correspondence, and the last heard of the high Lama was that he was in a prisoners' labour camp.

Fifteen years after the final news from Tibet, the former abbot was declared dead, and sought for in the form of a young reincarnation. Six years after the presumed time of death, the lamas found a two-year-old lad in Dalhousie (Darjeeling), who was consecrated as Drugpa Rimpoche in 1975 at the age of twelve. The lad had an aged mentor named Dungsey Rimpoche, and the time up until the consecration of the boy was spent in intensive studies and disciplines.

While living with the monks, I could not help noticing a tall man of about thirty years of age, who was clearly not of Tibetan origin but, judging from his facial features, from somewhere in the West. As I found out the young man was an Australian; he was interested in my research and was able to serve as an interpreter for me when I was with the Holy One, who only spoke Tibetan. We entered a magnificently decorated low-roofed room, in which a dignified old man was sitting in the pose of a Buddha on a small throne. Before him was a richly ornate silver teacup upon a low stand. After bowing to him with folded hands, in the customary manner, I was permitted to sit before him on the carpet. His alert and shining eyes emanated goodness and wisdom from a smiling face adorned with sculptured wrinkles and a thin white beard. I showed him my letter of introduction, and attempted to convey to the old man how important these texts could be for the whole of Christendom.

With an indulgent smile, the wise lama instructed me to find the Truth for myself, before attempting to convert the world. At that time I found his words obscure. The Australian only translated a fraction of what the lama told me. Finally, the old man informed me that the scriptures in question had been sought for, but could not be found.

This piece of news struck me like a bolt from the blue, and somewhat confused and disappointed, I took my leave. It seemed very much as though the monastery was to keep its precious secret for many years yet.

Later I was able to make use of the knowledge that an old diary of Dr. K. Marx, a 19th c. specialist on Tibet, was to be found in a mission of the Moravian Church in Leh. The Marx diary confirmed Noto-

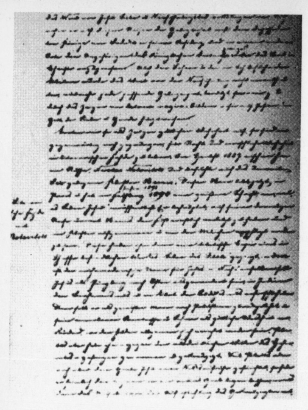

One page out of the missionary Dr. Marx's diary wherein the attendance of Notovitch because of a tooth-ache is mentioned.

vitch's stay at the monastery in Hemis (see illustration). Further confirmation of the texts in question appeared in the travelogue of Lady Henrietta Merrick, published in 1931, entitled *In the Attic of the World*.

In the 1890's, the renowned Oxford Indologist, Max Müller, (born in Dessau 1823), attempted to "expose" Notovitch's discovery as a fraud. Müller, who had never been in India himself, claimed that through contact with British colonial officials in Kashmir, he had ascertained that *no mention was on file* of an European with a broken leg ever having been in one of the local monasteries. One can best grasp the intellectual tradition from which Müller emerged by looking at a letter he wrote in 1876 to a friend:

"India is riper for Christianity than Rome and Greece were at the time of Saint Paul . . . – . . . and I should like to see if I can take part in the mission whose goal it is to destroy the perfidious Indian priesthood and to open the gates for Christian teachings."[29]

Sir Francis Younghusband, the British crown's ambassador to the court of the Maharaja of Kashmir at the time, recalled having met Notovitch on the Zoji-la-Pass. In *The Heart of a Continent*, Younghusband writes (pg. 214) that the two men had spent the night in a common camp while Notovitch was en route from Kashmir to Skardu.

But the texts are verified by others. After reading *The Unknown Life*, Swami Abhedananda, of the Ramakrishna Mission in Calcutta, set off for Hemis in 1922. Being very sceptical of Notovich's claims he wanted to see for himself. To his surprise, he found the papers in question, and, being fluent in the Pali language, he made his own direct translation. He later published his findings in his Bengali book of travels, *Kashmiri O Tibetti*.

The Russian professor and artist, Nicholas Roerich, also visited the monastery in 1925 and published his account of the manuscript in his book *The Heart of Asia*.

And long before Notovitch had been to Hemis, as early as 1854, a Mrs. Harvey wrote of the existence of the scripts on Issa in *The Adventures of a Lady in Tartary, China and Kashmir* (Volume II, pg. 136).

Immediately after returning from Leh, I looked for this mission of the Moravian Church, which had been founded by the German lay-brothers' Order of the *Herrnhuter* in 1885.

Zealous Christian missionaries had come to Tibet long before that date. Capuchin monks had resided in Lhasa from as early as the fourteenth century in the hope of converting Tibetans to Christianity, an endeavor that was not to meet with success. For when the Christian missionaries told the Tibetans that Christ had sacrificed himself on the Cross for the redemption of humanity and was finally resurrected, the Tibetans accepted the entire story as a matter of course and exclaimed enthusiastically, "That is he!"

The pious Buddhists were completely convinced that Christ was an incarnation of Padmasambhava, in fact the same person. The missionaries finally had to give up their attempts to convert the population, not because they encountered too much resistance, but on the contrary, because their teachings were merely interpreted as a further confirmation of the teachings that had been proclaimed by Sakyamuni, Padsambhava and other Buddhist saints[30].

Today there are only 185 Christians in the entire population of Ladakh. Father Razu, the director of the Christian mission, a native Tibetan, received me cordially and related the history of the mission to me over tea and fresh pastries. Father Razu was unable to show me the diary that was actually the occasion of my visit, because it had mysteriously disappeared three or four years ago. At the time, a delegation from Zurich had been staying in Leh, and the grandson of the celebrated Dr. Francke (Dr. Marx's partner) had also spent some time in the house. The friendly priest was unable to explain the disappearance of the book, but he recalled that a certain Professor Hassnain from Srinagar had made photographs of the relevant pages

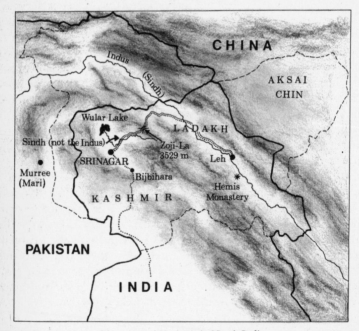

The Indian province of Jammu and Kashmir in North India.

four years before (see illustration). Hassnain was the professor who had supplied the reporter of *Stern* magazine with information for the report that appeared in 1973.

After looking into the matter of the missing diary at the municipal library and the library of the near-by village for Tibetan refugees, Chaglamsar, I resolved to end my stay in the "moon-land" of Ladakh and to cross over back to the idyllic "happy valley" of Kashmir. While going through the village of Mulbek, one passes a half-relief of Maitreya, the Saviour of the Buddhists, whose future advent was promised by Sakyamuni, chiselled into a vertical wall of stone, a full twelve metres high. The name Maitreya appears to be related to the Aramaic *"Meshia"*, the Messiah that the Jews continue to hope for as their saviour.

Kashmir is called India's Switzerland because of its fertile valleys with their large, smooth lakes and clear rivers, lying at the foot of the "Roof of the World", surrounded by wooded mountains. This paradise has attracted people from far-off regions ever since ancient times, and especially during the Golden Age of Kashmir, when pilgrims came to the green valley from all parts of the world in order to study the teachings of Gautama Buddha at the feet of the widely renowned scholars of Kashmir. Kashmir is regarded as the centre of Mahayana Buddhism, and as a place of the highest spiritual values and cultural endeavours. The storming fires of Islam have left scanty remnants of the extensive monasteries, temples and teachings of the ascetics.

Despite its idyllic location, Srinagar is a turbulent, loud and hectic city, humming with business activity. The city lies amidst a lavish spread of several lakes, on the left bank of the large Dal Lake (Dal = lentil) and is interlaced by a number of water-ways that have given Srinagar the atmosphere of a Venice of the East. A considerable part of the population lives in the houseboats that lie in great numbers on the canals of the old town, or which are moored to the banks of the lakes amidst the "floating gardens". The houseboats vary greatly in design, from simple "Dongas" to artistically carved and luxurious floating palaces with every conceivable comfort and convenience; all depending, of course, on the wealth of the owners. A short distance out of town, on a small lake, I found accomodation on an old but quaint little boat, which was to serve as my domicile for the whole season. From this boat one could be taken to any point in the city, by small, covered paddle-boat "taxis". A veritable fleet of boats run by

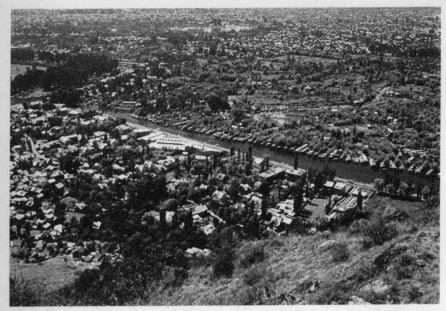

The view from the 'Throne of Solomon' to Srinagar with its houseboats and 'floating gardens' along the banks of Dal Lake.

merchants delivered all the necessities of life. Even a small post office on water would make its daily rounds. Needless to say, such an idyllic setting was most delightful, and many Europeans and Americans are enticed to spend longer periods of time in such houseboats, be it to learn the Sanskrit or simply to enjoy the lovely atmosphere.

From my abode I was able to reach the modern University of Kashmir in ten minutes by foot. I was to spend a great deal of time at the university, where I became absorbed in a wealth of interesting literature pertaining to my field of study. Finally I visited Professor Hassnain in his office.

Professor Hassnain is a scholar of international reknown (Doctor of Indology and Archaeology), the author of several books, and at the time guest professor in Japan and the United States, director of the "Kashmir Research Centre for Buddhist Studies" and a member of the International Conference for Anthropological Research in Chicago. At the time he was executing the duties of director of all the museums, collections and archives in Kashmir from his office. After I had informed him of my wishes and plans, he began to tell me with great enthusiasm about his own research, postponing all other appointments until the next day. After several hours of lively conversation, he closed his office and invited me to visit him at his home. Despite his high position, Professor Hassnain has remained a simple, modest and congenial person.

In the course of our conversation, I learned of all that he had uncovered during the past twenty-five years about Jesus' stay in India. Most of his knowledge was based on the pioneering work, *Jesus in Heaven on Earth*, the fruit of ten years of labour by the erudite lawyer, Al-Haj Khwaja Nazir Ahmad, and published in 1952 in Lahore.

All the historical facts, findings, connections and proofs remain incomprehensible and apparently absurd hypotheses, unless they are dealt with in the light of the most recent research about the life of Christ. Not until one establishes an irrefutable foundation for the

The author with Professor Hassnain in his garden in the Kashmiri capital of Srinagar.

historicity of Christ, will one be able to ascertain whether it is possible that Jesus did in fact go to India in his youth, and whether he survived the crucifixion and did not immediately depart to heaven in the ascension, but returned to India and died on at an old age.

Without such a foundation, anyone raised in the Christian tradition would dismiss the possibility of Jesus' having lived in India with an amused if rather sympathetic smile. It is hard indeed to divert the current of almost 2000 years of deeply-rooted tradition. Nevertheless, just because a story has been told for two thousand years, it need not necessarily be the true or complete account of those ancient facts.

Perhaps one can begin by taking a closer look at one aspect which has hardly succumbed to the mists of myth and legend, and which yet has surprising significance for our question of "Jesus in India". I refer to the presence of Jewish tribes east of Israel, even in Kashmir. We will start by taking another look at the impressive Biblical figure of Moses, the great Old Testament prophet. Let us try to widen our context, and so understand his significance better.

Chapter Two

Moses and the Children of God
The Origins of the Hebrews

   Modern researchers are of the opinion that a certain Abraham, patriarch of the Hebrews, was in fact a historical individual, and was born around 1700 B.C. . God Jahwe commanded him, "Get thee out of thy country, and from thy kindred, and from thy father's house, unto a land that I will shew thee;" (Genesis 12,1) Where, though, was the original home of Abraham's forefathers? One theory, represented by Blavatsky, holds that the first Semitic languages derive from the early phonetic corruptions of the ancient Indian language, Sanskrit. The word Adima is Sanskrit for "the first person (adi = first of all)", and *Hava* or *Heva* would signify "that which makes life complete" (hava = sacrificial offering; hevakin = devoted to, absorbed in). In *The Secret Doctrine*[1], H. P. Blavatsky shows how the Hebrews were descendants of the Chandalas, those Indians of humble status who did not belong to any of the castes. Many of them were ex-Brahmans, who had sought refuge in Chaldea, in Aria (Iran) and in the Sindh, and who belonged to the a-brahmana, the non-Brahmans, from as early as 8000 B.C. At a very early stage in their history, the Abrahm had protested against the inhumanity of the caste system. But they were unable to assert themselves against the ruling Brahman caste, so that in the end their only chance lay in emigration. According to Chapter 29 of Genesis, Abraham's son, Jacob, went to Laban, in the land of the "Sons of the East". Moreover, in the book of Joshua, the patriarchs of the people of Israel are said to have originally come from the East (i.e. east of Israel).

   "Thus saith the Lord God of Israel, Your fathers
   dwelt on the other side of the flood in old times,
   even Terah, the father of Abraham, and the father
   of Nachor: and they served other gods. And I took
   your father Abraham from the other side of the
   flood, and led him throughout all the land of Canaan,
   and multiplied his seed, and gave him Isaac"
   (Joshua 24,2–3).

Several passages in Genesis state that Abraham's real home was in the region of Haran. According to Genesis 11,32, while Abraham was living in Haran he was commanded by God to leave his home. Abraham sent his eldest servant "unto my country, and to my kindred," in order to find a wife for his son Isaac (Genesis 24). Haran is generally assumed to have been a place in lower Mesopotamia now called *Eski-Chârran*. Yet there is a small town in northern India called Haran, a few kilometres north of Srinagar, the capital of Kashmir, in which the remains of ancient walls have been excavated and dated by archaeologists back to long before the Christian era. Although it is no longer possible to reconstruct the wanderings of the nomadic tribes, full consideration of all factors does permit one fairly evident conclusion, that in c. 1730 B.C., the nomads under the leadership of Jacob began to wander towards Egypt.

The Egyptian priest and historian Manetho has left us the following account: "Unexpectedly, people of humble origins appeared from the East, courageously came into our country and took possession of it by force, without encountering any serious resistance." Murals in Egyptian burial chambers clearly depict the conquerors as having light skin and dark hair.

Wall paintings from an Egyptian tomb: An Egyptian official is receiving semitic nomads. The semites are depicted having brighter skin and a different profile than the Egyptians. With a group like this Joseph came to Egypt.

The Sermon of Saint Stephen in The Acts, Chapter 7 supplies a brief account of how Abraham, the patriarch of the Jews, was compelled to go to the land that the Lord of Glory wished to show him. He went from "the land of the Chaldaeans, and dwelt in Haran", travelling through Mesopotamia. It is conceivable that the nomadic families led by Abraham named the place in northwest Mesopotamia where they temporarily settled, after their home. Driven on by hunger, the group finally moved to Egypt, for Abraham's son Jacob had heard that "there was corn in Egypt". However the group was soon forced to return to Palestine. Although there was a good deal of strife among Abraham's sons, Isaac, Esau and Jacob, the family had become a unified tribe by the next generation.

Jacob's twelve sons crossed over into Egypt again during the time of the Hyksos dynasty, again because of a famine. The emigrants first settled in the province of Goshen. A Semitic settlement on the northeastern Nile delta has been found and dated in that era. To begin with, the Hebrew population spread rapidly throughout the entire land and gained wealth, influence and power. Before the close of the Hyksos dynasty in 1583 B.C., however, their position had already deteriorated due to internal disintegration and disunity.

Thus we find that the expression "Hebrew" was not originally applied to a national or ethnic group, but to any persons without permanent abode and rights, whose fate was to serve the Egyptians as a form of cheap labour (later even as forced labour), as can be seen in sources from the thirteenth and fourteenth centuries B.C. Exact accounts in Exodus (I,11) in which the ancestors of the Israelites are conscripted for the construction of the towns Pithom and Ramses, lead one to the conclusion that Ramses II (1301–1324 B.C.) was the oppressive Pharaoh in question. At that time some of the Semitic tribes then left Egypt under the leadership of Moses in search of the land of their fathers, the blessed land which had been promised by God Jahweh.

Manu – Manes – Minos – Moses

Things can be made easier and clearer if we take representative figures or "figureheads" from some of the main cultural lines of the Orient. 19th century Indologists probed the parallels in some depth. Thus the man who laid down political and religious laws in ancient India was called Manu. The lawgiver of the Egyptians was called Manes. The Cretan who went to Egypt to study laws which he intended to institute in Greece was called Minos. The leader of the Hebraic tribes and the proclaimer of the Ten Commandments was called Moses. Manu, Manes, Minos and Moses were to change the whole world. All four stood by the cradle of peoples destined to have enormous influence in the history of the world. All four laid down the laws that were to remain valid in the future and were to form the foundations of priestly and even theocratic societies. They all proceeded according to one archetypal pattern, which is evident in more than the mere similarities in the names and institutions they created.

Manu is Sanskrit for "A man of excellence, the lawgiver". All four names have a common Sanskrit origin (root man = *thought know* . . .; *also the base for man, mind etc.*).

At the beginning of every developing civilization, certain men are called upon to do greater deeds than others; they impress the masses and act to bring about progress or to rule. Instead of allowing themselves to be impressed by mere power, which serves as the highest law to the uneducated alone, cultural and spiritual leaders seek to wield their power in harmony with the one supreme Being, which exists in the consciousness of every man. Such men are endowed with an aura of mystery, and their origins and lives become wreathed in legends. They are deemed "prophets" or "emissaries of God", and they reformulate the obscure revelations of the past which they alone can explain. In their skilled hands, every physical reality can be transformed to become a manifestation of a heavenly power, which they can evoke or appease as they desire. Magicians of both Israel and India could, for instance, by putting a snake into a catatonic state, show it around as if it were a staff, and transform it back to its original condition; this has remained a popular trick in the repertoire of Indian fakirs.

Literal adherents of the verses of Manu, who joined with the Brahmans (the most influential caste) including the priests in order to topple the social structure of the Veda, were the cause of the decline and ruination of their people, who were to suffocate under the corrupt rule of the priesthood. Similarly, the scriptural preservers of the oral tradition of Moses simply took over the despotic role that his predecessors had played when ruling the people of Israel (or children of God).

Who was Moses?

The etymology of the name Moses is a matter of dispute. In Egyptian, mos *simply means child, or literally "is born" (e.g. Thut-moses)*. According to another interpretation, based on the Hebraic, the name derives from *mo*, water, and *useh*, save, which corresponds to the legend of Moses' having been found in a floating basket of reeds (Exodus 2,10). It is impossible to establish a consistent picture of the historical personage, and tradition has left many questions unanswered and created further mysteries. Historical research into the Old Testament has shown that Moses could not possibly have been the author of the five books attributed to him. The Pentateuch is the product of centuries of oral and written tradition. An inconsistency in diction, a great many of contradictions and repetitions, and irreconcilable variations in basic theological tenets give reason enough to believe that a variety of sources was used. Even if the darkness of aeons past has obscured a great deal, we can nonetheless be certain that Moses was in fact an historical figure. It is safe to assume that he grew up in the royal court, was raised by priests, attained a high level of education, and was influential as a civil servant in all spheres of the state. Moses made use of a peculiar mixture of pure doctrine and curious magical practices, a mix suffused with Vedic elements as well as elements of Egyptian idolatry. His intention was to proclaim the existence of a unique God, the God of Israel, and to end worship of all other gods; and he was compelled to resort to "miracles" to assert God's (his own) will. Greek and Roman mythology have been rejected as the religious roots of Christian belief, and the accounts of Moses have been accepted as such, – as difficult as it should be to accept that the vengeful God depicted by Moses as a devouring fire is the same God of the New Testament.

Whosoever opposed Moses in his drive for power was destroyed without mercy. Fire was a motif in such liquidations and was frequently used to demonstrate power; for Moses often used to illustrate his point in a rather incendiary manner. He evidently had a great variety of magic tricks at his disposal. Following his appearance before the magicians of Egypt (Exodus 7,8–13), Moses even gained renown as a great sorcerer among the ancient Greeks. In the early Christian era, apocryphal writings appeared, which complemented the Pentateuch, associating the magical content of the Pentateuch with Moses' authority. Editions of the "sixth and seventh Book of Moses", disseminated after the birth of Christ, returned to the Egyptian tradition, offering a series of magic words, sorcery, magical prayers and texts containing secret doctrines of various origins.

In *The Biblical Moses,* which appeared in 1928, Jens Juergens[2] proved that Egyptian priests were able to produce gunpowder and use it in fireworks and as a kind of Bengal light as early as six thousand years ago. Moreover, a clear implication of the research of the English archaeologist Professor Flinders Petri (Researches in the Sinai, 1906) is that Moses not only enjoyed authority over the Egyptian temples, but also over the royal mines in the Sinai and therefore the sulphur mine "Gnefru" which had been in operation from ca. 5000 B.C. Moses had learned about the production of gunpowder from the secret writings of the priests, and the composition of gunpowder (sulphur, saltpetre and charcoal) proved to be simple enough from a technical point of view. So when his subjects refused to obey him, (and he did preach a great deal "from the morning unto the evening" (Exodus 18,13ff.)), he called forth a devouring inferno, which was certain in its effect (Exodus 19,Il: 24,17: 33,9. L Deuteronomy 4,11; 4,24; 4,33; 4,36; 5,4; 5,5: 5,23; 9,3; 32,22).

As the authorized representative of his God of fire, Moses was able to command according to his every desire, and if the people resisted the sacrifices demanded of them, a simple demonstration of divine power was all that was needed to restore the peace. The incident on Mount Sinai (Exodus 19), the deaths of 250 people in a fire following the rebellion of Korah (Numbers 16,1–35), and the deaths of several thousand in a fire-storm when they rose against Moses (Numbers 16,36–50) are well-known instances of such demonstrations of power. When the sons of Aaron experimented with a "strange fire" that the Lord "commanded them not" in the tabernacle, they were fatally injured (Leviticus 10,1–7). Even Moses suffered from such severe burns, evidently the result of an explosion, that his face was horribly deformed and he was obliged to wear a special bandage (Exodus 34,29–35).

Moses continues to be regarded as the great lawgiver, but the Ten Commandments are in fact nothing more than a summarised excerpt of laws that had been valid among the peoples of the Near East and India long before Moses was born, and were even current in Babylon seven hundred years earlier. The famous laws of the Babylonian King Hammurabi (1728–1686 B.C.) contained all of the Ten Commandments, and these laws had themselves been based on the Indian Rig-Veda, which had already existed for millenia. The thought of an omniscient, invisible, single God, the father of the universe, a being of love and of goodness, the father of mercy, humanity and faith, existed in the Veda and in the Nordic Edda long before Moses. Even the Lord Zoroaster was expressly proclaimed as unique.

The papyrus of Prisse (ca. one thousand years before Moses) recounts that God said of himself: "I am the hidden one, the creator of Heaven and of all beings. I am the great God who is created by himself and without equal. I am yesterday and I know tomorrow. I am the law for every being, and the essence." The principle of a divine unity was referred to as "the unspeakable" in Egypt long before Moses spoke of "the nameless". "Nuk pu Nuk = I am who I am." (compare this with accounts in Exodus 3,14: "I am that I am.")

There is no longer any doubt that Moses actually existed as an historical person. His heroic deeds are nonetheless based for the most part on much older legends, for instance the legend of the ancient god Bacchus, originally Arabic, who had been rescued from the water like Moses, was able to cross the Red Sea with dry soles, wrote laws on slates of stone, had armies that were led by columns of fire, and emitted rays of light from his forehead.[3]

The Rig-Veda contains an account of Rama, who led his people into the heart of Asia and finally to India at least five thousand years ago. Rama, too, was a great lawgiver and a powerful hero. He caused springs to gush forth from deserts (cf. Exodus 17), showed his people a kind of manna for nourishment (cf. Exodus 16), and quelled an epidemic with the holy drink of soma, India's "water of life". Finally he conquered the "promised land" (India and Ceylon) and invoked hails of fire against the king. He was able to reach Ceylon via a bridge of land that had been exposed at ebb, at a place which is still referred to as the Bridge of Rama. Like Moses, Rama is also depicted with rays of light proceeding from his head, (the flames of enlightenment; see illustration).

Like Moses, Zoroaster (Zarathustra) also had holy fire at his disposal, with which he could perform the most extraordinary variety of tricks. According to the Greek writers Exodus, Aristotle and Hermundorius, Zoroaster had lived some five thousand years before Moses. He was of royal blood like Moses and was taken from his mother and left exposed. After completion of his thirtieth year, he became the prophet of a new religion. Heralded by rolls of thunder, God appeared to him clothed in light. Seated on a throne of fire on the holy mountain of "Albordj", encircled by flames, God announced his sacred law. Zoroaster also wandered with his supporters to a far-off "promised land", came up against the banks of a sea, and separated the water with the help of his God, so that God's chosen people might cross the sea with dry feet.

The Jewish accounts with which we are most familiar begin with the emigration of the tribes of Israel under the leadership of Moses from Egypt, and the search for another land for settlement as a new, independent people. The land of Goshen (Gosen), where the Israelites initially settled, has not yet been located beyond all doubt, but it must be on the east side of the Nile delta. Passages in the Bible mention a change of Pharaohs at the time. This coincided with the

Moses with ray-like protuberances similar to Bacchus and Rama.

expulsion of the Hyksos at the beginning of the eighteenth dynasty under Achmosis I. The direct route towards the north-east would have been from the Sea of Reeds to Palestine. The Philistines were blocking the route, however. It remains a mystery why Moses did not take the route to Beersheba, the longest standing refuge for the Israelites. At any rate, he escaped to the south. In the third month of the Exodus, the people arrived at Mount Sinai. Very probably the impressive demonstration of Moses' God of fire, Jahweh, took place on the mountain that is today referred to as "Jebel-Musha", the mountain of Moses. According to biblical tradition, the Israelites remained on Mount Sinai for eight months and then tried to move further into the promised land. The attempt failed, however, and the people of Israel had to wait at the oasis of Kades, according to the Bible for forty years (but forty is a symbolic number indicating a very long period).

At this point, Moses realized that he was not to be in the world much longer and that he would not be able to lead his people to the end of their long path (see Deuteronomy 31,1). He therefore proclaimed those laws that were to be regarded as sacred in the promised land, gave instructions for the transitional period following the crossing of the Jordan, made all other final arrangements, delivered a farewell speech and finally left with a few companions to reach the paradise "where milk and honey flow", and to die there (Deuteronomy 34,1–7). His place of burial remained unknown, for ". . . no man knoweth of his sepulchre unto this day."

Because a very detailed description of the place exists, it is all the more surprising that Moses' grave could not be found.

"And Moses went up from the plains of Moab unto the mountain of Nebo, to the top of Pisga . . . over against Beth-peor . . ."

It seems equally improbable that the people of Israel should not have arranged for a place of burial worthy of their great saviour and leader, traces of which should at least be in existence. There are, in fact, traces of such a grave, but nowhere near Palestine. They are in the north of India.

Moses' Grave in Kashmir

The Bible contains five points of orientation for Moses' place of burial (cf. Deuteronomy 34): the plains of Moab, Mount Nebo in the Abarim Mountains, the peak of Mount Pisga, Beth-peor and Heshbon. The "promised land" had been expressly reserved for the children of Israel alone, and not for all Hebrews (Numbers 27,12). The land must be beyond the Jordan. If it is possible to find the places mentioned in the texts, it should also be possible to locate the "promised land".

The literal meaning of Beth-peor is "a place that opens", for instance a valley that opens out into a plain. The river Jhelum in the north of Kashmir is called "Behat" in Persian, and the small town of Bandipur at the point where the valley of the Jhelum opens out into the broad plain of Lake Wular was once called Behat-poor. Beth-peor became Behat-poor, which is now Bandipur in the region of Tehsil Sopore, 80 kilometres north of Srinagar, the capital of Kashmir. Only approximately 18 kilometres northeast of Bandipur lies the small village of Hasba or Hasbal. This is referred to as Heshbon in the Bible (Deuteronomy 4,46), and is mentioned in connection with Beth-peor and Pisga. On the cliffs of Pisga (now: Pishnag), north of Bandipur and only 1.5 kilometres northeast of the village Aham-Sharif, there is a spring famous for the healing quality of its waters. In the Bible, the valley and the plains of Mowu are called the plains of Moab, ideal pasture land, about five kilometres northwest of Mount Nebo. Mount Nebo is a single mountain in the range of Abarim and is always mentioned in the context of Beth-peor'. All five names are to be found within close proximity to one another. Mount Nebo, also called Baal Nebu or Niltoop, offers a splendid view of Bandipur and the entire highlands of Kashmir.

> "And the Lord said unto him, This is the land which I swore unto Abraham, unto Isaac, and unto Jacob, saying, I will give it unto thy seed: I have caused thee to see it with thine eyes, but thou shalt not go over thither. So Moses the servant of the Lord died there in the land of Moab, according to the word of the Lord. And he buried him in a valley in the land of Moab, over against Beth-peor: but no man knoweth of his sepulchre unto this day" (Deuteronomy 34, 4–6.)

It is just possible to reach the village Aham-Sharif, about twelve kilometres from Bandipur, by car. From Aham-Sharif one must proceed by foot if one wishes to reach the little village of Booth at the foot of Mount Nebo. One climbs for about an hour on a continuous incline along a barely visible path, moving westwards. The mountain's form and the luxurious vegetation are strongly reminiscent of the hills of Europe. After crossing several fields, one comes across the small hamlet of Booth directly beneath Mount Nebo, which is also called Baal Nebu by the locals. The "Wali Rishi" is the authorized grave watchman, and he leads strangers to a place with a sort of unfenced garden above the village, upon which a small mausoleum has been constructed. The humble hut serves as the burial place of an Islamic saint, Sang Bibi, a female hermit and two of her followers. Somewhat to the side, in the shadow of the little wooden building, one can barely make out a stone in the shape of a column, pushing about a metre out of the soil and almost completely covered with grass: *the tombstone of Moses.*

The Wali Rishi explains that the Rishis have been tending the grave for over 2700 years out of deep reverence. And in fact, the grave is near the plains of Moab, near the top of Pisga, on the mountain of Nebo, across from Beth-peor, and from this place one has a splendid view of a fresh and blossoming land, forever green, in which "milk and honey flow", a true paradise. In this area, as in other parts of Kashmir, there are numerous places with biblical names, some of them called the "Muquam-i-Musa," i.e., "the place of Moses". To the north of Pisga lies the small village of Pisga, (Deuteronomy 4,44–49), which is today called Hasbal; and south of Srinagar, at Bijbihara, a place on the banks of the river is still referred to as "Moses' Bath". There one can see a magic stone, called Ka-Ka-Bal or Sang-i-Musa (Stone of Moses). The stone weighs approximately 70 kilogramm, and according to legend the stone is supposed to rise through its own power and remain suspended at about one metre, if eleven people touch it with one finger and speak the magic formula "ka-ka, ka-ka" at the same time. The number eleven and the Stone itself represent the tribes of Israel.

Another place named after Moses is near Auth Wattu (the eight paths) near Handwara Tehsil. The cliffs near the confluence of the rivers Jhelum and Sindh (not the Indus), north of Srinagar near Shadipur, are called Kohna-i-Musa, "the cornerstone of Moses". It is

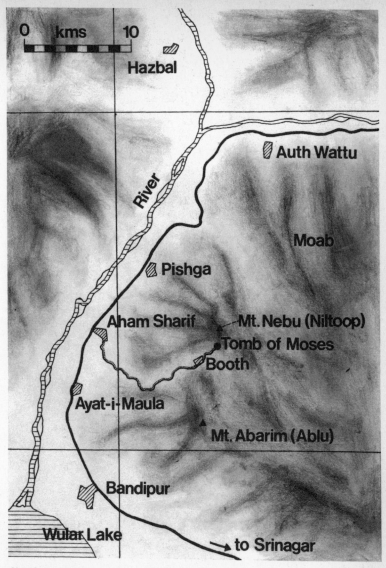

0 kms 10

Hazbal

River

Auth Wattu

Moab

Pishga

Aham Sharif

Mt. Nebu (Niltoop)

Tomb of Moses

Booth

Ayat-i-Maula

Mt. Abarim (Ablu)

Bandipur

Wular Lake

→ to Srinagar

Sketch showing the area around the Grave of Moses: the mountain Nebo, the slopes of Pisga, the mountains of Abarim (Ablu/Abul), Bandipur (Beth-peor), Hazbal (Hesbon), Auth Wattu, Ayat-i-Maula, Moab and Aham Sharif.

believed that Moses rested on this rock. Ayat-i-Maula (Aitmul = the sign of God), about three kilometres north of Bandipur, is another places where Moses was said to have rested.

From Conquest to Exile

Following Moses' death, the twelve tribes of Israel gradually increased their hold over Canaan, achieving total hegemony under the leadership of Joshua in the thirteenth century B.C., after which the land was distributed by lots. The process of the acquisition and adaptation of the land took place over a period of 150 years. In the song of Debora (Judges 5,8) the population is estimated at forty thousand Israelites, ruled by strong dictators, the judges, in accordance with the laws of Moses. But the power of the judges did not last long enough to transform the inconstant nomads into a united people. The Israelites needed a king to lead them with a firm hand. Samuel, the last of the judges, finally anointed Saul as King of Israel at the end of the eleventh century B.C. But not until the reign of King David (around the first half of the tenth century) did Israel finally become a unitary state with its capital in Jerusalem. Under the reign of David's son, Solomon, the famous temple was constructed.

Solomon has attained fame throughout the world by virtue of his wisdom. But the biblical texts attributed to him were certainly written after his time. It is unfortunate one does not know to which teachers he owed his wisdom.

Helena Petrowna Blavatsky wrote the following about Solomon in *Isis Unveiled*:

> "Solomon, celebrated by posterity (according to the historian Flavius Josephus: Antiquities, Volume VIII, Chapters 2 and 5) for his arts of magic, attained his knowledge in India through Hiram, the King of Ophir, and perhaps through Sheba. His ring, usually known as the 'seal of Solomon', famed for its influence over many spirits and demons in old folk legends, is also of Indian origin."[5]

Blavatsky then quotes from the chapter on the natural history of Travancore[6] in Dr. Mateer's book, *The Land of Charity*. While relating the background of the name of a bird, the peacock, the writer sheds new light on the holy scriptures. King Solomon sent a fleet to Tarshish that returned years later, laden with "gold, and silver, and ivory, and apes, and peacocks" (1 Kings 10,22).

The word used in the Hebraic bible for the peacock was "tukki". Because the Jews did not, of course, have their own word for the beautiful bird before King Solomon introduced it to Judea, "tukki" was undoubtedly simply adopted from "toki", the word for peacock in the southern Indian language of Tamil. In Hebraic, the word for ape is "koph", – in Indian, it is "kaphi". Ivory was available in surplus in southern India, and gold is to be found in the rivers of India's west coast (Karnataka delivers up to today 90 % of the total gold production of India). Solomon's ships were accustomed to voyages to the East. One might add that in addition to "gold, and silver, and apes, and ivory, and peacocks", King Solomon and his friend Hiram also brought another exotic souvenir home with them: their "magic" and their "wisdom".[7]

In the first Book of Kings, it is written that Solomon presented Hiram, King of Tyrus, twenty cities, among them Kabul, once part of the greater Indian empire. On the mountain above the city of Srinagar stands a small temple, called "Takht-i-Suleiman", the throne of Solomon. According to an inscription, the "new temple" was restored in 78 A.D. by King Gopadatta (also called Gopananda) on the foundations of the old, delapidated building. Tradition tells us that Solomon visited the land (Kashmir), and that it was he who divided the mountain of Barehmooleh, thereby creating an outlet for the water that was later to form Lake Dal, and that he constructed the small building (Takht-i-Suleiman) that is still known as the throne of Solomon[8] (See illustration).

The local Moslem population still knows another name for Kashmir: "Baghi Suleiman", the Garden of Solomon. When Solomon died in around 930 B.C., his son, Rehoboam, succeeded him. Almost immediately after he mounted the throne, a revolt broke out under the leadership of the exiled Ephraimite, Jeroboam, because of the high taxes demanded by the royal house. As a consequence of the revolt, the tribes of the north gained independence and the empire was split in two. The ten tribes of the north made Jeroboam their leader and called their empire the Kingdom of Israel. The two remaining tribes of the south were ruled by the house of David, and called their kingdom Judah. The two brother states existed as enemies alongside one another for more than 250 years, and the population grew to about 300,000 during the 400 years in which the Hebrews remained settled. During the so-called Age of Kings, neither state succeeded in

Takht-i-Suleiman, the Throne of Solomon on the mountain Barehmooleh, which was restored in A.D. 78 by King Gopadatta of Kashmir.

mastering internal unrest and attacks from neighboring states. During the royal dynasty of Jehu (845–747 B.C.), Israel was first occupied by the Assyrians under Shargon II for three years, and finally destroyed during the conquest of the capital of Samaria in the year 722. Judah was able to survive for another hundred years as a vassal state subject to tribute, until the Babylonian king Nebuchadnezzar took Jerusalem and destroyed the city in 587 B.C., signifying the end of the state of Judah. The conquerors expelled the population by use of brute force. The two tribes of Judah and Benjamin, which comprised the southern kingdom of Judah, were spared at the onset and sent by Nebuchadnezzar into exile in Babylonia. The King of Persia, Cyrus II, later allowed about half of the exiles to return to their homeland, after 50 years of exile, in 535 B.C.

Those who had been deported from the northern state of Israel 130 years earlier had a very different fate altogether. The ten tribes that had been driven out by the Assyrians, the greater part of the population, moved eastwards and were never heard of again. "So was Israel carried away out of their own land until this day" (2 Kings 17,23). They entered history as "the ten lost tribes of Israel", and until today have been regarded as having completely vanished and as untraceable. Numerous undeniable clues indicate that most of the "lost tribes", after centuries of wandering and political confusion, arrived at the promised "praised land", the "land of the fathers", northern India, where they found peace and tranquillity unto this day.

The Children of Israel
The Flood took place in Kashmir

According to the genealogy of the Bible, Abraham was a direct descendent of Noah, God's chosen one, who alone was granted the grace of surviving the flood with his family. The Biblical legends give no indication as to the origins of Abraham's father, and simply relate the family tree of humanity up until Noah and the natural catastrophe of a great flood. Archaeologists came across a clay layer of two to three metres in depth while excavating in the region of Ur in Mesopotamia; sherds were found both above and below this deposit. But the clay layer merely proves the occurrence of a local flood in the region of Ur. A document in cuneiform from Nineveh portrays the end of the catastrophe:

"And all mankind turned to clay. The land became as flat as a roof."

This layer of clay has been used as evidence for the flood of the Bible; and it would fit into the biblical history very nicely indeed, if archaeologists had not estimated that the date of this flood was approximately 4000 B.C. One can state with certainty that Semitic shepherd tribes had not yet arrived in the land of the two rivers at that time[9]. Hence, they could not have survived the flood and later given testimony as eye witnesses. The flood in the biblical accounts must have been a different one.

The Flood is a part of universal tradition, and is recounted in the mythology of various peoples. There have been many ice ages on earth, and unheard of floods with various causes have undoubtedly been equally numerous.

In the Sumerian Epic of Gilgamesh, discovered at around the turn of the century in the ruins of the ancient library of Nineveh, written in cuneiform on slates of baked clay, the hero Utnapishtim survives a flood. Utnapishtim is the Noah of the Sumerians, and the flood is depicted as an arbitrary act of the gods. In this account, as in the Bible, a man builds a ship according to the advice of the gods and thus survives a flood that destroys all life around him.

Alexander von Humboldt mentions that the Peruvians have the same legend, and in an account of the flood from Polynesia, the hero is even called Noa. There are more than 250 accounts of the legend of the flood in the world. Which, though, is the flood of biblical accounts?

Because the Indian Vedas are certainly the oldest of revelations about the history of man, it would seem logical to assume that the account of the flood in the Vedas was the first in existence. The flood appears as a legend in Hindu scriptures, but is not sacrosanct. The Mahabharata (the Great Song) portrays the event in the following manner: True to the predictions of the Lord, the Earth was populated by Man, and the progeny of Adamis and Hevas soon became so numerous and wicked that they were no longer able to live in peace with one another. They forgot God and his promise and even rebelled against Him. The Lord (Brahma) thereupon decided to punish his creatures in a manner to serve as an example for generations to come. He looked for the man most worthy of being saved for the preservation and continuation of the species. His choice was Vaivasvata, and he let him know his will. On the holy bank of the river Virim, Vaivasvata saved a small fish that later proved to be an avatar (an incarnation of a god) of Vishnu. The fish warned the just man that the end of the world was near, and that all of its inhabitants were doomed. Vishnu, in the form of the fish, then ordered Vaivasvata to build a ship for himself and his family. When the ship was ready and Vaivasvata and his family inside with the seeds of every plant and a pair of every species of animal, the big rains began and the rivers began to overflow. Then a great fish with a horn on its head placed itself at the bow of the ark, and the holy man fixed a sail to the horn. The fish then pulled the ship safely through the furious elements, until the ship landed intact on the peaks of the Himalayas (cf. Genesis 6).

The number of days of the flood accords with the number in the accounts of Moses (40 days).

The German designation for the Great Flood, "die Sintflut", has an obscure etymology. Traditional scholarship maintains that in Old High German, "Sint" simply meant a "great flood", which was later transformed to "Sündflut", – the flood of sin, – a rather dissatisfying explanation!

There is, however, a more credible explanation. Sindh is simply the old name of the mighty river to which the entire subcontinent of India owes its name: the Indus. In ancient times, India referred to a land that extended far beyond its current geographic borders. Tibet and Mongolia also belonged to India, and in the West Iran of today was also included. Seen from the West, the Sindh-Indus is the most powerful river to be crossed in order to arrive in India. Running from north to south, the Indus flows through Pakistan and flows through a formidable delta into the Arabian Sea. "The other side of the flood", Abraham's place of origin, could certainly have been in the land beyond the Indus (cf. Joshua 24,2–3), which serves as India's natural barrier to the West.

Today, Sindh designates the province in the valley of the Indus in southeast Pakistan, which runs along the border of India's Punjab, the land of five rivers, with its capital in Karachi. The region is 140,000 square kilometers in area and extremely fertile due to constant flooding.

In the northern Indian province of Kashmir, there is yet another river with the name Sindh. The other Sindh is less conspicuous than its big brother, the Indus, but perhaps at least as significant in explanation of the term *Sintflut*. This Sindh flows northwards from the city of Srinigar through the region visible from the mountain, Nebo, from which Moses beheld paradise before his death. The source of the small Sindh is near the Cave of Amarnath, the goal of great pilgrimages during full moon in the month of August every year. According to legend, the Hindu God Shiva was supposed to have let his wife Parvati into the secret of the creation on this spot. If one follows the course of the river downstream, one arrives after three days of hiking at the village of Sonamarg, still 2,600 metres in altitude, "the golden meadow" that Notovitch crossed on his way to Ladakh across the Zoji-La pass, more than 3,500 metres in altitude. The path, along the river, leads from Sonamarg onwards to Srinagar, 84 kilometres further on, by way of a route over ancient wooden bridges, through small villages with luxuriant green meadows, apricot, pear and apple trees. Artistically carved window frames and decorated wooden roofs are evidence of the prosperity of the region. The closer one comes to Srinagar, the more fertile the valley appears in its depths. After the village of Kangan, the valley opens into vast terraces of rice and corn fields that extend to Gandarbal on the left bank of the Sindh.

All in all, Kashmir appears to be an enormous Garden of Eden, and the enormous marshy areas and large, shallow lakes bear witness to a gigantic flood in times long past.

Is Kashmir the "Promised Land"?

According to the Bible, Paradise, the place of the creation, lay eastward. "And the Lord God planted a garden eastward in Eden; and there he put the man whom he had formed" (Genesis 2,8). The following passage specifies the position of the Garden of Eden by mention of four rivers: "And a river went out of Eden to water the garden: and from thence it was parted, and became into four heads" (Genesis 2,10). In Mesopotamia, the land between two rivers, usually considered the Garden of Eden, there are only two rivers, als the name suggest.

In contrast to this, northern India can boast today five great rivers, all tributaries of the Indus (Sindh), giving the country its name: the land of five rivers, the Punjab. Since 1947, the province has been politically divided into an Indian and a Pakistani region. The five tributaries of the Indus, all on the left side of the river, are called Jhelum, Chenab, Ravi, Beas and Sutlej. The Punjab was the region with the earliest civilization in India (the Indus culture dates from ca. 3000 B.C.), and archaeologists have found traces of a civilization going back 50,000 years in Kashmir.

In 1983 the renowned Syrian historian Prof. K.S. Salibi published his book "The Bible came from Asir" in Germany. In it he proves with scientific accuracy that Palestine could never possibly have been the country of origin of the biblical history. In his linguistic investigations Salibi concludes that only *a handful of the thousands of biblical geographical names could be located in Palestine.* (p.35)

"For more than a century traces of the Hebrews have been searched for in Mesopotamia and also those traces showing the path of their assumed migration from there via Northern Syria to Palestine, but never have been really discovered." (p.35)

"The reconstruction of the early Jewish history in Palestine is not possible from the canonical texts of the Hebrew Bible nor from other sources."

Salibi also found out that in the Old Testament animals and minerals were mentioned which cannot be found in Palestine at all.

Kashmir means "Paradise on Earth" in the language of the land. The etymology can, however, be interpreted in various other ways.

Kush was a grandson of Noah, whose descendants were to populate the earth, naming the countries in which they settled after themselves. According to the accounts of the Creation, "And the name of the second river is Gihon; the same is it that compasseth the whole land of Kush." (Genesis 2,13). All the names mentioned in the Bible have been subject to a great number of changes due to the influence of a great variety of languages and changes in language. "Kush" of the Bible could easily have become Kash, and "Mir" has a great variety of meanings: in Russian, "Mir" is the region of a community, in Turkish, "Mir" is an honorary title, and in Persian, "Mir" means something of value, a jewel. Noah's descendants and the regions that they settled in were recorded in Chapter 10 of Genesis, which also tells us, "and the border of the Canaanites was . . . even unto Lasa" (Genesis 10,19). Lhasa is the capital of Tibet.

Another interpretation is based on the Hebrew word, Kaser (also Kashir or Kosher), which means "flawless", particularly when applied to food. According to Jewish law (Leviticus 11, Deuteronomy 14), only animals that have been slaughtered and bled ritually can be eaten. People who submitted to such stern regulations, and thus distinguished themselves from the rest of the world were called Kasher, as was the land that they populated; later Kasher turned into Kashmir.

A further interpretation goes back to the name of a saint "Kashyapa" who is supposed to have lived in the region ages ago. Kashyap means "turtle" in Sanskrit. In the ancient Indian world view, the Earth was equated with the back of the turtle swimming in the water, and "Kashyap" was the name of both God and His divine people that

63

inhabited the Earth. The "children of God", called "Israel" in Hebrew, are called "Kashyab" in Sanskrit. "Kashyab-Mar" (God's land) finally became Kashmir.

The Ten Lost Tribes of Israel

Not until the nineteenth century, and then evidently as a consequence of colonisation, did the West begin to take a more profound interest in the countries of the Middle East. At that time, surprising reports began to arrive about tribes in remotest north India that were evidently of Jewish descent.

The minister Joseph Wolff, a scholar in both law and theology, reported in his two-volume work *Account of a mission to Bokhara in the years 1843–45*, Volume 1, page 13[10]: "All the Jews in Turkistan claim that the Turkmenes are descendants of Togarmah, a son of Gomer, who is mentioned in the Old Testament (Genesis 10,3)." And on page 14: "In Bokhara there are around 10,000 Jews. The chief rabbi has assured me that Bokhara means Habor, and that Balkh is Halag (2 Kings, 17, 6). During the reign of terror of Gengis Khan, all written accounts were destroyed."

The account continues: "There are ancient legends in Bok that say that some of the ten lost tribes of Israel went as far as China. I asked the Jews about this important fact in particular" (page 15).

"Some Afghanis maintain that they are descendants of Israel. According to these accounts, Affghaun was the nephew of Asaph, the son of Berachias, who built the temple of Solomon. The descendants of this Affghaun were led away to Babylon by Nebuchadnezzar, because they were Israelites. From there they were led to the mountains of Fores in Afghanistan and later converted by force to Islam. They possess the book *Majmooa Alansab*, a collection of genealogies in the Persian language" (page 16).

"I was surprised to hear that Sergeant Riley considered the Afghans as a people of Israelite ancestry" (page 19).

And finally, on page 56, Wolff wrote: "I spent six days with the children of Rachab, Bani Arbal. Children of Israel from the Dan tribe, who live with Terim Hatramawl, were also there."

A much-travelled French scholar, G. T. Vigne (a member of the Royal Geographical Society) wrote in "A personal account of a voyage to Chuzin, Kabul, in Afghanistan"[11]: "The father of Ermiah was the father of the Afghans. He was a contemporary of Nebuchadnezzar, called himself Beni Israel and had forty sons. But a descendant in the thirty-fourth generation was called Kys, and he was a contemporary of the prophet Mohammed."

Stone with aramaic inscription found in Sirkap near Taxila.

Drs. James Bryce and Keith Johnson note on page 25 of their "Comprehensive Description of Geography"[12] under the heading "Afghanistan" that the Afghanis "trace their lineage back to King Saul of Israel and call themselves 'Ben-i-Israel'."

According to A. Burnes, the legends of Nebuchadnezzar confirm that they were transplanted from the Holy Land to Ghore, in northwest Kabul. They remained Israelites until 682 A.D., when the Arabian sheikh, Khaled-ibn-Abdalla, converted them to Islam.

There is a great deal of additional literature on the settlement of Afghanistan and the surrounding areas by the Hebrews. One of the most important works is *The Lost Tribes* by Dr. George Moore[13], who found numerous Hebrew inscriptions on archaelogical sites in India. Near Taxila, in Sirkap, currently Pakistan, a stone was uncovered bearing Aramaic inscriptions, the language that Jesus spoke (see illustration).

In the middle of the nineteenth century, a society was founded in England that dealt exclusively with the rediscovery of the ten lost tribes of Israel, – the Identification Society of London. Most of the works on the topic by British authors have come from this society. It would be superfluous to list all the authors and works, around thirty in number, that prove that the Kashmirian population is of Israelite descent. One could list more than three hundred names, of tribes, clans, families, individuals, villages, regions, estates and other geographical terms of the Old Testament, that are closely related linguistically to the same or similar names in Kashmir and its environs.

Name in Kashmir	Biblical name	Biblical reference
Amal	Amal	1 Chron. 7,35
Asheria	Asher	Genesis 30, 13
Attai	Attai	1 Chron. 12,11
Bal	Baal	1 Chron. 5,5
Bala	Balah	Jos. 19,3
Bera	Beerah	1 Chron. 5,6
Gabba	Gaba	Jos. 18,24
Gaddi	Gaddi	Numbers 13,ll
Gani	Guni	1 Chron. 7,13
Gomer	Gomer	Genesis 10,2

. . . and so on!

Places in Kashmir	(Province) name	Biblical	Reference
Agurn	(Kulgam)	Agur	Proverbs 30,1
Ajas	(Srinagar)	Ajah	Genesis 36,24
Amonu	(Anantnag)	Amon	1 King, 22,26
Amariah	(Srinagar)	Amariah	1 Chron. 23,19
Aror	(Awantipur)	Baalpeor	Numbers 25,3
Behatpoor	(Handwara)	Bethpeor	Deut.34,6
Birsu	(Awantipur)	Birsha	Genesis 14,2
Harwan	(Srinagar)	Haran	2 Kings 19,12

. . . and so on!

The inhabitants of Kashmir are different from the other races of India in every respect. Their appearance, their physiognomy, their way of life, their behaviour, their morals, their character, their clothing, their language, mores, customs, and habits are typically Israelite in origin.

The profiles of these two young men clearly show the difference between the races of North India - Aryan descent (with turban, right); semitic descent (left).

The Kashmiris never use fat or greaves for frying or baking; like the Israelis, they only use oil. Most Kashmiris prefer boiled fish, called "Phari" as a remembrance of the time before their exodus from Egypt; "We remember the fish, which we did eat in Egypt freely" (Numbers 11,5).

Butchers' knives in Kashmir are in the half-moon shape typical of the Israelites, and even the rudders of the boat people (Hanjis) are in the typical heart shape.

The men wear the same unusual caps in the characteristic jewish form (jarmulka) and the clothing of the old women of Kashmir (Pandtanis) is very similar to that of old Jewish women; both also wear head-scarves and belts. Like young Jewesses, the girls of Kashmir practice the custom of standing in two facing lines with linked arms, and moving together forwards and backwards to a given rhythm. Such songs are called "Roph".

After bearing a child, a woman of Kashmir waits forty days to bathe; this, too, is a Jewish custom.

Many of the older graves in Kashmir lie facing the west; Islamic graves always point from north to south. A great number of such graves are to be found in Haran, Rajpura, Syed Bladur Sahib, Kukar Nagh and Awantipura. At the cemetary of Bijbihara, the place where the bath and stone of Moses are to be found, there is an old grave with an inscription in Hebrew. Sixty-five kilometres to the south of Srinagar and just a few kilometres from the "Bath of Moses", one can see the Temple of Martand. Despite the figures of various Hindu divinities chiselled into the outside walls of this ancient and formidable building, the construction of the temple is clearly quite different from conventional Hindu architecture. The construction is in fact much more similar in its vestibule, its steps, its pillared hall and sacred interior, to a typical Jewish temple.

Is this not perhaps this temple that a stranger showed to the prophet, Ezekiel, during the time of the Babylonian exile (586–538)? In fact, the Temple of Martand does stand on a "very high mountain", unknown to Ezekiel, – the Himalaya: and at its side, a spring gushes forth that flows into the Jhelum farther downstream. (Cf. Ezekiel, Chapters 40–43.)

The relation between ancient Israel and Kashmir can most clearly be demonstrated linguistically. Kashmirian is different from all the other Indian languages, the origins of which are Sanskrit. The development of the language of Kashmir has been greatly influenced by Hebraic. Abdul Ahad Azad writes: "The language of Kashmir derives from Hebrew. According to tradition, in ancient times Jewish peoples settled here, whose language changed into the Kashmirian of today. There are many Hebrew words that are quite obviously connected with the language of Kashmir."[14]

I have chosen a few particularly notable examples among myriads of others:

Hebrew	Kashmirian	Meaning
Akh	Akh (-ui)	single
Ajal	Ajal	death
Arah	Arah	saw
Asar	Asar	plague
Awn	Awan (on)	blind
Aob	Aob	ample
Ahad	Ahad (ak)	one
Aaz	Aaz (az)	today
Ahal	Hal	belt
Awah	Awah	agree
Aosh	Aosh	tears

. . . and so on!

The Spread of Buddhism

The world-wide spread of Buddhism long before the pre-Christian era can essentially be attributed to the initiative of one of the greatest rulers, not only in the history of India, but in the history of the world: the Emperor Ashoka, who lived from 273 to 232 A.D. Ashoka was simply one of the most significant political, moral and intellectual personalities of all time. During his reign the first war between Rome and Carthage took place in Europe. Having experienced the monstrosities of war in his youth, the Emperor firmly condemned it and instead turned entirely to the peaceful teachings of Buddhism.

69

Many of his beneficial laws and human decrees have been preserved until today in inscriptions on buildings and temples. In one decree, the Emperor commanded that all living beings be protected: "All people are my children. Just as I should wish my children to enjoy the salvation and happiness that this (earthly) and that (heavenly) world offer, so do I wish the same for all people."

Ashoka had more than 84,000 Buddhist monasteries built in India, and throughout his enormous empire he constructed hospitals for people and animals. He provided the incentive for the second Buddhist World Council of Pataliputra (today = Patna), the capital of his empire, in which thousands of monks took part. In accordance with the duties prescribed by Buddha, Ashoka organised the propagation of the Buddhist teaching and thus caused the spread of the spirit of India to the farthest countries. He fulfilled the concept of missionary activity by sending Buddhist missionaries not only to all the towns of India and Ceylon, but also to Syria, Egypt and Greece via the Silk Road.

The spreading of the law of Buddha was one of the obligations that the Buddha Sakyamuni had himself imposed on his followers. "Go, oh monks, and rove about, for the benefit and welfare of the many, out of sympathy for the world, to the advantage and for the welfare of the gods and of men. And may not two of you take the same path. Preach the teaching that is beneficial . . . preach it in its spirit and in its letter; present the practice of religious life in the fullness of its purity." Those monks and other followers thus moved out and about, each one of them dependant upon others. The monks lived as beggars and were reliant on the alms of their lay following. They possessed nothing other than the clothes they had on their backs. Their lives were defined by their renunciation of all worldly goods, – but their renunciation had none of the ascetic severity of other movements. Their principal occupation was to meditate on the teachings of Buddha and to gradually free themselves from the passions of the world. The act of going out into the open (pravrajya) was a requisite for joining the community; this was the symbolic act of leaving the house, the symbol of the life of the layman in order to enter the order of wandering monks (the second meaning of the word, pravrajya), and lead a life without shelter.

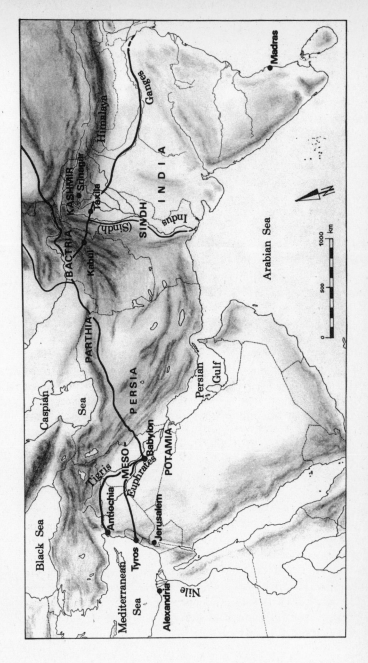

The Silk Road provided a bridge from the Far East right across to the Mediterranean even in prehistoric times, with a flow of goods and philosophical ideas.

71

For the purpose of fulfilling the admission requirements, it sufficed to don the yellow monk's clothing, to have one's head shaved and to utter a threefold incantation. The mandatory minimum age was seven, which had been the age at which Rahula, the "son of the exalted", entered the community.

At the ordination, the novice is informed of the four fundamental rules of monastical life:
— to nourish oneself by alms alone;
— to dress oneself in clothes taken up from the dust;
— to tarry at the foot of trees;
— to heal one's wounds with the urine of cows.

Without exception, the monks led a nomadic existence. Canonical accounts report of Buddha and his followers traversing the entire Ganges basin while meditating and preaching Buddhist teachings, alone or more often in groups – from town to town and village to village.

A remarkable parallel between the lives of the Buddhists and of Jesus' followers is evident; Jesus also sent forth his disciples to wander and preach the word, from village to village, in one last, desperate attempt to convince the people of Israel of his message. Mark VI, 7: "And he called unto him the twelve, and began to send them forth by two and two; and gave them power over unclean spirits; (8) And commanded them that they should take nothing for their journey, save a staff only, no scrip, no bread, no money in their purse: (9) But be shod with sandals; and not put on two coats. (10) And he said unto them, In what place soever ye enter into an house, there abide till ye depart from that place. (11) And whosoever shall not receive you, nor hear you, when ye depart thence, shake off the dust under your feet for a testimony against them. Verily I say unto you, It shall be more tolerable for Sodom and Gomorrha in the day of judgement, than for that city. (12) And they went out, and preached that men should repent. (13) And they cast out many devils, and anointed with oil many that were sick, and healed them."

Here, as in Buddhism, conversion by force is quite out of the question. The salvation of the many can only be achieved by preaching as described in Chapter 53 of Isaiah. Documents in Singhaleseien indicate that after the Council of Haran (now Harwan, near Srinagar), which took place at the time of Kanishka, missionaries were again sent forth to Kashmir, Gandhara, Mahisamandala, to Vanavasi, to Yonarattha ("Land of the Greeks") and to Ceylon.

Incidentally, it seems that Buddhism, which was far less political and far more flexible than Brahmanism, was well able to deal with the various elements that had penetrated and were settling the Indus basin, the upper Ganges basin, and the Deccan. Such conquests had been undertaken by the Greeks of Bactria in the second century B.C., and by the Scythians and the Parthians in the first century B.C. The great conqueror Menander engaged in peaceful discourse with the Buddhist monk Nagasena in *Milindapanha*. The Scythian rulers in particular, the founders of the Kushan dynasty, turned out to be great fosterers of Buddhism after their conversion. The most famous of that dynasty, Kanishka, became a Buddhist whose zeal was to rival that of Ashoka.

The Council of Haran was exemplary for its time. According to various sources, it took place under the rule of Kanishka during the second half of the first century A.D. in Kashmir. Like the Council of Pataliputra during the reign of Ashoka, it seems to have been attended by only a part of the Buddhist monastical community, probably in this case the Sarvastivadin, who were particularly numerous in north-western India. Regardless of Kanishka's own personal contribution on the occasion, it is likely that the Saravastivadin of Kashmir deemed it necessary to submit their Tripitaka (= the "triple basket" of the teaching) to thorough inspection in order to discuss the diverging, reformistic tendencies that had evolved in the community. It is impossible to establish the actual outcome because of contradictions in the sources.

Was Jesus an Orthodox Jew?

The fact that Jesus can be said to be the perfect embodiment of the ideal which sprung up in India in the budding Mahayana Buddhism of his time is of special importance. Even in the minutest details, he represented the characteristics of a Bodhisattva ideal as it had just been formed in the third century B.C. when Buddhism changed from the more selfish monks' religion of Hinayana to a universal and popular religion. The earthly existence of a Bodhisattva is completely determined by his commission as a saviour who has to guide all souls

73

onto the rightous path so as to give them salvation from earthly sufferings.

In spite of all attempts to obscure the true origin of the teachings of Jesus and despite the rigorous canonziation of the gospels we do still find *far more than one hundred passages* which give a clear indication that their roots go back to the older Buddhist tradition.

Before we go to that point, it is first necessary to point out that Jesus never was the traditional orthodox Jew he is so often represented as. Death, family, women, children – four examples, four realities which can serve us as criteria as to how radically the alleged "product of ancient religion" differed from it in several decisive factors.

Jesus is said to have demythologized all that was sacred to the Jewish culture. This is pre-eminently true of death and the family. In four successive verses St. Luke reports how Jesus prefers liberty and love to the unimpeachable burial rites and customs: "And he said unto another, Follow me. But he said, Lord, suffer me first to go and bury my father. Jesus said unto him, Let the dead bury their dead; but go thou and preach the kingdom of God." (Luke 9,59–60). But family relations, too are of secondary importance: "And another also said, Lord, I will follow thee; but let me first go bid them farewell, which are at home in my house. And Jesus said unto him, No man, having put his hand to the plough, and looking back, is fit for the kingdom of God." (Luke 9,61–62) Wherever Jesus' teachings and behaviour touch upon family matters, they tend to hurt the Jewish feelings, as the Jew Montefiore remarked. "If any man come to me, and hate not his father, and mother, and wife, and children, and brethren, and sisters . . . he cannot be my disciple." (Luke 14,26). "He that loveth father or mother more than me is not worthy of me: and he that loveth son or daughter more than me is not worthy of me." (Matth 10,37). "While he yet talked to the people, behold, his mother and his brethren stood without, desiring to speak with him. Then one said unto him, Behold, thy mother and thy brethren stand without, desiring to speak with thee. But he answered and said unto him that told him, Who is my mother? and who are my brethren? And he stretched forth his hand toward his disciples, and said, Behold my mother and my brethren!" (Matth 12,46–49). This very Jesus in whose name so many "crusades for the family" have been undertaken, had to escape from his own family that was trying to keep hold of him.

And it is Matthew at all, the evangelist for the Jews, who quotes a sentence from Jesus which is unique for the whole of antiquity and scandalous for Jewism: "I am come to set a man at variance against his father, and the daughter against her mother, and the daughter-in-law against her mother-in-law." And in curious anticipation of Freud he adds: "And a man's foes shall be they of his own household." (Matth 10,35–36). Today there is a widely shared belief that the attitude of Jesus towards family relations and his rejection of their sacrosanct unimpeachability within the culture of his day represents a unique phenomenon. But is not this exactly the teaching which alone leads to complete detachment from egoism and self-complacency in thought and action? In order to gain salvation man has to liberate himself from all personal and individualistic tendencies and to transcend all such egoistic limitations. As long as man is unable to free himself from all earthly greed and desires, he remains attached to the cycle of rebirths. Jesus does not care the least about meaningless, useless and empty laws and frequently violates Jewish legislation. The demonstrative neglect of the Sabbath laws finally leads directly to his crucifixion.

Buddha and Jesus – a Comparison

Before his descent Buddha exists as a spiritual being among the godheads in heaven. He comes down to earth for the benefit of the earth of his own free will. Like the biblical Christ he is born in a miraculous way. Angels announce him as the saviour and predict his mother: "All joy may come over you, Queen Maya, rejoice and be happy, for this child which thou hast born is holy!"

There is a Buddhist Simeon, too. The saintly aged Asita prophesies the birth of the Buddha in the same way as the old god-fearing Simeon predicts that of the Messiah. Instructed by God, the seer shortly before his death comes to the newborn child, takes it in his arms and, full of bliss, prophesies thus: "This one is incomparable, the most pre-eminent among men . . . The peak of enlightenment will be achieved by this boy; he who sees what is the purest will set moving the wheel of the teachings, he who feels compassion for the welfare of many men. His religion will spread wide." Simeon, too, takes the child in his arms and says: "Lord, now lettest thou thy servant depart

75

in peace, according to thy word: For mine eyes have seen thy salvation, which thou hast prepared before the eyes of all people; a light to lighten the Gentiles, and the glory of thy people Israel." (Luke 2,29–32). Even cautious scholars are convinced that this motif has directly derived from Buddism.

At school the prince is already conversant with all kinds of scripts. He makes a short journey, gets lost and is found in deep meditation. The analogies with the twelve-year-old Jesus found in a learned discussion with the scribes in the temple while being sought after by his parents are too obvious to be neglected.

At about the age of thirty, i.e. the same age as the biblical Christ, Buddha starts his spiritual career. While keeping fasts and doing penances, he is tempted by evil in just the same way that Jesus is tempted by the devil after his forty days' and nights' fast. A similar temptation story is known about Zoroaster and the same motif, which is quite popular in the Orient, appears again in the saga of Christian saints.

Like Jesus Buddha roams about with his disciples in deliberate poverty, communicating with them in maxims, images and parables. Like the biblical Christ Buddha, too, has twelve main disciples. His first followers are two brothers, again in complete concurrence with the first followers of Jesus. Buddha's first companions are sitting under a fig tree (a symbol of Buddhism) when called by him, and Jesus, too, meets one of his first apostles under a fig tree. Both Buddha and the biblical Christ have one favourite disciple and one traitor. And Buddha's traitor Devadatta, whose plot, however, fails, like Judas finds a miserable end.

As fiercely as Jesus criticizes the Pharisees, the orthodox believers in the Thora, Buddha criticizes the externalized ritualistic legislation of the Brahmins, the orthodox believers in the Vedas. "Offspring of the learned trade, the priests spin their net of maxims and are present wherever evil is being bred." Similarly, Jesus says about the Pharisees: "They bind heavy burdens and grievous to be borne, and lay them on men's shoulders; but they themselves will not move them with one of their fingers. But all their works they do for to be seen of men." (Matth 23,4–5). In the same way as Buddha brands the Brahmins: "Inside you are a wild wood, while smoothing your outer appearance", Jesus unmasks the hypocrite Pharisees: "You are like unto whited sepulchres, which indeed appear beautiful outward, but are within full of dead men's bones and all uncleanness." (Matth 23,27). Just as Buddha rejects the blood sacrifice of the Brahmins, Jesus rejects the blood sacrifice of the Jews. And just as Buddha condemns ritual washings as well as superficial notions of purity and impurity, Jesus exactly shares these misgivings.

Buddhist Thought in the Teachings of Jesus

The close relation between the ethical teachings of Buddha and Jesus is well-known. Both prohibit killing, stealing, lying and illegal sexual relations. Both demand the veneration of the elder. Both praise the peaceful in heart. Both want to overcome evil by good, both preach the love of one's enemy, advise one choose not to heap up unnecessary treasures on earth and mercy instead of sacrifice. The parallels are numerous and there are passages which coincide almost literally. Buddha called himself "Son of Man" like Jesus and is likewise called "Prophet", "Master" and "Lord". The denominations of Buddha as "Eye of the World" and "Unequalled Light" correspond to those of Christ as "Light of the World" and "the True Light".

Buddha's understanding of himself and his role is hardly below that of the biblical Christ. Thus Buddha says: "I known God and his kingdom and the way which leads to him. I know him als well as one who has entered the brahmaloka (kingdom of God) and is born therein." Or else: "Those who believe in me and love me are certain to gain paradise. – Those who believe in me can be sure of salvation." This is remarkably similar to the promise of the Christ of St. John: "He that heareth my word, and believeth on him that sent me, hath everlasting life . . ." (John 5,24). Or else: "He that believeth in me, he shall live." (John 11,25).

Buddha says to his disciples: "Those who have ears to hear, let them hear." Miracles happen through him, the sick are healed trough him, blind regain their eyesight, the deaf their hearing, the crippled become erect. He strides across the flooded Ganges as Jesus does across the lake. And when Jesus' followers perform miracles, they have their predecessors in the disciples of Buddha. For instance, St. Peter's walking on the water, was first achieved by a follower of Buddha. And in the same way as Peter begins to sink, as soon as his belief starts wavering, Buddha's disciple sank when waking up from

77

his deep meditation in Buddha. And such as St. Peter is saved by the Lord, Buddha's disciple is saved by the renewed faithful thought of his Master. That the New Testament has adopted these incidents becomes evident through the fact that the idea of the ability of strong believers to walk on water is totally unknow to the Jews but old and wide-spread in India.

Buddha as well as Jesus never performs miracles in order to create sensations. Thus Buddha says to a yogi who, after twenty-five years of mortification, has acquired the ability to cross a river without even wetting his feet: "So you really have been wasting your time on a thing like that, while nothing more than a coin was needed for the ferryman to take you over in his boat." Later on, however, in Mahayana Buddhism the miracle plays the same dominating role as in the Christian church and in Islam. The masses in every religion are prone to be impressed by magic, miracles and outer guarantees rather than spiritual essence, the ethos. They want that something should be done for them but not through them.

At this point, I would like to refer to one of the most astonishing parallels between the Indian scriptures and the New Testament, that of the "widow's mite". In the Buddhist narration, rich people give precious donations in a religious congregation. A poor widow, however, owns nothing but two coins. This is all she has got and yet she donates it with pleasure. The priest recognizes her noble attitude and praises her without recognizing the gifts of others. And this is the parallel in the gospel of St. Mark: "And Jesus sat over against the treasury, and beheld how the people cast money in the treasury: and many that were rich cast in much. And there came a certain poor widow, and she threw in two mites, which make a farthing. And he called unto him his disciples, and saith unto them, Verily I say unto you, that this poor widow has cast more in, than all they which have cast into the treasury: For all they did cast in of their abundance; but she of her want did cast in all that she had, even all her living." (Mark 12,41–44)

Apart from the correspondence of the basic idea the following striking details may be mentioned: in both cases, the story is about a woman; both women are poor; both sacrifice in church; both sacrifice together with rich people; both give all they have; both own two coins; both are praised by some by–stander; the sacrifice of both is much more appreciated than the donations of the rich. Here, too, the

The books in the library of the monastery consist of loose leaves, bound together with coloured silk and protected by wooden covers.

Above: The excavations at Haran, 12 km north of Srinagar.

Opposite: The Tomb of Moses, and the keeper or Wali Rishi whose features are typically Jewish.

Below: The plain by the town Bandipur (Behat-poor) where the valley opens towards the marshy Wular lake.

Above: the 'Bathing-Place of Moses' in Bijbihara (46 km south of Srinagar), with a stone lion that is c. 5000 years old.

Below: the so-called 'Stone of Moses' or Ka-Ka-Bal, on which Moses is said to have demonstrated his magical skills.

conclusion of a dependence of the biblical text on the earlier one is hardly avoidable.

The analogies between Buddhism and Christianity continue after the deaths of their founders. Myths and legends idealized their personalities. Buddha and Jesus are soon after deified and raised above all other gods. A boundless craze for miracles springs up. In both creeds, there is no organized church in the beginning but only a congenial community. A doctrinal dispute soon setting in between sthaviras and mahasamghikas, the rigorous conservatives and the progressive forces within the larger Buddhist congregations, is equalled by the struggle between conservative Jewish Christians and the progressive heathen Christians. In both religions, apostle councils are called in, one in Jerusalem and one in Rajagriha. And as the orthodox Buddhists fixed their dogma in the Council of Pataliputra (241 B.C.), about 250 years after Buddha's death, thus in the same way the orthodox Christians fixed their dogmas in the council of Nicaea (325), about three hundred years after Jesus' disappearance.

Chapter Three

Eastern Wisdom in the West
The Wise Mens' Star

In the second chapter of the Gospel according to Matthew, it is written:

"Now when Jesus was born in Bethlehem of Judea in the days of Herod the king, behold, there came wise men from the east to Jerusalem, Saying, Where is he that is born King of the Jews? for we have seen his star in the east, and are come to worship him" (Matthew 2, 1–2).

If some extraordinary astronomical event did indeed occur on that night, this would have been recorded in the secular documents. Furthermore, any special constellation that appeared among the planets then should be easy enough to ascertain today (by computer). Johannes Kepler began such speculations, reckoning that the star of Bethlehem must have been a nova ("new star") that appeared as a result of the conjunction of Jupiter and Saturn in the year 7 B.C. The theory of a nova was rejected by later astronomers. The conjunction that Kepler thought was the cause of the generation of the nova, has itself come to be regarded by many as the star of Bethlehem. In the course of the year 7 B.C., a conjunction of Saturn and Jupiter in the constellation of Pisces occurred three times (Pisces, the fish, is a symbol of Christ, and was the secret sign of recognition for early Christian communities). Such an encounter in this astronomical constellation occurs only once every 794 years, and all observers were captivated by the impressive sight of two planets in such close proximity as to appear against the night sky as a double star of great brilliance[1]. In 1925, the Orientalist Paul Schnabel succeeded in deciphering a cuneiform slate, almost 2000 years in age, found at the observatory at Sippar on the Euphrates. The clay slab contained an exact description of the astronomical event of the year 7 B.C.: the great conjunction of the planets Jupiter and Saturn in the constellation Pisces[2].

Towards the end of 8 B.C., Jupiter and Saturn became visible after twilight in the western sky. They lay approximately sixteen degrees

84

apart, Jupiter in the constellation of Aquarius and Saturn in the constellation of Pisces. In February of 7 B.C., both planets disappeared and remained invisible for several weeks in the rays of the sun. The Oriental astrologers expected the first appearance of Jupiter at early dawn (the heliacal rising) to be a significant event on the occasion of the thirteenth Adaru of the year 304 of the Seleukidan era, i.e. March 16, 7 B.C. by our reckoning. They observed how Jupiter came increasingly near to Saturn, until the two planets finally "joined" at the end of the month of Airu (May 19th, 7 B.C.). The conjunction, in which Jupiter and Saturn stood at twenty-one degrees to Pisces with a separation of only one degree in declination and precisely the same azimuth, was to repeat itself twice again in the same year in a similar manner, on October 3rd and December 5th.

Both planets were visible from evening until morning, and shone high in the meridian at around midnight. When the sun sank in the west, the planets rose in the east; and when they disappeared westward, dawn made its entrance from the east. At the beginning of the year, the pair of planets rose heliacally (i.e. with the sun), and at the end of the year, they sank heliacally. During the entire course of the year, Jupiter and Saturn were visible and never left one another's company by more than three degrees. This spectacle in the constellation of Pisces was not to repeat itself for another eight hundred years.

In the Gospel according to Matthew, the star is mentioned just three times. The wise men say, "for we have seen his star in the east . . .". In the original Greek text, reference is made to the *anatole*. Linguists have discovered that the word *anatole* had a special astronomical significance when used in the singular. It meant the heliacal rising of a star, i.e. its appearance from the east, at a certain point on the horizon shortly before the sun. Used in the plural, the same word has a geographical connotation, and indicates the Orient. The three wise men did indeed follow the heavenly apparition from the east to the west.

The second mention of the astronomical event in Saint Matthew's gospel also bears a special meaning in Greek: "Then Herod, when he had privily called the wise men, enquired of them diligently what time the star appeared" (Matthew 2,7). The verb "appeared", when applied in astronomy, was a special term that designated the first appearance of an ascending star. According to the popular belief then current, a person's star rose at the moment of the person's birth.

What Herod's question implied was that the birth must have occurred a good while before. According to the Babylonian calendar, Jupiter had appeared in the ascendant in the last month of year 304 of the Seleukidan era. The year 305 (6 B.C.) began with the spring month of Nisan, which also marked the beginning of the Jewish New Year. When the wise men arrived in Jerusalem, Jupiter would have already been in the second year of its conjunction with Saturn, and Jesus, having been born probably in 7 B.C., would have been an infant almost two years old at the time. This could perhaps be the reason why Herod had all the children up to the age of two in certain areas slaughtered, according to the legend.

What drove these mysterious sages of the east (the Greek word *anatole* being in the plural in this case) to undergo the trials of a voyage lasting months or even years, at such great cost? Where did they really come from, and why did they persevere in their search for a small boy with such zeal? Theology alone provides no answer to the identity of the three wise men.

Who Were the Three Wise Men
Or: How to Find an Incarnation?[3]

In the original Greek text, the wise men are called *Magoi* (Magus refers to a Zoroastrian priest of Persia; hence our terms magic, magi).The Magi of the Bible story were first elevated to kingship in the sixth century by Caesarius of Arles. In the ninth century, the wise men were given the names Caspar, Melchior and Balthasar. The early sources do not specify how many Magi had been present. Their number has been given as three since the days of Origen[4], perhaps because of the three gifts. They were (of course) well-versed in "magical" practices, being experts in the methods of astrology, and were certainly not poor.

Any account of the "star" having stood precisely over a rustic little stable, in which a new-born infant lay, is just a pious representation. It is far more likely that the child of almost two years of age was found and visited in the protection of people who appreciated the divine stature of the boy. These people obviously did not enjoy the favour of Herod, because when the king heard what the three Magi were seeking, he was exceedingly upset; and "all of Jerusalem along with him". Whether or not the child was to be the coming Saviour of the secret sects of Qumran, the Nazarenes or the Essenes, will be the topic of discussion later in this book. Today it is known that the monastery of Qumran by the Dead Sea was deserted for ten years during the rule of Herod the Great because the secret sect had been banned during those years. Those circumstances might have been behind the king's wrath, and his resolution to have the child killed.

In the apocryphal gospel of the Nazarenes[5], one can read the following passage:

"When Joseph looked out with his eyes, he saw many wanderers accompanying him and coming towards the cave; and he said, 'I wish to rise and go to meet them'. Yet after Joseph had gone out, he said to Simon, 'It appears as though those people are soothsayers; for behold, they are forever looking up into the heavens and conferring among themselves. They also appear to be foreign, for their appearance is very different from our own; their clothing is very rich and their skin dark, and they are wearing caps on their heads, and their gowns appear soft to me, and their legs are also clothed. Behold, they have stopped and remain standing, looking at me; now they have begun to move again and are coming here'".

Did the members of the forbidden sect perhaps have ties to their brethren in India, to the lost tribes of the House of Israel? It can hardly be proved from the sources that the Magi did come directly from India. It is nonetheless astonishing to what extent the story of the three wise men corresponds to accounts of the practice whereby the reincarnations of high Buddhist dignitaries are found in Tibet after their demise, even to this day. The ancient and traditional procedure for such a search is described in the Dalai Lama's accounts[6] of his own "discovery" as a little boy, and also in a book by the Austrian Heinrich Harrer[7] who spent seven years at the court of the god-king in Lhasa. It is a fascinating story. It also provides a good point of comparison between Christian and other eastern traditions, so we will tell it now in some detail.

Shortly before his death in 1933, the thirteenth Dalai Lama had given some clues as to the place and time of his next incarnation. His corpse had been placed in the Potala Palace, facing southward in the traditional Buddha posture. But one morning, his face was found facing eastwards. And on a wooden pedestal at the north-east of the shrine on which the body was positioned, a star-shaped fungus plant had mysteriously appeared. After receiving these clues, the head lamas performed a magic ritual, questioning a monk in a trance condition, whose task it was to act as an oracle (rather like in the old Greek temples). The monk drew a large curve eastwards through the air, while extraordinary cloud formations appeared to the north of Lhasa. After this, the lama magicians received no more clues for the next two years. Finally, the acting regent was inspired to make a pilgrimage to the holy lake of Lhamoi Latso, near Cho Khor Gyal, ninety miles away. According to Tibetan belief, one can see the future mirrored in the clear waters of this mountain lake. After days of preparatory meditation, the regent had a vision of a three-story monastery with gilded roofs, alongside a small Chinese farmhouse with beautifully decorated gables and green roofing tiles. Furthermore, the three Tibetan letters Ah, Ka and Ma appeared. A thorough description of the vision was committed to paper and kept strictly secret. Full of confidence and gratitude for the divine instructions, the regent returned to his palace in Lhasa, while he began preparations for the search.

Of greatest importance were the pronouncements of the astrologists, without whose calculations no essential steps were to be taken. In 1937, various expeditions were sent forth from Lhasa to seek the holy child according to the directions of the heavenly omens. Each group was composed of wise, noble Lamas (for this was in a unique theocracy),endowed with the distinctions of their high office. Each group took along servants and costly gifts, some of them from among the possessions of the deceased. The gifts were meant as tokens of worship for the Dalai Lama, and also as a test to verify the identity of the new incarnation. In theory the deceased might be born many thousands of kilometres from his former abode; and in the case of the fourteenth Dalai Lama, the search led well beyond the borders of central Tibet into the district of Amdo in the region of Dokham, all under Chinese administration. There were a number of monasteries in the area, because the reformer of Lamaism, Tsong Kapa, had been born there. The expedition found a number of boys, but none of them conformed to the details of the omens. Finally, in wintertime, the team arrived at a three-story monastery near the village of Taktser, the monastery of Kumbum, ornate with gilded roofs, which lay alongside a charming, small farmhouse having a green roof and carved gables. This tallied precisely with the regent's vision.

Two high and noble lamas disguised themselves as servants, and a young monk of their party acted as their master. The disguise was meant to conceal the actual purpose of their visit, so as to avoid unnecessary excitement and to allow the delegation to inspect the place in peace. The monks entered the house with two officials of the local monastery. The two high clerics (one of whom was Lama Kewtsang Rimpoche from the monastery of Sera in Lhasa), were led into the kitchen, in the role of servants, while the monk was shown into the living room. The children of the family were playing in the kitchen, and as soon as the disguised Lama Rimpoche took his seat in the kitchen, a little two-year-old boy hurled himself forward and plumped himself down on the lama's lap. The revered monk was wearing the rosary of the deceased Dalai Lama, and the lad seemed to recognise it and tugged at it as though he wanted to have it. The lama promised to give the boy the beads, if he could guess who the guest was; whereupon the lad immediately gave the answer *Sera-aga*, "The Lama of Sera", in the local dialect! The lad's ability to recognize a lama disguised as a servant was surprising enough; but that he was able to guess that the lama came from Sera astonished even these monks, who were relatively accustomed to miraculous events because of their tradition. The lama then asked the boy what their "master" was called, and he replied "Lobsang". The servant was indeed called Lobsang Tsewang.

The noblemen spent the entire day observing the child, and were obliged to restrain themselves from showing him the profound reverence that they were convinced was his due; for they were sure that they had at last found the incarnation. But they departed the next day, in order to return with the entire expedition. When the parents of the child saw the procession of the high dignitaries approach their humble home in all its splendour, they realised that their son must be an incarnation. In the neighbouring monastery of Kumbum, an incarnate lama had died, and the peasants believed that their child might be his re-incarnation. In fact an elder son of the peasant couple had already undergone such a test.

It is not all that unusual that reincarnations as children remember objects and people from earlier lives, and some are even able to recite scriptures that they had never been taught. In the isolated calm of

Tibet, there has always been a great deal of such proof of earlier lives. In the mechanised West, however, such accounts rarely appear in the press, because Westerners generally dismiss the possibility of the incarnation of a deceased person in a new body.

The four chief "Bonpos" of the delegation from Lhasa then proceeded to carry out the prescribed tests. First they offered the child two almost identical black rosaries, one of which had belonged to the thirteenth Dalai Lama. Without hesitating, the child chose the correct one, hung it around his neck and danced joyfully round the room. The test was repeated with various precious rosaries. Then the delegation offered the boy two different ritual drums, a large and precious drum decorated with gold, and a simple drum that had once belonged to the deceased Dalai Lama. The lad took the simpler of the drums, which he proceeded to beat in the exact manner of ceremonial practice. Finally, two walking sticks were presented to the child, and the boy first touched the wrong stick, paused, considered both sticks for a short while, and finally chose the stick that had belonged to the god-king. The Rimpoche told the spectators who had been surprised at the lad's prevarication how the second stick had also been used for a time by the thirteenth Dalai Lama before he gave it to Lama Kewtsang.

Thus one might draw a parallel between such a presentation of the deceased king's valuables, and the bestowal of the precious gifts that the Magi brought the young Jesus from the East. It is also clear that the child would normally have had to have attained a certain age before being ready for such a test.

The proof of this presentation of articles was complemented by an interpretation of the three letters that the regent had seen. It was surmised that the first letter, "Ah", stood for Amdo, the district in which the boy was found. The two letters "Ka" and "Ma" could have signified the small monastery, Ka(r)ma Rolpai Dorje, on a mountain above the village of Taktser, in which the thirteenth Dalai Lama had spent some time on his way back from China.

This visit of the thirteenth Dalai Lama had been a sensation for the entire region, and among the people blessed by their god-king was the father of the new incarnation, then just nine years old. Moreover, the former Dalai Lama was said to have gazed at the farmhouse where the incarnation was later found, and to have somewhat wistfully remarked how beautiful and serene the place was. And as many accounts would have it, the Dalai Lama had left a pair of boots in the small *lamasery*, – which might well, in retrospect, be considered a symbolic act.

After so much of confirmation, the delegates were quite satisfied that they had achieved their aim – they had found the true reincarnation. They telegraphed all the details of their discovery in a coded message to Lhasa via China and India, and received the order to arrange everything in the utmost secrecy, so that no dangers would be posed by any intrigues of the Chinese. Because the search had taken place on Chinese territory, it was necessary to deceive the officials, so that the young king would not fall into Chinese hands. The governor of the province, Ma Pufang, was told that the boy was to be taken to Lhasa because he was one of many possible successors of the deceased Dalai Lama. Ma Pufang first demanded one hundred thousand Chinese dollars for the child. After payment, the governor demanded a further payment of three hundred thousand dollars. The delegation feared that if they were to admit having found the true god-king, China might insist on sending its own troops to Lhasa "for his protection".

The parallel to the situation in Jerusalem is evident once again: there the divine child had to be smuggled out of the country in order to avoid the Roman governor of the province, Herod. "Then Herod, when he saw that he was mocked of the wise men, was exceeding wroth." (Matthew 2,16).

For security reasons, correspondence between Amdo and Lhasa was conveyed by messengers; this always required several months. It therefore took another two years before the caravan of the delegation, with the child and his whole family, could finally depart for Lhasa. It took months for the trek to the Tibetan border, where a cabinet minister and his entourage were waiting for the travellers to confirm the choice of the Dalai Lama with a letter from the acting regent. It was not until that moment that the parents of the boy realised that their son was no less a figure than the new ruler of all Tibet.

The Flight to Egypt

After the wise men of the Orient had found the child Jesus near Jerusalem, the father Joseph received the divine instruction: Arise, and take the young child and his mother, and flee into Egypt, and be thou there until I bring thee word: for Herod will seek the young child to destroy him" (Matthew 2,13). The flight probably took them via Hebron to Beersheba, and from there across the desert to the Mediterranean. The family could not have felt safe before reaching the Egyptian border. At the time about one million Jews were living in Egypt, with two hundred thousand in Alexandria alone. Traditionally the country was then a haven for the Jews, and there were colonies complete with synagogues, schools and everything else that a foreigner would need to make a place home.

The infanticide depicted in the gospels is freed from the clouds of legend and confirmed in a contemporary report, written during Jesus' lifetime by members of the sect of Essenes, who were the apparent object of Herod's attacks (and had therefore to work in secret in their own country). "The next king was impertinent and was not of the priestly class, an audacious and godless person. He killed both old and young, and the entire land was filled with a terrible dread of him" (Ass. Mos. 6,22)

According to Professor Hassnain Buddhist missionary schools were said to have even existed in Alexandria long before the Christian era. They were called Viharas, which is translated by the *Sanskrit-Chinese Dictionary* as a place "that is either an academy, a school or a temple and serves the study or practice of Buddhism. Such buildings were ideally constructed with red sandalwood (chandana), consisted of thirty-two rooms, each of which was eight 'Tala-trees' high; and contained a garden, a park, a bathing pool and tea kitchen, amply furnished and adorned with wall-hangings, and well stocked with beds, mattresses, provisions, and all the necessary comforts."[8] It is entirely conceivable that Jesus had been introduced to the wisdom of eastern philosophy from early childhood by Buddhist scholars in Alexandria. Such thorough scholastic instruction could, after all, help to explain why Jesus was able to astonish the priests in the Temple of Jerusalem with his wisdom as a mere twelve-year-old boy. "And all that heard him were astonished at his understanding and answers" (Luke 2,47).

In those days it was customary for a boy to be married off at about the age of twelve. Jesus certainly escaped the usual fate, though, for then he was old enough to continue his studies in the home of his real spiritual forefathers – in India.

Jesus was not able to return into the land of his birth without danger until years after the death of the hated usurper Herod (which was shortly before Passover in the year 4 B.C.) "But when Herod was dead, behold, an angel of the Lord appeareth in a dream to Joseph in Egypt, saying, arise, and take the young child and his mother, and go into the land of Israel: for they are dead which sought the young child's life. And he arose, and took the young child and his mother, and came into the land of Israel. But when he heard that Archelaus did reign in Judaea in the room of his father Herod, he was afraid to go thither (Archelaus was governor or Ethnarch of Judaea and Samaria from the years 4 B.C. to 6 A.D., that is until Jesus became 12 or 13 years old) : notwithstanding, being warned of God in a dream, he turned aside into the parts of Galilee: And he came and dwelt in a city called Nazareth: that it might be fulfilled which was spoken by the prophets, He shall be called a Nazarene." (Matthew 2,19–23)

Jesus the Nazarene

In almost all the Greek manuscripts Jesus bears the title "The Nazarene", which is generally falsely translated as "Jesus of Nazareth". Thus in many editions, Paul hears a voice that allegedly says, "I am Jesus of Nazareth, whom you shall follow." In fact the Greek manuscripts contain no such statement. The correct version, contained in the Jerusalem Bible, is "I am Jesus the Nazarene, whom you shall follow."

Was there perhaps some definite intention behind the alteration? If one intended to call Jesus according to his place of origin, one would have to call him "Jesus of Bethlehem" (none of the sources support the claim that Jesus lived in Nazareth). According to Saint Mark's gospel, his followers lived on the Sea of Galilee (Lake Tiberias), probably in Capernaum.

93

The Lutheran Bible simply states "and he came home". At any rate, "his own came out", in order to have him at home. If "his own" were to have come from Nazareth, they would have had to travel a distance in excess of forty kilometres.

In the accounts of the apostles, the first Christians are referred to as Nazarenes, and Jesus is called "The Nazarene" six times.

In the Gospel according to Saint John, Nathanael, an aspirant to the apostolate, asked the apostle Philip, "Can there be any good thing come out of Nazareth?" (John 1,46). Implicit in the question is the man's astonishment that anyone coming from such a tiny, insignificant place (that could not have consisted of more than a handful of huts in those days), could have such profound knowledge and the benefits of a thorough education.

The *Greek-German Dictionary on the Writings of the New Testament and other Early Christian Literature* (1963) openly admits that to find a connection between the actual word "Nazarene" and "Nazareth" is not possible.

The epithets Nazarene (nazarenos), Nazarite (nazoraios) and Nazorene (nazorenos) were all used to designate Jesus, which would suggest they were synonyms. It has generally been assumed that the epithets indicate that Jesus' origins lay in the town of Nazareth, which has led to the misleading title, "Jesus of Nazareth". As early as 1920, M. Lidzbarski proved in his work *Mandaic Liturgies* that for simple etymological reasons "Nazarene" could not possibly have come from the name of the town of Nazareth.

Before mention of the place in Matthew's gospel, Nazareth is not referred to anywhere, and could not have been more than a tiny village, miles from anywhere. Japha which was only 3 km southeast of Nazareth and was destroyed by the Romans in 67 A.D., was mentioned as belonging to the tribe of Zebulun, while Nazareth itself was not mentioned at all.

The word "Nazarene" derives from the Aramaic word *nazar* which means to keep watch, to observe, or to own. In a figurative sense, the word also means to vow or to bind oneself to serve God. Used as a noun, it means a diadem, the symbol for an anointed head. *Thus a "Nazarene" was a keeper or celebrant of the sacred rites.* The "Nazaria" were a branch of the Essenes (the Therapeutae or healers), and like the Ebionites, they were probably one of the first early Christian communities, all of which were referred to as "Nozari" in the Talmud. All these *gnostic* sects (Gnosis = knowledge) practiced "magic"; their members were initiates who led ascetic lives dedicated to the community in the spirit of the divine virtues. It is possible that the various spellings of the title originated from a community splitting into various groups, then retaining the common etymological origin but adopting very different interpretations of the teaching, and consequently having different styles of life. The designation Nazarene can be traced back to the Old Testament, and therefore its origins can be dated at some point well back in the pre-Christian era.

According to John M. Robertson, Samson was a Nazarite, (Judges 13, 5–7), who would not allow his hair to be cut and who drank no wine – an ascetic existence. The non-ascetics gave themselves the name "Nazarenes", in order to distinguish themselves from the ascetic "Nazarites".[9]

Jesus cannot be categorized as belonging to either camp with any finality, for he evidently refused to subordinate himself to any human code of law. Instead he took the same course that Buddha had taken, that of just doing the right thing at the right time. The tremendous geographical distance from India had widened the gulf between those sons of the common spiritual Fathers who lived according to the principles of Buddhist philosophy in India, and their brothers residing in Israel. Jesus could certainly be described as a reformer who had been sent to reestablish some unity in belief among the "lost sheep", who were in need of spiritual and emotional support in their struggle against Roman occupiers, Sadducees, Pharisees and Orthodox Jews.

Jesus was the divine personality whom many had longed for in a period of turmoils. He was greeted by two renunciants sent by John with the words, "Art thou he that should come, or are we to look for another?" (Matthew 11,3)

John the Baptist *(Jochanan)* was a Nazarene ascetic and a prophet, who was honoured with the epithet "Saviour" in Galilee. Josephus Flavius described the Baptist as "an honourable man, who aroused enthusiasm for the practice of virtue, for social justice, for piety towards God and for baptism among the Jews. Then God would show his favour, he announced; for baptism was used to heal physically and not in atonement for sins – atonement could only take place beforehand, by leading a just life. Throngs had assembled about John, stirred by his words . . ."[10]

The ritual immersion in water originated in India and continues to be practised daily by the Hindus with the same fervour as it was thousands of years ago. It is a tradition almost as old as the "Secret Knowledge" itself. The rite of baptism deviates from Jewish tradition altogether, and especially from the sacrifice of flesh, based on the crude premise that sins will be forgiven if blood is shed. Ceremonial cleansing is meant to symbolise release from the earthly of the one hand, and the "Rebirth" of the spirit in a pure body on the other hand. The second Book of the Laws of Manu, which deals with the sacraments, contains the injunction to pour holy water over a new-born baby before severing the umbilical cord, and then the baby should have a small, golden spoon with a mixture of honey, purified butter and salt passed over on his tongue, while holy prayers are recited (and such practices are still followed in families all over India today).

The Atharva Veda contains the passage, "Whoever is not cleansed after birth with the water of atonement from the Ganges as the holy invocations are intoned, will be subject to as many wanderings as years he spent in impurity" ("wanderings" refers to punitive reincarnations or spirit life).

In the case of John's form of baptism the rite seems to have been a sign of belonging to a certain community which had segregated itself from non-members through the introduction of various cult sacraments. This makes it evident that the Nazarenes were an independent sect that emerged with the Mysteries of a definite creed. And mysterious sectarians who act in secret have always been subject to mistrust and persecution by the ruling authorities. Paul faced the same hostility when he was tried by the governor, Felix, having been accused by the orator Tertullus of being "a pestilent fellow, an instigator of sedition among all the Jews throughout the world, and a ringleader of the sect of the Nazarenes." (Acts 24,5).

According to Pliny and Josephus, the Nazarene sect had existed on the banks of the Jordan and the east bank of the Dead Sea at least one hundred and fifty years before Christ's birth. Disciples were permitted to wear their hair long. John the Baptist is depicted with long hair, and wearing a "raiment of camel's hair, and a leathern girdle about his loins." (Matthew 3,4). A Roman patrician called Lentulus described Jesus' appearance in a letter to the Roman senate. The Lentulus epistle, one of the apocryphal texts, describes Jesus' hair as "loose and curly". It fell over his shoulders in waves, and was "parted in the middle of the head after the fashion of the Nazarites".

The word *nazar* can also be found amongst the languages of India (root *nas* = associate oneself with; *nasa* = nose, also applied in yoga to the point at the base of the nose *nasaanta*, i.e. between the eyebrows, where one concentrates). "In Hindustan, 'Nazar' means inner or supernatural vision, 'Nazar Cand' means fascination, and is an expression used in mesmerising and in magic; and 'Nazaran' is the word for 'to behold' or 'to have a vision'".[11] A detailed description of the sect of the Nazarenes is hardly possible today, because the texts at our disposal are very scant indeed. To determine the differences between the thoughts of Jesus the Nazarene and those of his orthodox contemporaries would be impossible but for the recent discovery of a great deal of information about the sect of the Essenes, who differed only superficially from the Nazarenes and who were clearly influenced by the teachings of Buddha and the Veda. The Essenes kept strictly to pure water, for example, though the Nazarenes (and Jesus) used oil (we will return to this point again later).

As long ago as in the last century, those familiar with accounts of the Essenes came to the conclusion that Jesus' community could only have been a branch of the Essenes. The Jewish historian H. Graetz even called Christianity "Essenism with foreign elements".[12] The Essenes were then known only through the indirect testimonies of ancient historians. The Jewish philosopher Philo of Alexandria (ca. 13 B.C. – 43 A.D.) called them "Athletes of virtue", and Josephus dedicated nearly an entire chapter (II,8) to them in his *Jewish War*. Both estimated the membership at around four thousand "men of excellent morals, who live throughout the land". Even the Roman author Pliny the Elder made mention of the sect of the Essenes.

Yet the full significance of the teachings of the Essene sect was to remain obscure until the discovery of the famous scrolls in Qumran by the Dead Sea. The realization that teachings of the Essenes had anticipated those of Christ placed Jesus himself in a completely different light.

The Essenes: Christianity Before Jesus

In the summer of 1947, a young Bedouin came across the entrance of a cave while searching the cliffs along the Dead Sea for a lost goat from his herd. His curiosity aroused, the shepherd boy entered, and noticed several sealed clay vessels among a pile of potsherds. In the hope of finding a treasure, the lad opened the vessels, but to his great disappointment found nothing more than a few musky leather scrolls. Yet the find was soon to prove the greatest archaeological sensation of the century. When the famous archaeologist William F. Allbright saw the scrolls in 1948, he called them the greatest manuscript find of our time. He dated them in the first century B.C., and had no doubts as to their authenticity.

In the course of the following years, researchers in the area of Chirbet Qumran found ten more caves with numerous scrolls, some of which have not yet been completely translated and interpreted up to this day. One fact was soon to emerge in all clarity: the similarities between the teachings of Jesus and those of the Essenes. Indeed, it was said the Essenes should be called the true precursors of early Christianity. The sensational similarities between these two movements can be seen in the recurrence of the same theological themes and religious institutions. This all confirms *the existence of a Christianity that preceded Jesus.*

Seven scrolls from the first cave are now on display in the "Manuscript Temple" of the Israel Museum in Jerusalem. The most extensive manuscript is the "Isaiah scroll of St. Mark" (designated 1 QIs). The complete book of the prophet Isaiah contains fifty-four written columns in Hebraic. The Isaiah scroll is the oldest relic among the finds (dating back to c. 150 B.C.) and bears an astonishing resemblance to early finds of Biblical manuscripts. In addition to this, fragments of a second Isaiah script (1 QIIs) and a commentary to the Book of the Prophet Habakkuk (1 Qp Hab) were found.

The most important find, however, was a leather scroll almost two metres in length, with the regulations of a religious sect. Today the document is called *Serek Hajjahad*, from its opening words meaning "Rules of the Community" or "Handbook of Instructions", *Manuale Disciplinae* (1 QS). The first part describes a "Bond of eternal love" that joins the members of the community to God. The second part describes "The two spirits in the nature of man", the spirit of light and truth, and its opposite, the spirit of error and of darkness (in Buddhism: Knowledge and Ignorance). The regulations of the order follow, with a detailed description of conditions for entry, and penalties for violation of the rules of the community. Finally a long hymn of praise and thanks concludes the scroll.

A second script, which had been rolled up with or even sewed to the rules for the celibate order of monks, was also found. The scroll was entitled "Rules for the Whole Community" (1 Q8a) and was directed at the lay branch of the community, for those members who were married.

Parallels to early Buddhist communities become very obvions at this point, for Buddhism also distinguishes between monks (Pali: bhikkhu) and laymen (upasaka).

Whoever belonged to the lay branch of the sect was instructed in all the teachings and regulations of the community from his eleventh year onwards. Jesus seems to have arrived at Jerusalem (from Egypt?) at about that age, and at that age he then disappeared and was not seen there again until he was a young man of about thirty. The men were not allowed to actually marry until they had turned twenty, and at the age of twenty-five they received a post and had a say in the community. At the age of thirty, they could aspire to all the chief offices, but remained under obligation to obey the priest and elders of the community. Honours were gained according to the importance of one's position and service. The officials were expected to retire from office in their old age.

Towards the end of the scroll, there is a description of the seating arrangement at a festive eschatological meal – the very matter that was the cause for debate among Jesus' disciples at the Last Supper. (cf. Luke 22,24).

Another scroll, which is very damaged in parts, contains both biblical and original "Essene" psalms. The forty psalms all begin with the words, "I praise thee, Lord", and are consequently called "Hochajot" – "Songs of Praise" (1 QH).

The scriptures discovered were evidently the remnants of what had been (perhaps fortuitiously) overlooked in the manuscript finds of bygone centuries. Origen, for example, mentioned that a translation of psalms had been found with other manuscripts in a vessel near Jericho. And the Nestorian patriarch of Baghdad/Seleukia, Timothy I

(† 823 A.D.) wrote in a letter of a find of Hebraic scriptures in a cave near Jericho. The texts were partly written in a secret code, and much discussion arose about a "New Covenant" (it is the term later rendered by Martin Luther as "The New Testament"), as well as a mysterious "Teacher of Righteousness".

In *Historia Naturalis*, Pliny the Elder mentioned a monastery that he had seen somewhere to the north of Engeddi on the west bank of the Dead Sea. He called it the Essene Monastery. Pliny described its inhabitants in the following manner: "... a lonely people strange among everyone else in the world, without any women, who have renounced human love and live quite penniless under the palms." (V, 17).

Less than a kilometre away from the cave in which the first scrolls were found, lie some remains which have been known for ages as "Chirbet Qumran" (The ruins of Qumran) and are thought to be the remnants of an ancient Roman fortress. In 1951, Lancaster Harding of the Jordanian Administrative Office for Antiquities, and Pater Roland de Vaux, the director of the theological institute of the Dominicans in Jerusalem, commenced with the first excavations on the field of the ruins. They found something that surpassed their widest expectations: the very Monastery of Qumran, in which the sensational scrolls had probably been written. During the next five years of work, the researchers discovered a large settlement protected by a fortified wall, with a square central building, several other buildings, a large dining hall, ritual baths, thirteen wells and a complicated network of water supply lines. They uncovered a cemetery with more than one thousand graves in which only men were buried. Moreover, they found a writing room with wooden tables and ink vessels, in which the greater part of the manuscripts had most probably been written. Today one knows that the monastery had been inhabited in as early as the eighth century B.C., but had been evacuated during the time of the Babylonian exile, and was not resettled until the second century (c. 175 B.C.). Josephus describes the manner in which the monks lived: "They despise money, and the communality of goods that they practice is so admirable that no one among them owns more than anyone else. For they have a rule compelling anyone wishing to join the sect to turn over his assets in their entirety to the community, so one sees neither abject poverty nor excessive wealth anywhere; instead, everyone disposes of the

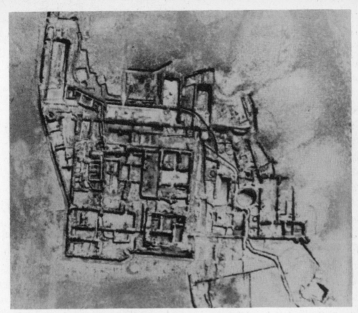

Aerial photograph of the excavated monastery of Qumran.

common property – that of all the individual members of the order, in the manner of brothers. They consider oil filth, and if one of them is anointed against his will, he wipes his body clean. For to have natural skin is considered by them to be honourable like the wearing of clean white robes" (Flavius Josephus, Jewish War II, 8,3).

There are obvious parallels between this description of the Essenes, the regulations of Buddhist monasteries, and Jesus' own style of life. Just as Buddhist monks owned no property beyond their clothing and a few small necessities, Jesus also led the existence of an itinerant teacher without property, and exhorted his follwers to join the community by the "Act of Departure into the Open" (Pali: pabbajja); by leaving house and family (agara), symbols of the life of the layman, and entering the class of wandering monks without fixed shelter (anagara). Only then would one be free of all earthly concerns, able to meditate whole-heartedly on the Teachings and gradually free oneself from one's deep-seated passions. For, "It is easier for a camel (a

101

rope of camel-hair) to go through the eye of a needle, than for a rich man to enter into the kingdom of God." (Matthew 19,24).

The replies of Jesus to questions from three of his disciples serve as a further demonstration of, and appeal for, freedom from all earthly concerns: "And a certain scribe came, and said unto him, Master, I will follow thee withersoever thou goest.

And Jesus saith unto him, the foxes have holes, and the birds of the air have nests; but the Son of man hath not where to lay his head. And another of his disciples said unto him, Lord, suffer me first to go and bury my father. But Jesus said unto him, Follow me; and let the dead bury their dead" (Matthew 8,19–22). The Gospel of Saint Luke adds the answer Jesus gave to the third disciple in the discussion: "And another also said, Lord, I will follow thee; but let me first go bid them farewell, which are at home at my house. And Jesus said unto him, no man, having put his hand to the plough, and looking back, is fit for the kingdom of God." (Luke 9,61–62).

One interesting rule in the Buddhist faith is that of forbidding the oiling of one's body, which it appears Buddha felt would call inordinate attention to the body and thereby pamper the ego. The sect of the Nazarenes was certainly not obliged to follow such strict injunctions.

The mention of a white robe has also been of significance for the critical analysis of the great supernatural events claimed in the Jesus story. Some eighteenth century philosophers of the Enlightenment regarded the crucifixion and resurrection as a clever spectacle produced by Essene monks, and some pointed out the likelihood that the white-robed boy who told the women of the resurrection at the empty grave was one of the Essenes, who customarily wore white robes. A hundred years ago, the theory was advanced that Jesus was the son of an Essene to whom Mary had given herself in religious ecstasy. The child was turned over to the Order, a customary practice of the Essenes according to the accounts of Josephus (see Albert Schweitzer's History of Research on the Life of Jesus). More extreme versions had appeared during efforts on the part of fanatic Jews to defame the early Christian communities.

As far back as in 1831, August Friedrich Gfrörer, the town vicar of Stuttgart and *Repetent* at the seminary in Tübingen, could write, "The Christian Church evolved from the community of the Essenes, whose thoughts they developed and without whose rules its organisation would be inconceivable."

The name Essene can be traced back to the Syrian word *hasen*, which means "the pious". Another version of the etymology is that it evolved from the Aramaic word, *assaya*, which means a doctor or healer (and this would tally with the Greek *Therapeutae*). Many of the monks, who showed extreme devotion to their ascetic practices of prayer and contemplation, achieved astonishing skills of extrasensory perception and action, similar to the yogis and fakirs of India.

The total silence about the Essene Order in the New Testament, – about this sect which was at least as significant in numbers as the Sadducees and Pharisees (whose membership Josephus estimated to be about four thousand), seems to have been in some way intentional.

Simple geographical considerations show how Jesus could not possibly have missed the monastery of Qumran. The place of Jesus' ritual baptism by John in the Jordan(which would enable him to enter the community of the moderate Nazarenes) was within sight of the monastery, a mere 7 km away. This obvious connection between the place of the baptism and Qumran becomes really striking when one sees with one's own eyes the proximity of the two sites in the clear air of the open mountain desert. From here one can clearly see the mountain where Jesus is said to have been tempted by the devil during his seclusion after the baptism (Luke 4,1–13), – at a distance of about 15 km.

John lived here in the desert, perhaps in the caves of Qumran; and immediately after being baptized, Jesus went there to practise the forty days of solitude. The settlers of Qumran referred to the area that they inhabited as "The Desert" in their writings. Jesus thus spent time "with the wild beasts; and the angels ministered unto him." (Mark 1,13). The Essenes had very extensive and strictly secret (oral) doctrines on the angels, who fulfilled the role of messengers.

Thus we can consider some parts of Jesus' life in the context of Essene practice. If Jesus did spend a kind of retreat in a cave outside Qumran, there would have been some contact with the monastery; perhaps the "angels" also meant the monks there.

In his chapter on the Essenes (in Jewish War II,8), Josephus Flavius wrote: "Whoever wishes to enter the sect is not granted admission immediately, but is obliged first to spend a year outside the order and lead the life of the members there, having been provided with a small

103

axe, a loin cloth and a white robe. If he passes such a test of moderation, he comes one step closer to entry into the community; he takes part in the purifying rites of consecration with water, but is not yet admitted to the common meals" (II,8,7).

The same procedure has been followed up until our times in Tibet. Before a simple monk is consecrated and becomes a lama (i.e. "the higher"), he has to complete a course of education and a number of tests. The aspirant is also expected to reside away from the community for a period, at a place where he might remain completely undisturbed, in order to devote himself completely to mystic meditation. The monastery of Hemis in Ladakh, like all the larger lamaist monasteries, has a second, far smaller and more austere building for this purpose on the peak of a high mountain and about 5 km distant from the main building. The practicants, lost in deep meditation in their single cells, receive only a little food twice a day from helpers.

In the year 31 B.C., an earthquake destroyed the entire settlement of Qumran. Evidence of gaps and cracks can be seen today. The level of the floor varies at some points by almost half a metre. After the earthquake, Qumran remained uninhabited for almost thirty years. It was not until the time of Jesus' Nativity that the monastery was revived and endowed with a new spirit.

In addition to the human graves, the grounds of the monastery also contained the buried remains of animals; the remains of sheep, goats, cows, calves and lambs had been carefully interred in clay vessels. It is therefore reasonable to assume that the Essenes valued the products of their domesticated animals but did not kill or devour the animals themselves, possibly because they considered the killing of all life to be an atrocity, as did the Buddhists. The monks cultivated fields and orchards, and numerous date stones confirm the existence of a palm plantation, in the shades of which the Essenes "tarried", as Pliny the Elder put it. Philo tells of the community's great interest in bee-keeping, which brings to mind John the Baptist's form of nourishment.

It is possible to establish the chronology of the settlement with extraordinary precision, by referring to the four hundred or so coins found in the monastery. A number date back to the time of Archelaus' succession to the governorship of Judea; he took over the office of his father in 4 B.C. The gap in the series of coins prior to this supports the theory that the monastery could not be inhabited again

'The Temptation of Jesus in the Wilderness' (by A. D. Thomas).

until after Archelaus had begun to rule. The reason for the absence of the members from this centre of their community was evidently the persecution of all Essenian sects at the hands of Herod, whose luxurious winter palace was only twelve kilometers away from the monastery, in Jerusalem. After the death of Herod the Essenes returned, and began with the reconstruction of their monastery. From then until the beginning of the Jewish-Roman war of 68 A.D., Qumran remained continuously inhabited. The grounds show evidence of a final violent end to the community. A layer of ashes suggests that the monastery was destroyed by a great fire.

The Teachings of the Essenes at Qumran

The members of the Essene community of Qumran did not refer to themselves with any one general name in their holy writings. They called themselves "The holy community", "The poor ones", "God's chosen ones", "Men of truth", or most often "Sons of Light". The Essenes surpassed the demands of Jewish law in their spirituality, but at the same time deviated so much from it that it is questionable whether the Essenes of Qumran can even be called a Jewish sect.

The Songs of Praise that were found announce the "Good Tidings" (evangelion) to the poor, in the fullness of God's compassion, and the desire of the Essenes to be "Messengers of the good news". The Essenes wanted to make a covenant with God (New Testament) and referred to themselves as the New Covenant, which was later said to have been founded by Jesus. The New Covenant was to last "from the day of the assumption of the one teacher until the Messiah of Aaron and Israel comes forth."

Astonishingly enough, the Qumranians did not pray facing the direction of the temple of Jerusalem, as prescribed by Jewish law, but turned eastwards in their prayers, which they said thrice daily. The focus of their prayer lay eastwards, towards the rising sun. Josephus writes that the Essenes "did not utter anything unholy before the sun rose, but said certain ancient prayers to the Sun . . ." This account makes it clear that the Essenes considered the sun to be a symbol for the Divinity. One of the Qumran psalms emphasises this in its praise of God: "And as the real Dawn you appeared to me at the break of day."; and further, "And you appeared to me in your might with the coming of the day."

The community rules require the faithful to recite a morning and an evening prayer. Followers of Pythagoras in Croton, very like Indian Brahmans, and followers of the Gnosis of Hermes Trismegistos, which had been influenced by the Pythagorians, practiced precisely the same rites. Both the direction of the prayer, the east, and the symbol of the sun, make one recall the Sun Temple of Martand in Kashmir.

A further remarkable fact is that the Essenes did not follow the calendar of the temple of Jerusalem – the lunar calendar – but had their own means of calculating the time. They followed the solar year, which is considerably more exact and which had been in use since the beginnings of Brahman rule. Not until the time of Gaius Julius Caesar was the solar calendar introduced in the entire Roman Empire, and to this day it has not been accepted by the Jews. In the Qumran calendar, the anual religious holy days always fell on the same day of the week, in contrast to official Jewish practice[13].

Even the division of the year into four seasons is not part of Jewish tradition. Ancient Greece only had two or three seasons, until Pythagoras brought the new division of the year, again apparently from India.

A further tenet of the Essenes points to the spiritual background and origin of Essene philosophy. They believed, as did the Indian sages and the Greek philosophers, in the immortal life of the soul, and that the spirit masters and survives its temporal prison, the body. Jesus added the new element of the teaching of ultimate resurrection. He spoke of the resurrection of the dead, without expressly referring to the resurrection of the flesh. He thus did not of course mean the resurrection of the human body, but the pure teaching of reincarnation culminating in total liberation in a complete divine form, the end of all "Samsara", as the Upanishads of the Indian Veda describe, which became a fundamental tenet of all religions in India. The Pythagoreans, the Orpheans, Empedokles, Plato and the neo-platonists to mention only a few – they all knew about the teaching of the rebirth of the soul in a new body besides the Essenes. This concept of *metempsychosis* (the word the old Greeks used) survived in the Gnostics and a few Islamic sects, and is a constituent of classical theosophy and anthroposophy.

107

Even in the last century, researchers recognised the influence of Buddhism in the teachings of the Essenes[14]. The Essenes also had a doctrine of Karma, which gave those of "understanding" the choice of reforming their ways, or continuing to sin only to find themselves lost on the Day of Judgement. They lived in awareness of the apocalypse and awaited the imminent heralding of the Kingdom of God.

Despite the numerous parallels between Jesus and the Essenes, the differences should also be pointed out. Comparing the two, one can see that Jesus appears to breathe new life into the hardened customs and habits with his magnificent stand of tolerance. "Ye have heard that it was said by them of old . . . But I say unto you . . ." (Matthew 5, 21–48). According to Jewish law, those who broke the Sabbath in spite of having been admonished were put to death. Yet the Damascus text of Qumran forbids the killing of anyone who breaks the Sabbath, and in the Gospel according to Saint Matthew, Jesus says, "For the Son of man is Lord even of the sabbath day . . ." (Matthew 12,8).

The difference becomes particularly clear in regard to Jesus' injunction to love one's enemy; the Essenes could still hate their enemies. Indeed, the people of Qumran valued their aloofness from the rest of the world very highly and were conscious of belonging to a kind of spiritual elite. In contrast, Jesus sought contact with sinners, so that he might aid those who were in real need. He stressed that he had been sent to "the lost sheep of the house of Israel". He expressly opposed any religious egoism, and the separatist claim of any religious institution to "unique" wisdom.

Jesus' use of oil or balm also clearly differs from the religious practices of the Essenes. Jesus himself was called "The Anointed" (*Chrestos*), a title and a specific epithet that at once set him apart from the rest of the Essenes. In ancient rites, anointment with oil served the purpose of magically banning and protecting oneself from demons. It healed the diseases of soul and body. The anointing was also used to "seal" the body of a follower, to bind him to the Deity whose protection he was under. Celsus mentions that the Ophitic Gnostics possessed a seal that transformed anyone into a "Son of the Father", provided he received it while reciting the words, "I have been anointed with white salve from the Tree of Life" (Origen contra Celsum VI,27). And in the apocryphal gospel according to Philip, one can read, "the Tree of Life is in the centre of Paradise, as is the oil tree, from which the oil of anointment (chrisma) comes; this chrism is the source of the resurrection" (Nag Hammadi Codex II 3; 121, 15–19).

If one thinks of the final rebirth of the free spirit in a divine body in this context, one can see the decisive new element which Jesus, as the Anointed, added to the teachings of the various Essenian sects. As Irenaeus wrote, anointing was a ceremony of deliverance for the "perfect", and was more highly esteemed than ordinary baptism. The anointing was generally administered on the head, especially the forehead, sometimes in the form of a cross. The tradition of anointment goes back to Vedic India, where ascetics (Sadhus) and the religious of various denominations can still be recognised by the sign of white horizontal (Shiva) or vertical (Vaishnava) stripes on the forehead, which they draw on with a mixture of oil and holy ash (vibhuti) or powder.

Gnostic beliefs can easily be recognized in early Christianity, particularly in the Pauline epistles, and most of all in the Epistle to the Ephesians (which hardly seems like the work of Paul). Strong Gnostic influence is also evident in the Gospel according to Saint John, in the works of Clement of Alexandria, Origen and the Origenists (lit. the origin-als). Few first-hand sources in Gnosticism have survived, due to the wholesale destruction of scriptures found "heretical" by the power-hungry institutions of the Church. The surviving Gnostic literature comprises the Pistis Sophia (Gk: Pistis = belief, Sophia = wisdom), the books of Jeu, and the texts of the coptic library of Nag Hammadi, which were compiled in the fourth century A.D., and rediscovered in 1945, in a manner similar to the discovery of the famous Dead Sea Scrolls.

At this stage in our explorations we have gathered a convincing body of evidence for the wider pan Asian background of the advent of Jesus and the course taken by the early Church. Still, some of the most direct and impressive links can be found while examining the actual life of Jesus and his words in the New Testament, as we will do now.

Chapter four

The Secret of Jesus

Any attempt to describe the historical figure of Jesus Christ can be likened to the attempt to locate an atomic particle and to determine whether it is positively or negatively charged. The particle itself cannot be directly seen, but in the process of experimentation, one can make out lines, the tracks of larger particles in motion. If one traces these back to their common origin, one can calculate the force necessary to move the particle. One can thus reconstruct and describe the invisible cause. In the case of Jesus, there are two complicating factors. The first is that the Church has destroyed almost all the evidence that could be used in reconstructing the historical events of the life of Jesus; the other is that Jesus was compelled to keep his secret (his real identity) throughout his life in order to evade the grasp of his enemies. His personage is covered by a mysterious veil. A mist hangs over the events of his life, leaving much room for speculation.

So much of ambiguity finally leads to a state of general resignation. Our idea of the nature and personality of Jesus Christ is based not so much on documented biography and a historical understanding of the man, as on a concept that transcends history (but which has nonetheless been passed down through history). Invariably, we come up against the limits of what is for us natural and comprehensible. All our questions ultimately boil down to the same central question that had been posed by contemporaries of Jesus: *"What manner of man is this?"* (Mark 4,41).

The reason for such a great variety of interpretations of Jesus lies in the nature of the historical figure of Jesus, which has been the subject of an extraordinary, intense dialectic, with its veilings and unveilings. Jesus' exhortation to silence, the inability of even the disciples to understand him, and the fleeting words of the Son of Man have all played a role in this dialectic. For the very disciples who surrounded Jesus were not able to interpret him correctly or grasp his message in its entirety. He appeared strange and enigmatic, and he evidently did not see any great need to make himself more comprehensible to the public. The disciples were even expressly commanded to keep silent. In the Gospel record, Peter admits that Jesus "charged them that they should tell no man of him" (Mark 8,30). One encounters the same urging to secrecy when Jesus heals people. In numerous accounts, Jesus forbade those who were healed to spread the news of their healing. He sent away a leper whom he had cured with the words, "See thou say nothing to any man" (Mark 1,34 ff.). And as for those present at the awakening of the daughter of Jairus, "he charged them straitly that no man should know it . . ." (Mark 5,43). Jesus sent home the blind man of Bethsaida, whose sight he had restored, with the command, "Neither go into the town, nor tell it to any in the town." (Mark 8,26). In spite of all this, the miracles could not be kept secret and were spread throughout the land. For instance after the healing of the dumb: "And he charged them that they should tell no man: but the more he charged them, so much the more a great deal they published it." (Mark 7,36).

Jesus even commanded silence to the demons who recognised God in him (cf. Mark 1,25 and 5,7). He "suffered not the devils to speak, because they knew him" (Mark 1,34). The "unclean spirits" fell down before him when they saw him, crying "Thou art the Son of God", upon which Jesus "straitly charged them that they should not make him known" (Mark 3,11 ff.).

Thus the disciples, the healed, and even demons were forbidden to publicize his deeds, and were expressly told to keep silent about them. "And he would not that any man should know it" (cf. Mark 7,24;9,30). Evidently this also applied to the disciples. It appears that a great gulf separated Jesus from his disciples, who simply could not understand him. This becomes all the more clear with the master's repeated expression of dissatisfaction and anger about their incomprehension. For instance, when the ship is tossed on the sea by a storm, he asks his disciples, "Why are ye so fearful? How is it that ye have no faith?" (Mark 4, 35–41). Or following the miracle of the loaves, "And when Jesus knew it, he saith unto them, Why reason ye, because ye have no bread? perceive ye not yet, neither understand? have ye your heart yet hardened? Having eyes, see ye not? and having ears, hear ye not? and do ye not remember?" (Mark 8,17–18). "And he said unto them, How is it that ye do not understand?" (Mark 8,21).

When the disciples unsuccessfully attempted to cure a boy possessed by a "dumb spirit", Jesus harshly admonished them with the words, "O faithless generation, how long shall I be with you? how long shall I suffer you? bring him unto me" (Mark 9,19). One might interpret the last question as an indication on Jesus' part that he had always regarded his stay in Palestine as temporary and that he foresaw to return one day (to India).

His first public appearance in Jerusalem is also puzzling. Why should this man of plebeian origin be given such a splendid reception in the city, if he had been planing beams in his father's carpentry shop until after his thirtieth year, during which time he would have undoubtedly been a familiar face, well known among the local population? His enthusiastic reception by the people of Palestine suggests that he had returned after a prolonged absence from far away, with new, unknown teachings and extraordinary practices, such as the ability to perform miracles and to heal the sick. This theory would add further meaning to the question of the Nazarene Baptist, John: "Art thou he that should come, or do we look for another?" (Matthew 11,3).

Reincarnation in the New Testament

There are several places in the New Testament where obvious reference is made to reincarnation, but they are rarely considered, and remain deliberately misunderstood. Belief in reincarnation was a central tenet of early Christian communities until it was declared heretical and forever banned from Christian theology at the Second Council of Constantinople in 553 A.D. Clear evidence for the belief in the rebirth of the soul in another body can be seen in the Old Testament. Friedrich Weinreb tells of a punitive reincarnation in the form of cattle, described in the book of Jonah, as well as a reincarnation of Nimrod. Weinreb explains the Jewish concept of the divine soul "Nshamah" as being the divine spirit which is equally perfect in all men, and from which from time to time this or that character trait emerges[15].

Meyer's Konversationslexikon, a famous German encyclopaedia of 1907, contained the following passage on the topic of "Reincarnation in the Jewish Talmud": "Jews at the time of Christ held the general belief of the transmigration of the soul. The Talmudists assumed that God had created just a finite number of Jewish souls which would return as long as there were Jews, with occasional punitive reincarnation in an animal form. They would all be purified on the day of resurrection and arise in the bodies of the just in the promised land (Volume 18, p. 263)."

The Old Testament in fact ends with the prophecy of the reincarnation of Elijah, (as presaged in around 870 B.C.): "Behold, I will send you Elijah the prophet before the coming of the great and dreadful day of the Lord" (Malachi 4,5).

A few centuries later, a messenger comes to Zechariah and announces the birth of a son: "But the angel said unto him, fear not, Zechariah: for thy prayer is heard; and thy wife Elizabeth shall bear thee a son, and thou shalt call his name John, And thou shalt have joy and gladness; and many shall rejoice at his birth. For he shall be great in the sight of the Lord, and shall drink neither wine nor strong drink; and he shall be filled with the Holy Ghost, even from his mother's womb. And many of the children of Israel shall he turn to the Lord their God. And he shall go before him in the spirit and power of Elias, to turn the hearts of the fathers to the children, and the disobedient to the wisdom of the just; to make ready a people prepared for the Lord" (Luke 1,13–17).

Jesus later expressly replied to the questions of his disciples whether John the Baptist was Elijah: "Verily I say unto you, Among them that are born of women there hath not risen a greater than John the Baptist: notwithstanding he that is least in the kingdom of heaven is greater than he. And from the days of John the Baptist until now the kingdom of heaven suffereth violence, and the violent take it by force. For all the prophets and the law prophesied until John. And if ye will receive it, this is Elias, which was for to come." (Matthew 10,10–14).

We never learn where John the Baptist spent his youth. We have only the one pregnant sentence in the Gospel of Saint Luke: "And the child grew, and waxed strong in spirit, and was in the deserts till the day of his shewing unto Israel" (Luke 1,80)

It is conceivable that John was recognised as a high incarnation and therefore given an education in India. If this were the case, "preparing a path for the Lord" could be given more than a figurative interpretation.

At another point, Jesus asked his disciples: "Who do men say that I the Son of man am? And they said, Some say that thou art John the Baptist: some, Elias; and others, Jeremias, or one of the prophets. He saith unto them, But whom say ye that I am? And Simon Peter

answered and said, Thou art the Christ, the Son of the living God."
(Matthew 16,13–16). And the disciples asked Jesus, "Why then say
the scribes that Elias must first come? And Jesus answered and said
unto them, Elias truly shall first come, and restore all things. But I say
unto you, That Elias is come already, and they knew him not, but
have done unto him whatsoever they listed. Likewise shall also the
Son of man suffer of them. Then the disciples understood that he
spake unto them of John the Baptist." (Matthew 17,10–13).

According to the Gospels, then, Jesus himself confirmed that the
soul of Elias had been incarnated in John. Elias (Greek form of Elijah)
had tried to make monotheism the official religion at court, and
taught that God does not manifest himself in violent power and
destruction but in "a quiet whispering", in silent workings, and in
forbearance. Elias was a typical wandering monk who dressed in
rags, was nourished miraculously, and who performed miracles
himself, such as multiplying food and awakening the dead. He was
authorised to anoint others, spoke of having been sent, and attracted a great flock of followers. Finally he disappeared in a mysterious
manner (ascension) and was sought by fifty men for three days but
could not be found.

The followers of Jesus were aware that he was an Incarnation, but
were unsure of who Jesus could have been in his previous incarnation
and began to speculate. Jesus himself gave no hard and fast statement,
but he did confirm the disciples' views indirectly and with tact, by
encouraging them in their inquiry, "But who do you say I am?". In an
account of Jesus healing a man who was born blind, the disciples
asked: "Master, who did sin, this man, or his parents, that he was
born blind?" The idea that someone could have been born blind
because of previously committed sins can only be based on the
premise of a previous life and subsequent rebirth. The question also
implicitly suggests the sublime concept of Karma, in which the deeds
of a previous life determine one's next existence.

In the third chapter of Saint John's Gospel, the concept of reincarnation emerges quite clearly. When Jesus meets the Pharisee Nicodemus he greets this Jewish ruler with the following words: "Verily,
verily, I say unto thee, Except a man be born of water and of the
Spirit, he cannot enter into the kingdom of God." Nicodemus, who
obviously knows obviously nothing about the teaching of rebirth,
replies in astonishment: "How can a man be born when he is old?

Can he enter a second time into his mother's womb, and be born? Jesus answered, Verily, verily, I say unto thee, Except a man be born of water and of the Spirit, he cannot enter into the kingdom of God." (John 3). This would of course suggest the final birth into the pure spiritual life after so many "animal" births.

In 1900, James Morgan Pryse, an American, listed such places in the New Testament in which the doctrine of reincarnation is implicit[16]. According to Pryse, Jesus' teaching was simply a fresh continuation of the wisdom of the ancient philosophers and the fundamental tenets of the ancient world.

The fact that the spiritual priciple in human existence and the spiritual principle of the entire universe (microcosm-macrocosm) are in essence identical means that all elements, forces and processes are inherent in man, both materially and in a divine sense. This understanding of the world implies the spiritual unity of all beings and the inseparability of Nature and God. It stresses God's omnipresence, – his presence everywhere and always, in every particle of the entire universe. In his physical form, man is a manifestation from the region of the undifferentiated, limitless and timeless divine Unity, which materializes Itself through the cycles in all the various forms of existence. The original and real Being is eternally immutable; nature and the universe are, in contrast, in a state of continuous change, – the state of becoming.

Accordingly, the soul or spirit of man is imperishible and is subject to a continuous sequence of causes and effects in its continuous comings and goings (reincarnations). To finally return to his divine state, man must become conscious of this principle, and transcend the material field of his action. After a long series of lives, the karmic encasement in bodily existence is transcended, and in a final state of perfection, the inner and spiritual self merges into the eternal Unity. This is the original doctrine of reincarnation in a brief summary.

It is possible to transcend the narrow limits of physical existence and become conscious of one's own divine nature while still on earth, through knowledge, perception, devout meditation, discipline and renunciation.

The goal has been formulated for us in the Gospel according to Saint Matthew: "Be ye therefore perfect, even as your Father which is in heaven is perfect" (Matthew 5,48). But the path to perfection is paved with many incarnations through which man must evolve, before finally awakening to the Truth of the Son of God, and living as Jesus lived. "Believe me that I am in the Father, and the Father in me; or else believe me for the very work's sake. Verily, verily, I say unto you, He that believeth on me, the works that I do shall he do also; and greater works than these shall he do . . ." (John 14,11–12).

Miracles – of Jesus and in India

Seen in isolation, the miracles Jesus performed seem unique and unprecedented at first glance. In fact, people have always believed in superhuman, supernatural and inexplicable powers lying behind stupendous, extraordinary, spectacular and inexplicable realities, which might be valuable and benefical or dangerous and accursed. From the evolution of the first cult forms of primitive religions, man has dedicated himself to such inexplicable phenomena, and he continues to do so. Jesus' magical abilities were hardly considered worthy of mention by contemporary historians. When Jesus was alive, performers of miracles, healers and even quack anointers could be found in many places; the difference in Jesus' case was that he did not practice his arts in order to become famous or to increase his wealth.

The accounts of miracles in the New Testament, approximately thirty in number, are largely the product of the theologies of local congregations, and therefore not verifiable as historical. Accounts about Jesus' occupation as an exorcist are older, however, and were certainly current while Jesus was alive.

For thousands of years, the question of whether miracles were in fact possible was never posed; it was first asked when the world and its contents became the object of scientific analysis. Not until the seventeenth century did anyone attempt to explain rationally the acts of miracles described in the Gospels. Rationalists, however, are only prepared to accept phenomena that are in accordance with natural law and are deemed valid from the perspective of scientific analysis. Miracles are phenomena whose causes cannot be grasped and explained. Every day, technologists discover new rules in natural processes and solve puzzles that were inexplicable and a source of wonder the day before. Theologians define Christian miracles as "the suspension of a law of nature by God himself".

In contrast, occultists do not believe in the suspension of a law, but maintain that miraculous phenomena are subject to more complex

116

laws that have not yet been discovered and described. Everything that happens in the universe occurs in accordance with some law and is explicable. The so-called miraculous powers of the initiate or adept can be simply attributed to his exact knowledge of the play of laws that rule the inner cosmos of the consciousness. In both the Old Testament and the New Testament, the concept of "miracles" is unknown; instead, "signs", "power" or "great deeds of God" are described.

For instance, the Hebraic word *el* (elohim) which can be traced to the Semitic root *alah* (= to be strong) means "the great power". The designation for the holy power of magic is thus equated with the concept of God.

The same connection exists in the Indo–Germanic languages: the Sanskrit word, *brahman,* can be traced back to *brh* (= to be strong/to illuminate).

In performing miracles, Jesus' speciality seems to have been healing the ill, the deranged and the lame. But he evidently performed other miracles, such as transforming water to wine, multiplying loaves, making himself invisible, awakening the dead and walking across water.

The accounts of the miracles in the New Testament, like other accounts about the historical deeds of Jesus, have parallels and literary precursors in the East. Pliny relates that the Greek doctor Asclepiades (born 124 B.C.) healed people miraculously; Tacitus and Sueton write of healings performed by the Emperor Vespasian. Even the early Christian apostles were able to heal the sick and perform certain miracles, and in the first century A.D., Apollonius of Tyana performed similar miracles and a great many more. The attempt to find the earliest reports of miracles similar to those performed by Jesus inevitably leads to the legendary miracles of Krishna in the Vedic literature. Krishna is Hinduism's saviour and the eighth avatar of Vishnu. Vishnu (from the Sanskrit *vís* = to penetrate) is the second figure in the Hindu trinity (Trimurti) of Brahma, Vishnu and Shiva. In the Rig-Veda, Vishnu is not portrayed as a god incarnate, but as a manifestation of solar energy. An avatar (from the Sanskrit *ava* = downwards and *tri* = to cross over) is a person who has been filled with the light of divine spirit and thus represents a divine incarnation. This divine higher being has transcended the need of rebirth, but is nonetheless incarnated in the simple form of a mortal body in order

117

to help humanity attain salvation out of compassion for humanity.

The story of Krishna's birth, childhood and life has exact and even detailed parallels in the accounts of the New Testament (the infanticide is one instance). Krishna and Christ are the two most distinguished performers of miracles in the Holy Scriptures. Bhagvan Dass has established seven categories of miracles that Krishna performed[17]:

1. creating visions;
2. seeing things at a great distance;
3. multiplying small amounts of food or other things;
4. appearing at several places at the same time;
5. healing the ill by touching them;
6. awakening the "dead";
7. destroying the demonic

Some miracle workers can perform one or two kinds of miracles, others more. There have always been people of divine powers, healers or prophets of various grandeur and fame.

At any rate, India is the home of the miraculous. In his book *The Holy Science,* Sri Yukteswar defined the sense of human existence as the aspiration to unite self with God. Yukteswar regards such an endeavour as "essentially the same as nature's own play in the only real being, God, the powerful father and highest guru of the universe. An inevitable consequence of such an assumption is that all things are composed of the same one thing. This means that God himself, who appears as a multiplicity because his essence is expressed in a variety of ways, is everywhere and in everything. The Bible describes the principle in Psalm 82, Verse 6: "Ye are gods; and all of you are children of the most High." And according to the gospel according to Saint John, Jesus replied to the Jews' accusation that he was trying to make a god of himself, "Is it not written in your law, I said, ye are gods?" (John 10,34).

The same conceptual tendency is apparent in Yukteswar's work[18], which explains that the consecrated, having attained absolute supremacy over the material world, find their God or salvation in their own selves and not in their external surroundings. Such god-people finally obtain mastery over life and death and almost become world creators, capable of anything. They achieve the eight ascetic attainments (Aiswaryas), through the power of which they are capable of performing

1 Anima = to make matter as small as one desires;
2 Mahima = to make matter as large as one desires;
3 Laghima = to make matter as light as one desires;
4 Garima = to make matter as heavy as one desires;
5 Prapti = attain the desired through "Apti";
6 Vasitwa = to attain power over all things through "Vasa";
7 Prakamya = to fulfill all wishes through the strength of one's will;
8 Ishitwa = to become Isha (= Lord) over all things.

When Jesus' disciples failed to exorcise an unclean spirit, he was blunt in explaining why: "For verily, I say unto you, If ye have faith as a grain of mustard seed ye shall say unto this mountain: Remove hence to yonder place; and it shall remove; and nothing shall be impossible unto you" (Matthew 17,20).

The phenomenon of levitation has had an uninterrupted tradition both in and outside the Church. Two hundred and thirty Catholic saints were known to have possessed the more or less voluntary ability to levitate.

In the last century, the medium Daniel Douglas Home convinced thousands of spectators on various occasions of his ability to "fly". Among the spectators were persons as famous as Thackeray, Bulwer Lytton, Napoleon II, Ruskin, Rosetti and Mark Twain. Such performances were put on repeatedly over a period of almost forty years and were inspected and confirmed in their authenticity.

In his reports on the most varied forms of phenomena, Francis Hitching[19] cited more than twenty-five cases of levitation. Even the most recent past has provided examples of levitations. The followers of the Transcendental Meditation of Maharishi Yogi claim that almost anyone can learn to levitate, provided that they stick strictly to the technique of the master; photos of levitating followers were circulated among the world press as proof of this.

Levitation seems to be produced by unusually heightened control over bodily functions through concentration or meditation, or by a temporary suspension of gravity in moments of religious ecstacy.

Such minor miracles can evidently even be performed as a means of earning money, satisfying the demand of the sensationalist public. The truly great masters would, of course, always refuse to perform miracles out of such base motives.

The Indian miracle performer, Sai Baba, claims (as Jesus also said), that every person has divine power in himself, which can be augmented by training and conscious living. Whoever uses his powers to sow the seed of evil, however, will reap evil. And whoever uses his powers to his own advantage will lose them. Sometimes powers have been limited, either in their effect or in time, particularly when practised without goodness, wisdom and piety.

Today, just as thousands of years ago, miracles remain legitimate means for bringing the divine message closer to the doubter and those who are chained to the material world.

Almost everything that has ever been said about Jesus has parallels in ancient Indian legends. Widespread ignorance of the similarities between the Indian and Christian tradition can partly be attributed to the inability of almost all Europeans to read the Sanskrit of ancient texts; not until recently have translations begun to arouse interest in the Western world.

None of the known incarnations of God seem to have been able to prove their legitimacy to the unbelieving people without heavenly signs and miracles. Every son of God must be able to demonstrate his status to sceptics by means of superhuman attributes.

In the Indian trinity, the son of God is called Krishna, whose very name shares its roots with that of Christ (H. P. Blavatsky always used the more obvious spelling, "Christna"). "Christ" descends from the greek word *chrestos,* meaning "anointed with oil". Christos can be traced back to the Sanskrit word Krsna (Krishna = attracts all), which is colloquially pronounced "Krishto". "Krishto" means "attraction". This person who attracts everything is the highest personification of God.

Brahman tradition relates the following about Krishna: "Three persons emerged from the eternal, peaceful God without disturbing his unity. Brahma is the father (Zupitri), the all-creating God, the Son of God, who has become the word incarnate in Krishna, who came to the world as the shepherd of all people. Shiva is the Holy spirit, the third person. He is the Spirit that directs the eternal law of life and transition, is inherent in all living beings and the entire nature . . ."

Krishna is the eighth incarnation of the son of God, Vishnu, who was also incarnated in other forms. One such reincarnation was Buddha Gautama (Sakyamuni/Siddhartha), who is regarded as the ninth incarnation of Vishnu.

120

Krishna and Christ

According to the oldest available sources, Vishnu appeared as early as 4000 years B.C. in the presence of the virgin, Devanaki (= woman created for God), a member of the royal family, in the form of a man. Devanaki fell down in ecstasy and was "overshadowed" by the spirit of God, who joined her in divine and majestic splendour; she conceived a child. A prophecy in the Atharva-Veda depicts the event in the following manner: "Blessed art thou, Devanaki, among all women, welcome amid the holy Rishis. Thou hast been chosen for the work of salvation . . . He will come with a lightened crown, and heaven and earth will be full of joy . . . Virgin and Mother, we greet you; thou art the mother of us all, for thou wilt give birth to our saviour. Thou shalt call him Krishna."

According to the Bhagavad-Gita, the King of Mathura had been warned in a bad dream that his sister's daughter, Lakshmi, would bear a child who would be more powerful than the king himself. The virgin, Devanaki, hid in the fields with the new-born child in the company of some shepherds, and miraculously the child escaped the soldiers whom the king had dispatched to kill all new-born male babies.

According to the Atharva-Veda, which portrays the event somewhat differently, King Kansa of Mathura saw a falling star and asked a Brahman about its significance. The wise man replied that the world had become wicked, and that man's greed for money and his life of sin had moved God to send a saviour. The star was Vishnu, who had become flesh in the womb of his niece, Devanaki; the incarnation would one day avenge all crimes and lead humanity on new paths. Beside himself in rage, the king had the Brahman killed along with all new-born males.

There have been many accounts of Krishna's youth, poetry glorifying his power and qualities. Just like the baby Jesus in the apocryphical gospels, Krishna was able to perform all manners of miracles as a child. He thus survived many dangers prepared for him by his uncle Kansa. At one point, a snake crawled into his crib to strangle the child, but was killed by the lad with his bare hands (cf. the myth of young Hercules). Later, Krishna fought the many-headed snake, Kaliya, conquered it and compelled it to leave the river Yamuna. The

121

heroic deeds of the Indian child wonder would fill entire volumes. When he was sixteen, Krishna left his mother to spread his new teaching throughout India. He spoke out against the corruption of the people and the princes and said that he had come to earth to offer all people redemption from original sin, to drive out unclean spirits, and to restore the kingdom of good. He overcame monstrous difficulties, fought entire armies by himself, performed manifold miracles, awakened the dead, healed lepers, gave sight to the blind and hearing to the deaf, and healed the lame.

And finally, he collected a flock of disciples who supported him zealously and were to continue his works. Everywhere, people came to him to hear his teachings and to behold his miracles. He was honoured as a God and called the true redeemer, who had been prophesied by the fathers.

From time to time, Krishna would withdraw from the company, leaving his disciples alone in order to test them and only returning in times of difficulty. The growth of the movement displeased those in power, who unsuccessfully attempted to repress it.

Krishna, like Christ, did not wish to propagate a new religion, but simply desired to renew the religion that already existed and cleanse it of all its odious abuses and impurities. His teachings are in the form of poetic parables and aphorisms reminiscent of those of Jesus. The accounts and discourses have been recorded in the Bhagavad-Gita, which is an easily comprehensible presentation of the pure morality of Krishna's elevated world view. Krishna teaches his disciples brotherly love, self respect, to share with the poor, to do good deeds and to keep faith in the never-failing good of the Creator. He commands his followers to repay evil with good and to love one's enemy, and he forbids revenge. He consoles the weak, condemns tyranny and helps the unfortunate. He himself lives in poverty and dedicates himself to helping the poor and the downtrodden. He is free of personal ties and advocates chastity. Like Jesus, Krishna leads the life of an itinerant mendicant.

Krishna also undergoes transformation; the son of God shows himself in manifold divine forms to one of his favourite disciples, Arjuna, telling him, "Whoever does deeds for my sake, whoever devotes himself to me utterly, whoever is free of ties to the material world and of enmity to any beings, will come to me" (Bhagavad-Gita, eleventh song).

122

The legend of Krishna is probably the oldest source from which the mystical figure of Christ was drawn. Similarities with the legends of Dionysos (c. eighth century B.C.) are equally astonishing. But it was not just the high cultures of ancient Greece and Rome which affected Christianity; ancient Iran, with its figures of saviours and its eschatological and apocalyptical visions, also greatly influenced the Christian religion. The most prominent figures in the Persian religion were Zarathustra and Mithras, god-men who reformed the religous traditions which had become rigid. Before Zarathustra emerged, eastern Iran's religious outlook was practically identical to that of ancient India.

Chapter five

The "Death" of Jesus
Trial and Sentence

The political situation in Judea at the time of Jesus was confused, and marked by dramatic events. Herod the Great (37–4 B.C.) had been forced to deal with unrest and rebellion throughout his term of office. The "robbers" who fought Herod were fanatical patriots, who used all the power and means at their disposal to oppose Roman rule. Josephus gives an account of the rebel leader, Judas of Galilee, whose "band of robbers" must have really been religious men who were only attempting to defend the faith of their fathers from foreign influence (Jewish 18,I 1 and 6). Among the rebellious groups were the Pharisees, the Sadducees, the Rechabites, and the Essenes, who had the advantage of being organised as an Order and having an "élite", the Nazarites or Nazarenes. While the Sadducees and Pharisees compromised with Herod's successors and even accepted high office in the course of the years, the Rechabites rejected the changes that Rome sought to impose on them, and continued to live in tents outside the towns, as their forefathers had done.

As we have seen, when Herod's son Archelaus was removed from power, the Essenes and Nazarenes probably returned from their exile in Alexandria; in any case, at about this time the monastery of Qumran was resettled.

At the same time, however, during the office of Herodes Antipas, a bitter partisan war against Roman imperial rule began, conducted secretly and in hiding with Essene backing. While the Pharisees and Sadducees conformed and became integrated into the system, the Essenes and Nazarenes do not seem to have behaved so complacently and obsequiously. After the death of Herod the Great, the country went from one crisis to the next.

Under such circumstances, many were hoping for a Messiah who would revive the empire of David and Solomon, and free the land from hated foreign domination.

According to the Gospels of Mark, Matthew and Luke, the period in which Jesus was publicly active lasted about one or two years.

124

Only the latest of the texts, the Gospel according to Saint John, makes mention of three Passovers in Jerusalem at which Jesus is said to have been present. Thus one can safely presume that his residence lasted two to three years. During this period, Jesus often crossed the borders of the Palestinian provinces, and thus repeatedly withdrew from the powers of local jurisdiction. Why he went to Jerusalem afterwards and gave himself up to his persecutors is unclear and can only be the subject of speculation.

When the Nazarene entered Jerusalem, he was given a triumphal reception and celebrated as the king who would bring about the kingdom of God.

According to Christian tradition, the kingdom of God is the state of redemption which can only be attained by the individual through divine support and mercy on a purely spiritual level. But the masses in Jerusalem were awaiting something more worldly in nature. Jewish Messiah cults hoped to build the kingdom of God in the form of a new, purified and powerful state of Israel. Thus Jesus was expected to lead the state as David had once led Israel, and free the land from the Roman yoke. The reply of Jesus to such expectations was recorded in the Gospel of Saint Luke: "Neither shall they say, Lo here! or, lo there! for, behold, the kingdom of God is within you" (Luke 17,21).

Jesus' entry into the city of Jerusalem was an act of unprecedented provocation. Up to that point, the opposition was an entirely underground movement, and those involved had not shown themselves openly within the area of Roman jurisdiction. About a week before the great feast of Passover, Jesus decided to leave his place of hiding in the mountains of Ephraim and journeyed with his followers by way of a detour through Jericho to the capital, some forty kilometres distant (John 11,54).

The Gospel according to Mark tells of the dramatic decision: "And they were in the way going up to Jerusalem; and Jesus went before them: and they were amazed; and as they followed, they were afraid. And he took again the twelve, and began to tell them what things should happen to them, Saying, Behold, we go up to Jerusalem; and the Son of man shall be delivered unto the chief priests, and unto the scribes; and they shall condemn him to death, and shall deliver him to the Gentiles; And they shall mock him, and shall scourge him, and shall spit upon him, and shall kill him: and the third day he shall rise again" (Mark 10,32–34).

125

Five days before the great feast, they reached Jerusalem. When they entered the city gates, Jesus was given great ovations by the multitudes. Although Jesus was riding a donkey as a demonstration of his humility, modesty and peacefulness, the homage later turned into a tragic misunderstanding. "And when he was come into Jerusalem, all the city was moved, saying, Who is this?" (Matthew 21,10). Jesus' strongly-worded statements and particularly the real, physical conflicts at the clearing of the temple can hardly be interpreted allegorically. Jesus' appeal to the multitude could have easily been understood as a call to attack: "Think not that I am come to send peace on earth: I came not to send peace, but a sword" (Matthew 10,34). Or: "I am come to send fire on the earth: and what will I, if it be already kindled?" (Luke 12,49).

Jesus' first action in Jerusalem was a stronger attack on authority than had ever been dared before. Jesus remonstrated against the protectors of the law in the temple with incredible force. His sharply formulated denunciations (Matthew 23) finally settled accounts with his antagonists in front of a great number of enthusiastic pilgrims. According to the gospels, he even went so far as to castigate merchants and money changers and drive them out of the place of worship. Of course, such an attack on the authority of the officials of the temple could not simply be ignored. There existed a very real danger of a massive uprising. "And the scribes and chief priests heard it, and sought how they might destroy him; for they feared him, because all the people was astonished at his doctrine" (Mark 11,18).

Because of the possibility of uprisings and disturbances during the festival holy days, Pilate and his cohorts (five hundred legionaries) had marched in from Caesarea in order to intervene as soon as it seemed necessary. Such disturbances are only briefly alluded to in the Gospels. In the Gospel according to Mark, one does learn that Barabbas was taken prisoner with "them that had made insurrection with him, who had committed murder in the insurrection" (Mark 15,7). In this Gospel one can also read that the high priests and scribes "sought how they might take him by craft, and put him to death. But they said, Not on the feast day, lest there be an uproar of the people" (Mark 14,1–2). If Jesus was to be liquidated, great haste and caution were the order of the day. The Pharisees were the first to try to get Jesus to incriminate himself in public discussion. They asked him whether it was legitimate to pay the Roman Emperor taxes. If Jesus had replied in the negative, he would have been open to the charge of high treason; but he got out of the predicament through a stroke of genius (cf. Mark 12,14–17). The Sadducees then attempted to ridicule his doctrine of reincarnation. But his well-considered retorts quelled the attack (Mark 12,19–27).

The exact date of the Passion still poses a considerable problem. Neither the month nor the year is to be found anywhere in the gospels. Speculations range from 30 to 33 A.D. Although all the gospels agree that Jesus was crucified on a Friday, there are disagreements as to the day of the month. According to the Synoptics (Matthew, Mark and Luke), Jesus celebrated the Passover meal with his disciples on Thursday evening. According to the Jewish calender, Thursday was the fourteenth of Nisan, the day on which the Easter lamb was eaten; and the following Friday, the fifteenth of Nisan, the first holy day of the Jewish festival of Passah-Mazzoth. Now, it is quite inconceivable that Jesus was arrested and interrogated in front of the entire Sanhedrin (composed of seventy-one Jewish citizens) on that very holy night. Such a violation of holy Jewish law by its own protectors would have simply been impossible.

An alternative solution is to be found in the gnostic text of John. In John, the Last Supper was not specified as the Jewish feast of Passover and Jesus was crucified on the fourteenth of Nisan. In that case, Jesus must have celebrated without the prescribed unleavened loaves and the ritual cutlery, because these can only be obtained (even today) on the day immediately preceding Passover, the so-called day of preparation. This version of the John text seems logical enough, but it does necessitate the assumption that Jesus did not feel obliged to practice such customs anchored in Jewish law.

The very choice of where the Last Supper was held is an indication of Essene influence. "Behold, when ye are entered into the city, there shall a man meet you, bearing a pitcher of water; follow him into the house where he entereth in" (Luke 22,10). Yet to bear water was solely a woman's chore in the Jerusalem of those days. In this particular house, the customary practices of the day did not seem to be followed very strictly. And in fact the meal did not proceed at all according to the prescribed rites, but entirely in the Essene manner. It is expressly described how no sacrificial lamb was eaten; the participants ate bread, like the strictly vegetarian Essenes. In the apocryphal gospel of the Ebionites, Jesus' reply to his disciples' question of where

127

they should prepare the Passover meal was, "I do not wish to eat meat with you this Passover!" (Epiphanius, Haer. 30,20 4).

At this point, one comes up against this problem that has caused exegetes the greatest difficulties and still has not been satisfactorily solved, – how to establish the time of the Last Supper. The problem becomes quite simple when one considers that the Essenes had their own calendar upon which they based their festivals (cf. page 106). Because the solar calendar made it possible to divide the year into 364 days and 52 weeks, there was no time left over each year, in contrast to the official calendar. New Year's Day always fell on a Wednesday in spring. Accordingly, the Essene Passover always occurred on a Wednesday on the fourteenth of Nisan, and therefore took place two days before the Jewish Passover. Hence the John text is correct in asserting that Jesus was crucified on the fourteenth of Nisan; he is referring to the official calendar, according to which the day of crucifixion was one day before Passover. The entire events of the Passion take place over a period of three days and can be established logically and conclusively. – On Tuesday evening, the Last Supper, arrest at Gethsemane, preliminary interrogation by Annas, Peter's denial. – On Wednesday morning, the beginning of the trial in front of the Sanhedrin on the basis of religious law, examination of witnesses by the high priest Caiaphas; during the night, Jesus is kept in custody and ill-treated in Caiaphas' prison. – On Thursday morning, the Sanhedrin convenes to announce the judgement; Jesus is taken to Pilate for interrogation; and then taken to Herod Antipas for interrogation; and kept overnight in custody in the prison of the Roman garrison. – On Friday, the political trial continues in the presence of Pilate; flagellation, crowning with thorns, condemnation, crucifixion at about the sixth hour (twelve noon).

Something rather odd occurred during Jesus' arrest by the guards of the temple after the meal: "Then Simon Peter having a sword drew it, and smote the high priest's servant, and cut off his right ear. The servant's name was Malchus. Then said Jesus unto Peter, Put up thy sword into the sheath: the cup which my Father hath given me, shall I not drink it?" (John 18,10–11). Why was Peter carrying a sword?

The Sanhedrin (= the assembly) was the highest instance for religious law of the Jewish people; and before Roman rule, the institution had also had political power. This High Council was composed of high priests, the elders and scribes, all in all seventy-one men. The official high priest, Joseph Caiaphas (= the inquisitor) presided over the court. Among the elders of the assembly was Joseph of Arimathea, a rich and influential land-owner who, according to Luke, voted against the decision of the High Council to kill the Nazarene (Luke 23, 50 and 51). After detailed cross-examination of the witnesses, the High Priest Caiaphas concluded by posing the crucial question: "I adjure thee by the living God, that thou tell us whether thou be the Christ, the Son of God" (Matthew 26,63). When Jesus answers, "Thou hast said it", Caiaphas interprets this as confirmation. Whoever arrogated divine honour to himself was a blasphemer according to Jewish law and faced capital punishment. The execution was to take place by stoning, after which the corpse was to be hung from a tree, as the Jewish law prescribed. The reason why the execution of Jesus took place in a different manner was that the Sanhedrin had recently received the order from Rome not to condemn anyone to death without the confirmation of the Roman procurator, and not to convene anywhere outside the area of the temple. Trials were to take place during the day-time (between dawn and dusk!). If all seventy-one council members had been called in and the negotiations had taken place at night, the entire procedure would have been illegal from the onset. In Luke's Gospel, one can find confirmation that the session took place during the day (Luke 22,66). The assembly did not reconvene until the following morning (Thursday) to announce the judgement: "When the morning was come, all the chief priests and elders of the people took council against Jesus to put him to death; and when they had bound him, they led him away, and delivered him to Pontius Pilate the governor." (Matthew 27, 1–2).

Pilate seems to have been against the case from the very beginning (John 18,31). He said that he could not find Jesus guilty, attempted to obtain his release, and finally in a demonstrative gesture washed his hands of the matter (cf. Matthew 27,24). Pilate's attempt to transfer the delicate matter to the local Jewish ruler, Herod Antipas, who happened to be present, failed. For Jesus made no comment whatsoever and was sent back once again to the procurator who at last gave in to the will of the people (who had in the meantime been stirred up by Caiaphas), by turning over the Nazarene for execution.

Some of the contradictions and puzzling events described in the Gospels can be solved in an astonishingly simple manner when one

129

realises that (as we have suggested) the Nazarene had belonged to the "New Covenant" of the Essene movement as an "Observer of Rites" (cf. page 94). It becomes clear why Jesus was persecuted by the Orthodox Jews, and why he could be prosecuted in a political trial as well. With reference to the sources at our disposal, scant though they be, the events surrounding the historical figure of Jesus (as narrated here) can be convincingly and satisfactorily explained.

The problems arising from the popular views about the Resurrection from death and the Assumption of the body of Christ are far more difficult to solve. Available sources do not explain why Jesus was declared dead just a few hours after his crucifixion, although his legs, unlike those of his companions on the cross, had not been broken (which was a customary act to shorten decisively the torture which could otherwise last up to five days). Thus Pilate was very surprised when asked for the corpse: "And Pilate marvelled if he were already dead..." (Mark 15,44).

No one saw the resurrection – at any rate, we know of no one who claimed to have seen the resurrection. All pronouncements about the resurrection are the product of pure faith. Talk of resurrection only began in retrospect and was only an interpretation of what had happened'.

The matter might be left open as such: either one believes in the resurrection of Jesus or one does not. To turn the lamp of the historian on the matter would seem impossible after all these two thousand years, *if* . . . if it were not for a truly wonderful piece of evidence that has enabled us to examine the events surrounding the crucifixion in great detail *while using the most modern tests technology can devise*. This piece of evidence is the linen shroud from the tomb of Jesus.

"And now when the even was come, because it was the preparation, that is, the day before the sabbath, Joseph of Arimathea, an honourable counsellor, which also waited for the kingdom of God, came, and went in boldly unto Pilate, and craved the body of Jesus. And Pilate marvelled if he were already dead: and calling unto him the centurion, he asked him whether he had been any while dead. And when he knew it of the centurion, he gave the body to Joseph. And he bought fine linen, and took him down, and wrapped him in the linen, and laid him in a sepulchre which was hewn out of a rock, and rolled a stone unto the door of the sepulchre. And Mary Magda-

130

lene and Mary the mother of Jesus beheld where he was laid." (Mark 15,42–47).

From the other Gospels, we can gain further information about the course of events. Matthew and Luke note that Joseph was rich, Matthew and John report that he had been a disciple of Jesus (Luke says he awaited the coming Kingdom of God), and John adds that his discipleship remained a secret to the world. Luke observes that Joseph had disagreed with the counsel and deeds of the other Jews. Matthew, Luke and John confirm his request for and (Matthew and John) reception of the body of Christ from Pilate. Matthew and Luke refer to the linen shroud for the body of Jesus. From Matthew, we learn that the linen was pure, and from John, that there were linen wraps. Both Luke and John recount that the sepulchre was new, and that it had hitherto been empty. Matthew adds that the vault belonged to Joseph. Luke describes it as being carved into the rock, and Matthew says how Joseph rolled a large stone in front of the opening.

The linen mentioned here has actually been preserved to this day in Turin, and is an authentic document that has wondrously captured one of the most important moments in the history of the world for posterity, and this in a truly photographic manner.

The famed shroud of Turin is 4.36 metres long, 1.10 metres wide and shows the impression of a male body with astonishing clarity. One half of the shroud shows the back and, because the shroud was wrapped around the head at about its middle, the other side shows the front of a recently crucified man. It is an easy matter to recognize the head, the face, the thorax, arms, hands, legs and feet of the man in the impression. The colour of the impression is for the most part a sepia tone, though in some places grey. One can also clearly see traces of blood which appear as a pale crimson.

When one first beholds the entire shroud, one's eyes are led to two dark, vertical stripes, which extend to two large rhombus-shaped spots. These are burn marks which were repaired with lighter-coloured stitches. Their peculiar shape arose as a result of the shroud's being folded in forty-eight layers and preserved in a silver shrine after almost being lost in a fire in the chapel of Chambery (France) in 1532. When the silver container began to melt on one side from the heat of the fire, the heat and melted silver left the geometrically formed patches, burned into the folded material (see illustration). If the impression on this piece of material is really that of Jesus in person, and if that is proved, it should be considered not only a scientific sensation of the greatest significance, it would also serve as the only acceptable scientific basis for pursuing a question that has occupied so many until this day: did Jesus rise from the dead?

The Age of the Shroud

A first reservation might be that a textile could hardly have survived a period of almost two millenia with so little damage. There are, however, numerous pieces of linen that are considerably older and better preserved than the shroud of Turin. One can find well-preserved exemplars in the collections of the Egyptian National Museum in Cairo, the Egyptian Museum of Turin, as well as the Egyptology departments of museums in London, Paris, Berlin, Hildesheim etc., with some specimens going back 3500, even 5000 years. The dry climate of the Near East is very favourable for the long preservation of textiles and scrolls. The plant substance is mainly cellulose, a very stable molecule.

The word *sindon,* used by the Synoptics, designates a large linen cloth. The shroud is of linen, the fibres twilled together with a weave of three to one, creating a fish-bone pattern. At the time of Jesus, this was a rare form of loom work, requiring a great deal of technique, and probably very expensive. The only surviving examples of this kind of material that had been woven in the first century came from the Roman province of Syria, to which Palestine belonged at the time. Twilling was only introduced in the West in the fourteenth century.

While examining the strands with an electron microscope in 1973, Professor Raes of the University of Ghent in Belgium discovered a few traces of cotton, a substance which had not yet been cultivated in the Near East at the time of Jesus. In Syria and Mesopotamia, cotton imported from India was occasionally used for weaving, although the cotton had to be processed beforehand on a special loom.

Today there is a simple test to determine the age of all organic material, by measuring the amount of the radioactive isotope of carbon, carbon-14. Everything that lives and respires, absorbs carbon-dioxide from the air, using the carbon in its structure. As the organic life ceases, the radioactive carbon slowly diminishes; after c. 5730 years, one-half of the original radioactive C-14 is left. Measurement of the carbon isotope levels and calculations using the half-life (the time in which half of the carbon isotope disintegrates) allows us to determine the age of an archaeological find with a precision of $\pm$ 10%. One does need a fair quantity of the material, though, and it is completely destroyed in a combustion process. It goes without saying that one did not wish to have Christianity's most significant holy relic damaged by such wantonness. In any case, a carbon-14 test would have incorporated an error of $\pm$ 200 years for an object that is presumably two thousand years old.

The method of the Swiss botanist and criminologist Dr. Max Frei led him to sensational discoveries by using pollen analysis. Dr. Frei took samples of 10 to 20 cm from the surface of the shroud with the aid of adhesive tape, at twelve different points. Under the scanning electron microscope, he was delighted to locate, in addition to the dust and fibres, 1–4 grains of plant pollen per cm^2. Grains of pollen are between 0.0025 and 0.25 mm in size, and therefore not generally identifiable with the naked eye. But the tiny grains are surrounded by a double skin whose chemical composition has not been fully determined even today. The external shell is at any rate so resistant that under certain conditions the pollen can survive intact for several millions of years. Though it seems fantastic when one thinks of the fine yellow powder so familiar in spring, the tiny pollen grains of each variety of plant have their distinctive individual appearance so that it is possible to tell quite easily which grain originated from which plant. In a report on his research published in March of 1976, Frei announced that he was able to identify a total of forty-nine types of plants whose pollen had been found on the shroud. Many of the plants exist in all the areas in which the shroud is said to have been kept in the course of its history, as for example the Lebanon cedar (cedrus libani). The sensational news was, however, that pollen had been found from eleven types of plants which do not exist in Europe, but are among the halophytes of the Near East. Halophytes are plants that only flourish in soils with extremely high salt content, for example in the region surrounding the Dead Sea. Among them were special desert varieties of the species Tamarix, Suaeda and Artemisia. Because up to now the history of the shroud could only be traced back to the 14th century, a few researchers had presumed that it was produced in France at that time; one also knew that after that the shroud had only circulated in France and Italy. The pollen analysis proved that the linen had to have been in Palestine before its circulation in Europe. Moreover, one then found that the kinds of pollen identified on the shroud were also to be found in relatively high concentrations in those layers of sediment in the Sea of Galilee which date back to the time of Jesus.

Grains of pollen from eight further varieties of plants were characteristic of the steppes of Asia Minor, particularly the area around Edessa (today Urfa in Turkey). Dr. Frei could hardly have grasped the significance of this fact at the time.

We owe much of our ability to follow the history of the shroud back to its origins to the magnificent research of the English historian Ian Wilson[2]. With a great quantity of historical evidence at his disposal, he was able to prove that the shroud is the Edessa "Portrait", of which there have been accounts from as early as the first century, and which has been known as the "Mandylion" since the sixth century. The full history of the Holy Shroud gets as exciting as a good thriller. Indeed fact can be more wonderful than fiction!

According to the apocryphal gospel of the Hebrews, which was used by the Nazarites, Jesus gave the shroud described in the Gospels to the "priests' servant"[3] after the Resurrection. One can presume that the recipient was not an enemy of Jesus, or someone who had been attempting to have him killed shortly before. It is far more likely that the priests' servant received the priceless gift as remuneration for some special service.

In around 325 A.D. the Bishop Eusebius of Caesarea wrote in his *Historia Ecclesiastica* that the King of Edessa (Abgar V., Ukkama = the Black, who ruled from 9–46 A.D.), had sent a messenger to Jerusalem and invited Jesus to come to Edessa to heal him of a chronic rash. Eusebius refers to an alleged correspondence between Jesus and Abgar which he had acquired from the archives of the Edessan king, and which he himself translated from ancient Syrian (i.e. Aramaic) into Greek. According to the correspondence, Jesus was not able to make the voyage himself but sent a bearer of the Good News,i.e. one of the seventy disciples mentioned in the Gospel of Saint Luke (Luke 10,1). This disciple had the Greek name Thaddaeus, (though he was not the apostle of that name) and was called Addai in Syrian. Jesus sent him to Abgar with a mysterious portrait. Through the wondrous power of this portrait of Jesus, the king was healed instantly, and immediately converted to the teachings of Jesus.

In c. 1850, a number of ancient Syrian manuscripts were found in a monastery near Wadi el-Natrun (Natron Valley) in the lower Egyptian desert in which various confirmations of the story of Abgar were found. All the accounts agree that after the spectacular miracle, Addai/Thaddaeus delivered a sermon in Edessa, and most of the citizens then joined their king in converting to the "New Covenant".

Because a tomb shroud was actually considered "impure" in those days, it is easy to understand why it was referred to as a "portrait".

The word for the linen in the "Acta Thaddaei"[4], *tetradiplon,* means "four times folded". If one folds the shroud, which is over four metres in length, in the middle three times, the awkward piece of material is reduced to the handy size of about half a metre, showing just the *portrait of Jesus* in a very impressive manner. If preserved and displayed in this fashion, the true size of the *sindon* can hardly be suspected and was probably regarded as of little interest because of the lack of tonal contrast in the impression of the rest of the body.

In 57 A.D., Abgar's second son Manu VI., succeeded to the throne of Edessa, promptly reconverted to paganism, and persecuted the new Edessian community mercilessly. At this time the portrait disappeared and no more was heard of it for a while. The fate of the shroud thereafter can be gathered in great detail from the "History of the Edessan Portrait", which was written in 945 A.D. at the court of the Byzantine Emperor, Konstantin Porphyrogennetos. This version relates that the holy relic had been hidden in a hermetically sealed niche above the west gate of the town Edessa and was not rediscovered until 540 A.D., when the town wall had to be repaired (for there had been a catastrophic flood in 525 A.D.). It was identified beyond doubt as the original portrait that had, according to tradition, been brought to King Abgar. As early as 544 A.D., Bishop Eulalios declared that the portrait found was an impression, *achairopoietos,* "not made by human hands".[5]

The rediscovered picture was placed in "a large church" (the cathedral of Hagia Sophia), and was carefully preserved in a silver shrine under lock and key. From that point onwards the shroud was called "Mandylion", and regarded as so holy and valuable that it was rarely shown, only on very important holy days. A chronicle of the shroud from the tenth century relates that Abgar had fixed the picture to a board and "coated it with gold", leaving the face free of course. Curiously, various renderings of the portrait of Jesus before the

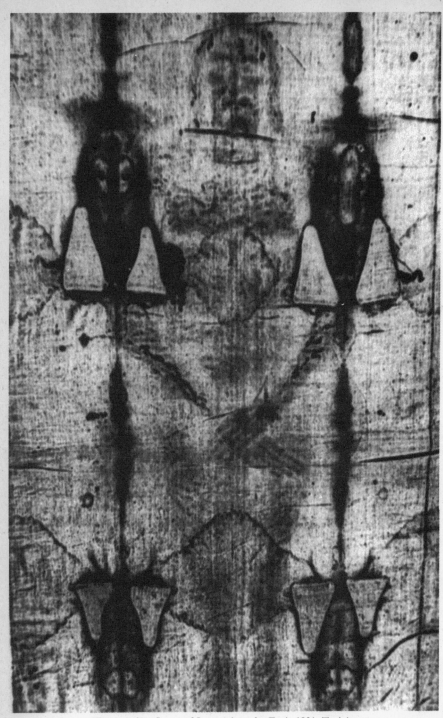
The complete figure of Jesus (photo by Enrie 1931, Turin).

thirteenth century show the image mounted on a rectangular support, which seems to be covered with a lattice material having just one circular opening to expose the portrait. Such pictures tally exactly with the format of the "four times folded" shroud. Furthermore, at no time in the history of art had a portrait been placed in a frame wider than it was high like this.

The Jesuit, Werner Bulst, believes that the word "Mandylion" derives from the Arabic word *mindil,* meaning towel⁶. In my opinion, a connection with the Sanskrit term *Mandala,* which means "circle" in Ancient Indian and is used to designate a mystical figure in circular form, is equally likely. Mandalas were used primarily by Tibetan Buddhists and represent a religious experience symbolically. They symbolise definite spiritual and cosmic relationships and are used in meditation as an aid for establishing unity with the divine. The verbal root of "Mandala" is also found in Greek and Latin.

At any rate, changes in the iconography of the image of Christ from the sixth century onwards are very noticable. Before the shroud had surfaced again, Jesus was portrayed as a teacher of the truth rather like ancient philosophers; or as a shepherd; or as an idealised, beardless and Apollonian youth, – youth being a symbol of the divine. As the Mandylion began to be worshipped, depictions of Jesus took on an astonishing similarity to the round picture on the shroud. It was as if Christians sensed they had before them a real image of their Lord. From then on, Jesus was generally portrayed from the front, with large, open eyes, long hair parted in the middle, a beard divided in two, a wide nose, mature in years; and the head always appears in front of a circular background, – a halo. Although there seem to be no original literary depictions of Jesus' personal appearance, he has been portrayed so consistently since the sixth century that anyone who sees a portrait never has any doubt as to the subject! It is therefore with good reason that Wilson believes the image of Edessa, the Mandylion, to be the "original" portrait, that has become the basis for all later portrayals.

Jesus as an adolescent Apollo (early 3rd c.). The authentic Mandylion portrait of Jesus was not yet known at this time.

In 943 A.D., the imperial Byzantine army besieged the town of Edessa and demanded the surrender of the Mandylion in exchange for two hundred prisoners and the sparing of the town. In order to save human lives, the people of Edessa accepted the demands, and secured immunity for their city and twelve thousand silver pieces from the Emperor. According to contemporary sources, the people of Edessa apparently tried twice to turn over a mere copy of the shroud. For Bishop Abramios from the neighboring city of Samosata, who had been instructed to bring the holy relic to Emperor Romanos in Constantinople, was not satisfied before receiving a third shroud.

A great number of accounts confirm that in 944 A.D. the shroud finally arrived in Constantinople to the great joy of the populace, where it was preserved in the Pharos Chapel for the next two and a half centuries.

In 1203 A.D., the French crusader Robert de Clari wrote that he had seen the shroud in the Church of the Holy Mary of Blachernai in Constantinople: ". . . the 'sydoine', in which Our Lord was wrapped, that was exhibited facing upwards every Friday so that the figure of Our Lord could be plainly seen".[7] Evidently the linen had been displayed in its entirety at the time; and that is the proof that Mandylion and Sindon are indeed one and the same.

In April of 1204, the crusaders who were camping in Constantinople plundered the wealthy city, destroying everything they could get their hands on. They robbed and plundered the valuables, and showed no restraint with Christian treasures and holy relics. In the confusion of events, the shroud disappeared and did not emerge again until 150 years later in France in the possession of members of the *de Charny* family, who displayed it in the West for the first time. In Rome, Genoa and Paris, various "Mandylions" were displayed at the time, though none of them were fraudulently intended to be taken for the original, they all having been copied by painters. The so-called "Towel of Veronica" is such a reproduction, whose name can be traced back to *Vera-Icon* (= true picture), an epithet used for the Mandylion.

In the late thirteenth century, the rumour began to spread that the powerful and influential members of the Order of the Knights of the Temple, who had helped to finance the fourth crusade, worshipped a mysterious "Idol" at the secret meetings of their masters. Such

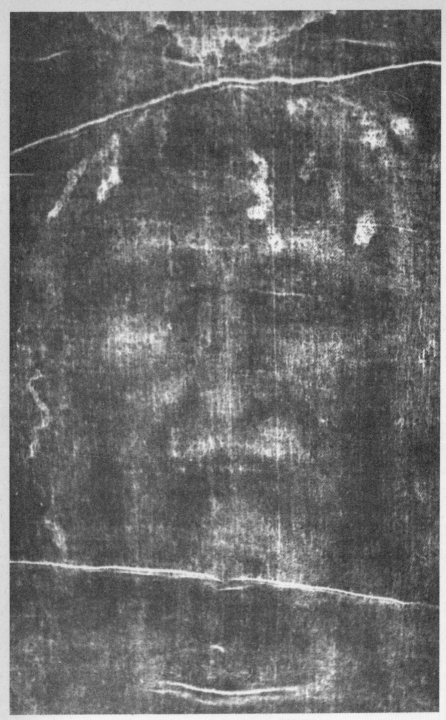

The Face of Jesus (photo by Enrie 1931, Turin)

image-worship was blasphemous in the extreme, and in 1307, Philipp the Fair of France used the rumour as an excuse to eradicate the Knights of the Temple on the charge of heresy. Various contemporary accounts and the protocols of the courts of the Inquisition confirm that the "Idol" of the Templars was a picture "on a plate", with a "very pale and colourless" portrayal of a life-size male head, "having a parted beard, like that of the Knights of the Temple", in which the Knights beheld the "unveiled countenance of God".

In some of the establishments of the Templars, copies of the idol were preserved. One of these was found in 1951 in a property that once had belonged to the order in *Templecombe* in Somerset. The picture is a copy of the Mandylion down to the finest detail.

In March 1314, two of the last remaining dignitaries of the Order were burned for heresy in Paris, although they protested their innocence and their faith in Christianity. One was the Grand Master of the Order, Jacques de Molay. The other, the Master of Normandy, – Geoffroy *de Charny*! Despite intensive search, their persecutors were not able to find the "Idol" of the Templars anywhere.

A few years later the shroud emerged once more, now in the possession of a Geoffroy de Charny, whom genealogists reckon to have been the grand nephew of the Knight of the Temple of the same name. Seen in this light it is understandable that the de Charnys were not able to declare how they had gained possession of the shroud. They were accused of displaying a counterfeit shroud at the Collegiate Church of Lirey by the two bishops of Troyes, Henri de Poitiers and Pierre d'Arcis. Although the bishops had never seen the shroud themselves, they took action against its public exhibition several times. After a series of intrigues against the de Charny family, Margareta de Charny succeeded in getting the shroud out of France; she bequeathed it to the pious Duke Louis of Savoy and received ample remuneration for "valuable services". The Duke paid off the canons of Lirey with fifty gold francs.

In 1502, the shroud was deposited in the chapel of the castle of Chambery, where it was almost destroyed in a fire in 1532, the traces of which can be clearly seen on the cloth. In 1578 it was finally brought to Turin, where it was destined to remain, in the possession of the House of Savoy.

Scientific Analysis of the Shroud

On the occasion of the fiftieth anniversary of the Italian nation in 1898, the shroud was once again shown to the public. The amateur photographer Secondo Pia then had the opportunity to photograph the shroud for the first time in its history. After several attempts, Pia succeeded in taking a reasonable picture of the shroud. As he developed the exposed glass plates in his dark room, he made a sensational discovery: the negative on the photographic plate shows a natural likeness of Jesus, as he must have appeared in real life. The countenance familiar to us as the portrait of Jesus on the Turin Shroud can only be created by reversing light and dark (although of course the blood stains are a slightly confusing feature, appearing on the negative as bright spots). This fact in itself shows that the impression cannot have been painted by any skilful artist. To create such a perfect inversion by hand would not even be possible with the most modern technology available today. The negative of the photograph taken by Pia was the starting-point for modern discussion about the authenticity of the linen. More recent photographs taken by Giuseppe Enrie in 1931 confirm that there are no signs to indicate that the image had been painted on the shroud. The newer, more exact photographs enabled viewers to make a number of completely new observations:

1. The body shown in the illustration is naked. In Roman law, criminals were castigated and executed in a state of nudity. An artistic representation of Jesus completely naked would have been an unforgivable blasphemy at every time.

2. This is very obviously the image of someone who was crucified by being nailed to a cross, rather than fixed to the cross with leather straps (also a common practice). Because crucifixions were frequent, this does not in itself serve to prove that the body was that of Jesus. However, since the first Christian Roman emperor, Constantine, had abolished such an inhuman manner of execution, the shroud must have originated prior to 330 A.D. .

3. The beard and hair-style of the portrayed person was not common anywhere in the Roman empire other than in Palestine and strongly suggests that the victim was a member of the Nazarenes and belonged to the Essene community.

4. The shroud bears perfect evidence of six main Stations of the Cross described in the Gospels. Firstly the medical specialists confirm severe swelling under the right eye and other facial wounds that were evidently caused by the hard blows to the face given by the soldiers.

5. Secondly, small but easily distinguishable marks in the shape of dumb-bells are distributed all over the back, some running round to the front of the body. There are over ninety such wounds in all, so that not only can one tell how many blows were delivered during the lashing, one can also ascertain that a Roman "flagrum" was employed. This special kind of whip had three leather straps fitted at the ends with pairs of small balls made of lead or bone.

6. The evidence for the third Station of the Cross is that the lash wounds in the shoulder-region were obviously smeared by a heavy weight, an indication that the victim of the crucifixion must have indeed had to carry the horizontal beam for the cross.

7. The fourth Station of the Cross is visible in the irregular stripes of blood on the forehead and the back of the head, evidence of a crown of thorns. It was not, however, a ring crown, as depicted in the Christian iconography by almost all artists, but must have been a hood that covered the entire head, similar to the crowns of the Orient. Any counterfeiter would simply have copied the conventional ring of thorns.

8. The fifth Station of the Cross, the nailing to the cross, is visible in the streams of blood on hands and feet. The direction in which the larger streams of blood flowed indicates that the arms had been stretched out at an angle of 55 to 65 degrees. One of the most surprising pieces of information supplied by the shroud is that the nails were hammered into the wrists, and not the palms as all the artists had assumed and is invariably seen in renditions of the crucifixion. Experiments of the French surgeon Bardet have demonstrated that hands nailed to a cross at the palm would not support a body weight of more than forty kilogrammes without tearing (because the finger bones extend into the palm). Which forger would have known that?

9. The sixth of these Stations of the Cross is recognizable in a wound of 4.5 cm on the right side of the body between the fifth and sixth ribs. The wound seems to have produced a fair amount of blood, which fits in with the account in Saint John's Gospel of a lance

injury from which a profusion of "blood and water" immediately flowed forth.

10. Neither thigh nor calf show any signs of a major injury, which suggests that the legs were in fact not broken.

The points enumerated above show that this was not just any crucifixion victim. The various characteristics and pieces of evidence that coincided with the Gospel narrative about the crucifixion could not have applied to any other man! The Jesuit and historian, Herbert Thurston, who was initially convinced that the shroud was a fake, writes, ". . . If this is not an impression of Christ, it was copied from the actual impression. These features, taken together, have never been shown by anyone else."[8]

Still more thorough examination, using the most modern scientific devices, was only possible after a commission had been formed for the scientific investigation of the shroud. In 1969, the Cardinal of Turin, Pellegrino, selected a number of scientific specialists, along with spiritual dignitaries, who were to investigate the shroud systematically. Initially, the group comprised only eleven specialists. In the course of the following years so remarkable were the finds that entire institutes, universities and even the National Air and Space Administration of America (NASA) became involved in the exploration of the linen!

Until 1969, all the research had only depended on photographs that had been made of the shroud. In 1969, for the first time the shroud itself was subject to investigations for two days for the first time. It seems extraordinary but the commission and its task were kept strictly secret; the names of the members were not made public until 1976. The results of these first experiments were rather scant. A number of colour photographs were produced, and parts of the shroud were examined under the microscope, in normal and ultra-violet light. A final report recommended full series of scientific tests and the taking of small samples for future research.

The Italian King Umberto II of Savoy, at this time the legal owner of the shroud, agreed with the demands of the experts from his residence in exile. In 1973, it was systematically examined and tested for three days as planned, after which it was shown "live" in a television broadcast with an audience of over one million, to whom Pope Paul VI delivered a speech.

144

A few years before this, a German sindonologist (= shroud special-ist!) had drawn attention to himself with several spectacular publica-tions claiming that the shroud proved beyond doubt that Jesus could not really have been dead when he was removed from the cross. Hans Naber (alias Kurt Berna, alias John Reban) announced in a loud voice to all the world that a corpse would not have continued to bleed in the manner the body under the linen of the Turin Shroud very evidently had bled[9]. Allegedly Naber had had a vision in 1947, in which Jesus appeared and authorised him to testify before the world that the subject of the crucifixion had only appeared to be dead, but was in fact in a kind of coma from which he awoke after three days. The publication of the said research results and the photographs of the shroud finally gave Naber the opportunity to prove his theories, and he succeeded in finding a number of shroud experts prepared to support his theory. The official representatives of the dogmatic tenets of the Church, of course, did not accept to such a thesis.

For the Fundamentalist theologian Professor Werner Bulst Na-ber's claims were "pure fantasy". Naber was accused of incompe-tence and a lack of education or "scientific training"[10]. Because Naber was able to find access to the world public, however, to just ignore him in the hope that the thing would blow over proved impossible. Even the Vatican saw the need to offer official explanations and refutations. Naber found himself subject to threats and great ill-will, which finally led to his complete physical, psychological and financial breakdown.

The widespread doubts in the wake of Naber seemed to have settled when the latest results of research came out in 1973. It is fairly simple to determine the presence of even the minutest quantities of blood by tests with chemical reactions in a modern, well-equipped scientific laboratory. The most common method is the so-called "peroxide reaction": even the smallest traces of the red blood pig-ment, haemoglobin, release oxygen from hydrogen peroxide, which in turn causes the colourless chemical benzidine to oxidize, and this results in a blue colour. Haemoglobin and the product of its decom-position, haem, are quite stable molecules that may continue to react normally even after many centuries. Several threads from the various blood stains were carefully taken from the material and examined by two independent laboratories in Italy. The result seemed to be quite a setback – all the results of the tests proved negative. Evidently the spots that looked like blood were not blood at all. Traces of blood on Jesus' feet could have sufficed to prove that blood had flowed after Jesus was removed from the cross, and that would have confirmed Naber's theories. Naturally it seemed far less problematical to confess that the shroud was the work of an ingenious forger than to admit that Jesus was still alive when he was removed from the cross.

The news of the "forgery" spread like wild-fire around the world after the publication of the commission's report in 1976. What was not published, though, was the fact that no substance was found that could have been used for any such forgery. The authorities also failed to mention that haem, although generally stable, loses its stability under the influence of high temperature, such as that caused by the fire of 1532 to which the shroud was exposed. In the presence of heat, haem decomposes and is then untraceable.

The question of the authenticity of the blood marks was not to be answered satisfactorily until several years after the investigations of 1973. In 1978, the shroud had been in Turin for exactly four hundred years, and to celebrate the occasion it was once again shown to the public. From August 28 to October 8, more than three million pilgrims saw the most valuable relic of Christianity with the most authentic picture of Jesus. Then, on the evening of the last day of exhibition, the linen was removed from its bullet-proof display frame and laid out on an adjustable bench. In a room in the Palazzo Reale, which adjoins the cathedral, two teams of top scientists were waiting to commence with a research programme that was to last two weeks. One group was predominantly European, including Turin's specialist for microscopy, Giovanni Riggi; the pathologist Baima Bollone of Milan; the physicist Luigi Gonella of Turin; and the criminologist Max Frei of Zürich. The other group consisted of twenty-five American specialists in the fields of photography, spectroscopy, radiography, computer technology, organic chemistry and physics, equipped with an extraordinary array of sophisticated instruments, some of which had been specially constructed for the projected analysis of the shroud.

In the fourteen days that followed, a great number of photographic negatives, special types of photographs, illustrations and tables of data were prepared, which were then evaluated with the help of large computers in America in a lengthy and elaborate procedure. The processing of all the material has not yet been completed. Since 1980, several intermediate reports have been released from the various institutes, mostly in scientific journals[11].

The shroud was first divided into a grid of sixty sections in order to make a spectral and photometric survey. Each of the sections was carefully photographed, using a variety of different filters. The negatives then served as the basis for a series of optical experiments. In NASA's photographic laboratory, the tonal (light-dark) values of the photographs were digitalised (i.e. converted into computer language), which made it possible to obtain a heightened clarity in the picture. Fine details, invisible to the human eye, became easily detectable. The method even made it possible to reconstruct a life-size, three-dimensional relief of the body in the impression. In the case of a forgery, such a feat of proportioning would have been inconceivable. On the basis of the relief it was possible to determine the actual size and weight of the body: *Jesus was approximately 1.8 metres tall and weighed about 79 kilogrammes.*

It was possible to calculate the distance between the body and the cloth at every point, using the tonal values. The impression was darker at the places of direct contact between body and shroud, and the greater the distance between the shroud and the body the lesser the darkening on the shroud (hence the 'negative' effect). The researchers then concluded that there was a direct relation between the image on the shroud and the distances between the shroud and the body; and that the impression must have somehow been formed by contact with the body. This confirmed earlier speculation on the origins of the impression. Investigations of the fibres under electron microscopes revealed that the image was not produced by any detectable particles of substance, but that the fibres of the shroud are themselves darkened on their surface where the image was visible.

One experiment that was performed on the cloth itself was the radiofluorescent spectral analysis, and this finally proved the authenticity of the blood stains. In this test part of the linen was subject to a high dosage of X-rays for a short period of time, and thus induced to radiate and fluoresce. Because every molecule fluoresces under the influence of high energy administered in a certain manner, the atomic structure of a material can be determined by means of a fluorescence spectrum. The marks showed significantly large amounts of the element iron, the characteristic component of blood.

147

The presence of iron was sufficient proof for the American chemist Dr. Walter McCrone to assert before the world press at the Annual Meeting of the American Association for the Advancement of Science that the Turin Shroud could not be genuine. For Mc Crone claimed that the iron in the spots was a sure indication that paint containing iron oxide had been used, – although such paints were not in use before the fourteenth century A.D. The chemist himself had never even seen the shroud! Such a rash dismissal was refuted by a different experiment in which particles of the shroud were treated with hydrazine and formic acid vapour, and subsequently illuminated with ultraviolet light. Under such conditions, porphyrin molecules turn a bright red. Porphyrin is produced in a stage of haem production, and is a sure sign of the presence of blood, even where the haem itself has been destroyed by strong heat. This method of ultraviolet fluorescence photography further revealed that there were two different kinds of burn patches. In 1532, the shroud smouldered in the fire in the palace chapel of Chambery, where there had been little oxygen. The reddish fluorescence of the singe marks confirmed the smouldering fire in the silver chest in which the shroud was preserved, known to us from its history. Other burn marks show a fluorescence of a different colour, suggesting a second burning, this time in an open fire (Mc Crone's "radioactive hypothesis" can easily be dismissed on the basis of this evidence).

Many sindonologists were of the opinion that the image on the shroud resulted from a kind of supernatural radiation; the body of Christ would have emanated some extraordinarily intense energy at the moment of resurrection which "burned" the impression of the entire body into the tissue. Because the body contours on the shroud do not fluoresce, the theory of heat radiation is not realistic. Moreover, any type of high-energy radiation would have gone right through the thin tissue. The image of the body is, however, only visible on the surfaces of the fibres. How then was the image produced?

To answer this question, an impressive number of fantastic and more or less speculative hypotheses have been developed since the discovery of the negative-positive phenomenon by Secondo Pia in 1898. But experiments have shown that there are quite simple, logical and natural means to produce an impression like that on the Turin Shroud. The results of the experiments of the American experts showed that the cause of the differing degrees of sepia coloration in the image was a change in the chemical structure of the cellulose of the linen. In laboratory experiments, it was possible to produce the same differences in colouring by decomposing the cellulose of the linen using various oxidising agents. Oxidation images grow even more distinct as they age.

As early as in 1924, the French biologist Professor Paul Vignon had great success with his experiments on the so-called "Vaporographic theory". Vignon proved that a sweating body laid out on linen that has been soaked in a mixture of light oil and aloe tincture (aloe medicinalis) produces the same coloration as that on the shroud because of the decomposition of chemicals of sweat to form ammonia vapour, causing an oxidation process in the cellulose. The coloration is strongest at the point of contact between the linen and the body, and becomes weaker as the distance between the body and the linen increases (this also explains why the impression resembles a photographic negative). Vignon explained that the impression on the linen is primarily caused by the ammonia vapour, which is released during the evaporation of uric acid and sulphur compounds from the body. The solution of aloe and myrrh absorbed in the linen reacts with this, and ammonium carbonate is formed, the vapours of which colour the linen fibres in the damp atmosphere between the skin and the linen. This happens in direct relation to the proximity of body and linen. The coloration of the blood marks, somewhat darker, was the result of a stronger chemical reaction. The Gospel according to Saint John mentions that use was made of great quantities of aloe in the preparations for the tomb of Jesus ". . . He came therefore, and took the body of Jesus. And there came also Nicodemus, which at the first came to Jesus by night, and brought a mixture of myrrh and aloes, about an hundred pound weight. Then took they the body of Jesus, and bound it in linen clothes with the spices, as the manner of the Jews is to bury." (John 19,38–40).

The experiments of Vignon, though convincing, became the object of harsh criticism when they were presented in 1933. This was simply because the body salts and body heat necessary for the evaporation and chemical reactions could not have been present in sufficient amounts in a corpse. Yet it had been established that mixtures of aloe and myrrh could indeed create permanent impressions of a body on a fabric in the presence of humidity. The experiments showed that the process could take place in as short a time as 45 seconds, creating a faint impression that can be recognized as a positive image when seen on a photographic negative.

Having established the vaporographic origin of the impressions, one would have thought it put an abrupt end to all further speculation. But three points have caused Church ministers to reject the theory:

a) According to the strict, legal regulations of Jewish burial ritual, a corpse has to be washed and purified before being embalmed. The impessions of the blood marks would have therefore been impossible.

b) If the body had been closely wrapped in the shroud as prescribed by the regulations, misshapen impressions, distorted crossways would have been produced, completely altering the portrait. (This argument can be safely dismissed because the soaked linen becomes rather stiff, so the material would not fold round every contour of the body, but only touch it at the more prominent parts.)

c) The third reservation about Vignon's explanation proved to be the decisive argument: corpses neither sweat nor emit body heat. Professor Vignon's theory, the result of forty-six years of research, was dropped on the strength of this objection. Because corpses in fact do not sweat. But had Jesus still been alive, the fever resulting from his wounds would have caused him to sweat more profusely than ever!

He did not Die on the Cross!

According to ancient accounts, the official Roman death sentence was "ibis ad crucem", "you will mount the cross". Crucifixion was the most ignominious and brutal way to die. Roman citizens were never condemned to this form of penalty, but in the countries occupied by the Romans, crucifixion was a popular means of keeping the rebellious people peaceful and obedient under the yoke of Roman rule. The Jews had been unfamiliar with crucifixion, and had only recognised stoning, burning, beheading and strangulation as legal death penalties. According to Mosaic law, however, a blasphemer who was already dead could be hung from a tree, "for he that is hanged is accursed of God" (Deuteronomy 21,23). That a crucifixion could never occur on the Sabbath is obvious; and the Sabbath begins on the evening of the preceding Day of Preparation, which was the day of the crucifixion.

150

The Romans were accustomed to tolerating the religious customs and habits of the Jews as far as possible in order to avoid trouble, so the execution was carried out in haste in order that it might end before evening fell. Crucifixions were torturous, painful and protracted. After all, their purpose was to deter other rebels and instigators.

If the entire body weight of the victim of a crucifixion were only supported by his wrists, death would result after five to six hours from gradual suffocation rather than loss of blood. Respiration in such a position would be so strongly impeded that the body would no longer take in enough oxygen to survive. In order to prevent such a "quick" death, a small stave was nailed horizontally onto the vertical post of the cross at the height of the feet so that the condemned person might support himself for as long as his strength held out. The nail wounds on the feet of the shroud victim do not prove that a stave had been supplied, but the nail alone would have given sufficient support to prevent asphyxiation. In Greek Orthodox art, the crucifix is always fitted with a small stave. Sometimes a "sedile", a small piece of wood that served as a makeshift seat, was placed behind the subject's rear, which may have lessened but prolonged the pain. Nero's court philosopher, Seneca, wrote in a letter, "Those condemned to such a death lost their life drop by drop" (Epistulae 101,14).

According to the Gospels, Jesus was nailed to the cross at the "sixth hour" or twelve noon, and died at the "ninth hour" or three o'clock in the afternoon. At dusk (the Gospel of Saint Luke notes that a triple star heralded the commencing of the Sabbath), at six o'clock in the evening at the earliest, the body, presumed dead, was taken down from the cross. If the accounts of the Gospels are correct, Jesus had been "dead" for at least three hours.

It was customary to place a board on the cross, usually under the feet, on which the name and the reason for condemnation were written for all to read. According to tradition, Jesus' board read in Latin, Greek and Aramaic, "Jesus, Nazarene, King of the Jews". In artistic renderings of the crucifixion, the board generally contains only an abbreviation of the Latin text, "Iesus, Nazarenus, Rex Iudaeorum", INRI. Evidently one charge against Jesus was that he was a Nazarene!

It seems all the more improbable that Jesus should have died after three hours on the cross, because the Nazarene (in contrast to the Essenes) was no ascetic (cf. Matthew 11,19: "The Son of man came eating and drinking, and they say, Behold a man gluttonous, and a winebibber . . ."). Jesus could hardly be described as lean and weak with a body weight of seventy-nine kilogrammes.

The death of the others who were crucified with Jesus is vividly described in the Gospel of Saint John: "The Jews therefore, because it was the preparation, that the bodies should not remain upon the cross on the sabbath day (for that sabbath day was an high day), besought Pilate that their legs might be broken, and that they might be taken away. Then came the soldiers, and brake the legs of the first, and of the other which was crucified with him" (John 19,31–32). The text implies that the two "robbers" died of suffocation within a few hours, not being able to support themselves because of their broken legs. "But when they came to Jesus, and saw that he was dead already, they brake not his legs . . ." (John 19,33).

The reason for Jesus' apparent death can be found a few verses before, verses 29 and 30: "Now there was set a vessel full of vinegar: and they filled a sponge with vinegar, and put upon it hyssop, and put it to his mouth. When Jesus had therefore received the vinegar, he said, It is finished: and he bowed his head, and gave up the ghost."

The question arises whether the vinegar was responsible for Jesus' immediately "giving up the ghost"; and if not, what could the substance have been? Vinegar has the same temporarily stimulating effect as smelling salts, and was even put to use for reviving galley slaves. The wounded were given vinegar to give them energy. But Jesus' reaction appears to have been the opposite: as soon as he inhaled the fumes or tasted the "vinegar", he spoke his last words and gave up the ghost. The reaction would be physiologically inexplicable.

To give a man condemned to death wine spiced with myrrh or incense in order to ease the pain by the slight narcotic effect, is completely in accordance with Jewish custom. In the Talmud of the Jews, one passage reads: "He who went out to be executed was given a small piece of incense in a beaker with wine, so that he might lose consciousness" (Sanh. 43a). The Roman soldiers not only tolerated narcotic drinks, one of them evidently helped administer the drink to Jesus (cf. Matthew 27,48, Mark 15,36, Luke 23,36, John 19,29). But all the Gospels write that *vinegar,* and not wine, was administered. The drink was some brew which tasted as sour as vinegar: the Latin

152

word for vinegar is *acetum,* and comes from *acidus,* meaning sour, and *acere,* to be sour.

There is another line of approach possible. The Persian cult of Mithras included a "Haoma sacrifice" very similar to the Christian Holy Communion. Professor Seydel writes: "The form of the sacrifice of Haoma was identical to the usual Persian sacrifices for the dead. Small round loaves, the size of a large coin, were offered up and consumed with the Haoma drink. Haoma was originally the pressed juice of the soma plant *asclepias acida,* with which the Vedic Aryans sprinkled the sacrificial fire. It was considered a symbol of divine life, a drink of the gods, and the drink of immortality . . ."[12] The holy soma drink of India enabled anyone familiar with the drug to appear dead for several days, and to awake afterwards in an elated state that lasts a few days. In such a state of religious ecstasy, a higher consciousness could speak forth, expressing newly acquired powers of vision. Asclepias acida and possibly hemp (cannabis indica) and other herbs were used to prepare the soma drink (similar to the known recipe for Zarathustra's drink). An illustration of the Indian plant appears by the graves of the first Christians in the catacombs of Rome. The plant is Asclepias acida, in a variety bearing longish fruits which is to be found nowhere in Europe.

The European variety of Asclepias acida is called swallowwort, in Latin, *Vincetoxicum hirundinaria.* Hirundinaria means swallowwort, and Vincetoxicum means "conquer the poison" (Latin vince= conquer, imperative of vincere, and Greek toxicum = poison), thus indicating an "antidote to poison". Of course, in order to use the plants correctly, one has to know how to mix the potion. The Essenes were known to be well versed in healing and therapy. Too strong a dose of the plant's poison would have endangered Jesus' life. The Greek physician and pharmacologist of the first century A.D., Dioskurides, called the plant "dog choker" in his Materia Medica, and wrote that the leaves mixed with meat could even kill dogs, wolves and foxes (Mat. Med. 4,80). Yet the poison could also be used as an antidote for the bites of poisonous animals (Mat. Med. 3,92). In a botany book written in 1563 (Mattioli, page 337) we find, "This is a splendid root against all poisons, of consummate substance and quality, which is why it is called Vince-toxicum in Latin, that is conqueror of every poison. Thus it is even used against the plague, and taken in wine, after which one sweats profusely." Extreme

Swallowwort/Soma/Celandine (Asclepias acida)

sweating and a dry mouth ("I thirst", John 19,28) are typical symptoms of poisoning. In Switzerland, swallowwort is called "master herb" (Zermatt, Wallis), and in Austria, Jewish herb (Linz, Tyrol) or White Cross herb (in Carinthia). Perhaps the ancient memory of the plant's wonderful significance is echoed in these names.

Such a magical potion with the property of putting living people into a cataleptic state resembling death is by no means unheard of, and has often been described in literary narratives. The best known example is Romeo and Juliet. This apparent death is a comatose state resembling deep sleep, where all signs of life such as respiration, heart beat and pulse are no longer noticeable.

154

The hypothesis that Jesus only appeared to be dead when he seemed to "give up the ghost" on the cross has been propounded often enough, but it has not been proved with any more certainty than Jesus' resurrection. Paul was able to make use of Jesus' death on the cross when he formulated his heathen doctrine of sacrificial redemption, which promised the saving of all mankind through a sacrificial death and the shedding of blood. Ostensibly, Jesus was a willing sacrifice. Yet Jesus' fear of death, mentioned several times in the Gospels, appears inexplicable in that context! In expectation of the coming events, Jesus prays at Gethsemane, "Abba, (Father) all things are possible unto thee; take away this cup from me: nevertheless not what I will, but what thou wilt" (Mark 14,36; Matthew 26,29; Luke 22,42). "And being in agony he prayed more earnestly: and his sweat was as it were great drops of blood falling down to the ground" (Luke 22,44). The martyr who was prepared to die would approach his death with a philosophical calm. But Jesus' final appeal, "My God, my God, why hast thou forsaken me?" is evidence enough that the crucifixion was hardly the fulfilment of his desire. In fact, Jesus was not as forsaken as his lament might have led one to believe (as later events were to prove). The three Synoptic Gospels state that Jesus uttered a loud cry before giving up the ghost. The loud cry would have been impossible in a state of absolute exhaustion or shortly before asphyxiation, which was the cause of death in the opinion of almost all medical experts.

But let us turn again to the shroud, which is more tangible than such speculation, and can throw fresh light on these historical questions 2000 years after the event. The historian Wilson concluded his book about the Turin Shroud (published in 1978) with the sentence, ". . . one cannot help but believe that the shroud still has a role to play and that its hour is imminent."[13]

Upon closer inspection of the impression on the shroud, one notices certain features that call for a new historical treatment. One of them is (as we have seen) the presence of blood stains on the linen. If Jesus had been interred according to the Jewish rites, the "corpse" would certainly have been washed with warm water beforehand. Following this, the body would have been anointed with salve and balsam, all the orifices would have been sealed to retard the process of decomposition, and finally the naked body would have been clothed once again. One explanation for this neglect is that the Sabbath was already in process, and to carry out the burial rites would have been unlawful. But this argument is invalid because, according to the Mishna Shabbat Tractate (XX III,5), it was expressly permitted to do "everything necessary" for the dead, even on the Sabbath. Evidently those involved in Jesus' interment did not pay any attention at all to Jewish regulations regarding burials.

The peculiar position of the body seen on the linen is also conspicuous. In a book refuting the authenticity of the Turin Shroud, Joseph Blinzler noted that it is ". . . hardly conceivable that the disciples placed the hands in such an unseemly and impractical position, as seen in the image of the Turin Shroud, while interring the Messiah".[14] Two objections can be raised to Blinzler's remark. Firstly, there is no mention anywhere that the disciples had then been in the sepulchre; and secondly, the position of Jesus' body is precisely that of skeletons found in the cemetery of the Essene monastical settlement of Qumran by the Dead Sea. "The position of the corpses in their graves is generally the same . . . As a rule, one can observe that the body is supine, with the head southwards, and the hands are crossed together over the abdomen, or lie at the sides of the body."[15]

Jesus was supposed to have hung dead on the cross for three hours. The consequences of this could be described with absolute certainty. According to the latest results of research in thanatology (the science of death), a process sets in after death whereby the muscles become rigid (rigor mortis). The process begins as early as thirty minutes after death and is completed in three to six hours, according to the temperature of the surroundings; higher temperatures accelerate the process. Rigor mortis is caused by complex biochemical processes, mainly through a decline in the level of ATP (adenosintriphosphate) after cessation of the heartbeat. The entire muscle formation around the skeleton rigidifies in the position of the body, and this condition only abates after four to seven days when the position of the body can once again be altered. Cases with animals have shown that an almost total rigor mortis can occur as early as a few seconds after death by poisoning; shortly after the last breath had been exhaled, the animals were completely rigid.

After Jesus lost consciousness while hanging from the cross, his body sagged from its upright position (supported by the nail through the feet), so that the legs were bent sharply. The entire body weight was then supported by the nails through the base of Jesus' hands. His head fell forwards and his chin lay on the breast. After three to four hours, his body would normally have become rigid in this position. But if one examines the impression on the shroud, one notices that both the back and head, and also the thighs and shanks of the "corpse" had been laid out quite flat on the shroud (see illustration).

In this position Jesus lay under the linen. The forehead and wrists are the highest parts of the body. The legs lie flat on the surface.

The same can be seen in the position of the arms. Jesus' arms would likewise have had the tendency to return to the position they had during the crucifixion. A few sindonologists have suggested that the arms were probably bound together at the wrists. However, if this had been the case, the bleeding at the base of the hands would have been covered over by the binding. Yet the blood can plainly be seen. Monsignore Giulio Ricci, a member of the Roman Centre of Sindonology, has offered a similar solution to the problem, suggesting that the shroud had been tightly bound round the rigid and crooked body with bands[16]. But this explanation is nonsense; for the impression clearly shows that the shroud had been spread out flat, both below and above the body. Otherwise extreme distortions would be visible across the impression. The fact that there was obviously no rigor mortis when Jesus was taken from the cross is proof enough that he was not dead.

Even more cogent evidence can be seen in the blood stains visible on the linen. One can clearly distinguish between two different types of bleeding on the shroud: blood that had dried up after it had flowed during Jesus' crucifixion, and fresh blood that left the body after Jesus had been laid down on the shroud in a horizontal position!

Let us first look at the bleeding on the head. The sharp prickles of the crown of thorns, pressed on Jesus' head in mockery, left small but deep wounds in the thin scalp. As long as the crown of thorns was on his head, the wounds of one to two millimetres in diameter were sealed fairly completely. The little blood that may have exuded around the thorns coagulated immediately to become encrusted in the hair, as can be observed from the marks on the shroud around all these smaller wounds. The impression on the shroud clearly shows numerous larger streams of dried blood running in all directions. This blood clearly did not come into contact with the shroud until after the thorns were removed, shortly before the body was laid out on the linen. The scalp only contains very fine blood vessels, supplied with blood from the intact circulatory system. . If the heart ceases to operate, the blood withdraws slightly from the capillary vessels under the surface of the skin (due to the negative pressure in the circulation, blood no longer rises above heart level). Thus the complexion becomes "as pale as death". Following death, blood no longer comes out of such small wounds because of the onset of intravascular coagulation.

If one inspects the image of Jesus on the front side of the linen, one notices a trace of blood on the forehead in the shape of a three turned on its side. This particular shape can only have resulted from a slight inclination of the head, for instance when resting on a small cushion. The viscous blood ran to a wrinkle on Jesus' forehead, after which it spread a little and ran on to a second wrinkle as the blood continued to flow from the wound. The wound on the forehead, also caused by the crown of thorns, is on the part of the body that was positioned the highest. Even if there are certain conditions which might allow blood to flow from larger wounds on a corpse, blood would certainly never flow from the forehead when it was the highest point of the body. Only during active circulation is such bleeding possible.

The hands, folded together, lie at a point which is almost as high as the forehead. Here one sees the most impressive evidence that fresh blood as well as clotted blood touched the cloth. At the base of the hand, three trickles of blood can be recognized (see illustration), running in various directions. Simple angle measurements provide information on how the streams of blood arose. The left hand lies upon the right hand, covering its nail wound, which is why the calculations only refer to the visible wounds on the left hand. Part of the blood also ran back into the furrow between the tensed muscles of the forearm, to finally drop downwards, in keeping with the law of gravity. The thin vertical lines of clotted blood run nearly parallel, and one can therefore calculate the angle of the arms to the horizontal beam of the cross – about 25 °. Two of the dried blood streams ran vertically, directly down from the hand wound, and they are at an angle of about 20° to one another, which must indicate the different angles of the forearm with the body in the erect and sagging positions on the cross (see illustration).

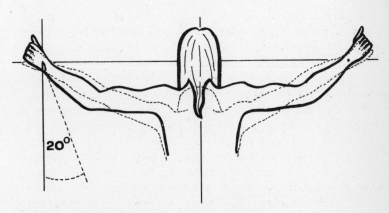

Due to the sagging of the body after exhaustion, the blood flowed from the nail wounds in two directions separated by an angle of 20 °.

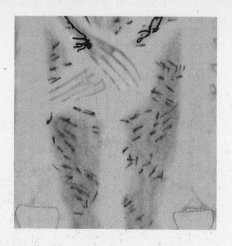

It is very strange that a third trace of blood visible here was not
mentioned by any of the recognized sindonologists[17]. Although the
third trace of blood is obvious and clearly recognizable for any
layman, it has simply been ignored! The reason is simple enough: the
third stream proves, by both its form and its direction, that the
bleeding can only have occurred after the nail had been removed
from the wound. Blood once again began to exude from the nail
wound, this time spreading out all round on the hand, which was
resting flat. Furthermore, one can clearly see that the boundary of the
third trace is far less sharp than that of the other two, particularly
clot 1. One can conclude that clots 1 and 2 had been completely dry
when the body was laid on the shroud, and were softened by the aloe
in the shroud. In contrast, the fresh blood of trace 3 shows serum
rings. Such serum rings are only produced when the fibrin present in
the blood is active. Blood which has previously clotted does not
produce them, but instead leaves an impression with clear contours.
Even the blood which flows from a corpse under special circumstances no longer contains active fibrin. The possibility of blood
flowing from this wound after death can be dismissed in any case

because the hand was lying above the body; only active circulation against gravity could have caused blood to flow from a wound at such a position.

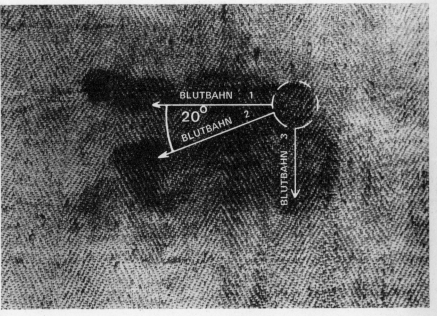

Streams 1 and 2 (= Blutbahn) are dried (sharp borders) and originated during the actual cruxifixion; but stream 3 only formed after the body had been placed in a horizontal position.

On the shroud, the right arm appears to be somewhat longer than the left. Such minor distortions on the front show that the linen had not rested as rigidly as a flat board on the body, but must have been slightly folded or pressed in. Were it not for this fortuitous mishap on the part of those responsible for Jesus' interment, it would not have been possible to view the wound on the side of the body. It is vividly displayed on the shroud. In the gospel of Saint John, the wound is attributed to the spear of a soldier: "But one of the soldiers with a spear pierced his side, and forthwith came there out blood and water" (John 19,34). It is significant that the lance thrust delivered by the warrior was described differently in translations from the original Greek text. Even the translators of the Vulgate misinterpreted the Greek text. For the Greek verb νύσσειν merely designates a slight scratch, graze or prick, and not a blow delivered with full force, still less a deep penetration of the body. The wound in the side, 4.5 cm in length, gives some clues as to how the injury was produced. The lance used by Roman soldiers at the time was generally a "hasta" or a "pilum", the small, thin blade of which measured 25 to 40 cm in length and only spread out at the base near the shaft (see illustration).

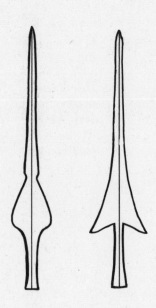

The lances of the Roman legionaries at the time of Jesus were generally shaped like these.

162

The Buddha Maitreya (the one to come), which marks the religious border between Islamic Kashmir and Buddhist Ladakh.

Above: the small river Sindh with the flooded Kashmir valley in the background.

Opposite: A Bodhisattva as the good shepherd.

Below: the Sun Temple of Martand (65 km southeast of Srinagar), a typically Jewish temple in Kashmir. Is this the temple referred to by Hesekiel?

Above: plaster cast of the 'footprint' relief of the prophet Yuz Asaf/Jesus. One can clearly see what the sculptor was trying to stress: the marks of the crucifixion are represented as crescents below the toes.

Below: in this building 'Rozabal' (=tomb of the prophet) the burial place of Yuz Asaf (=Jesus) is found in the centre of the old town of Srinagar.

With such a blade like a stiletto, one could easily inflict a minor wound to make sure that the crucifixion victim no longer reacted. The procedure served as a kind of official certification of death, and it is probable that the captain mentioned in the Gospels carried out the careful test himself. Had any experienced soldier wanted to deal Jesus a final blow, he would have certainly not have stabbed him from the right side right through to the heart, which is of course on the left; he would have pierced the heart with deadly accuracy from the front.

The exegetes have thought up a great number of explanations for the "blood and water" that gushed forth according to Saint John's Gospel. The water might just possibly have been blood serum that formed at the onset of the decomposition of blood. However, such decomposition does not begin until at least six hours after the death of the subject.

Another possibility is that an oedemic fluid might have been secreted from the space between the lung and the pleural membrane surrounding it. This theory can also be dismissed because if the chest had indeed been penetrated, the lungs would have instantly collapsed, creating a partial vacuum that would have prevented any fluid from emerging. A third possibility was that the water was fluid from the heart sac, which could in theory have followed the path of the lance back to the skin, after the lance's removal from the body following an injury to the heart. Both of the last hypotheses would presume that Jesus was extremely ill before being martyred, for otherwise such "water" would not have been produced.

But in fact, the words "blood and water" are merely an idiomatic expression used to emphasize the event. If someone "sweats blood and water", it does not mean that blood flows from his pores. The eye witness whose testimony of the crucifixion has been immortalised simply wanted to express his astonishment about the quantity of blood somewhat dramatically. At the beginning of the second century A.D., the author of Saint John's Gospel wrote of an unknown witness to the crucifixion: "And he that saw it bare record, and his record is true: and he knoweth that he saith true, that ye might believe" (John 19,35). The side wound of the "deceased" did indeed produce incredible amounts of blood. This is demonstrated very impressively by corresponding marks on the shroud. Blood from the wound collected in considerable amounts in a streamlet between the back and the posterior, even after the interment.

167

The most profuse bleeding was evident from the nail wounds on the feet. The blood left the wound, ran down to the heel, where it collected, and flowed off at the right, as fresh blood continued to be supplied (see illustration). The stream of blood, 17 cm in length, was interrupted at a point where the blood dropped into a fold in the shroud, after which it continued to flow towards the right. Blood from a corpse that has been dead for several hours never runs and coagulates in such a manner. The heart and circulation must have been completely unimpaired, even if respiration was hardly perceptible.

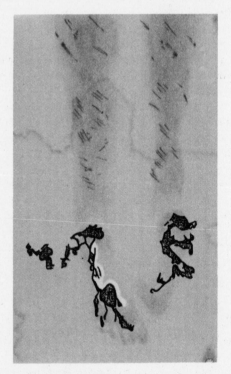

The blood traces on the feet most clearly show that the blood spread out in all directions on the surface of the cloth after the body had been taken down from the cross.

The blood rivulets, which show up as "positives" on the cloth, indicate beyond doubt that the blood did not come into contact with the shroud until after the interment. Because the cloth had been soaked in aloe, a resinous substance, the blood could not be absorbed by the material, and merely spread along its surface. During the subsequent coagulation of the blood, the blood's solid components clumped together within a border of clear serum.

The process can be easily observed in a drop of blood on a glass slide. The liquid serum surrounds the blood particles like an aureole. The dried blood-clots on the body, resoftened on contact with the soaked material, left an entirely different impression. In the case of those clots, there were no serum borders; this is especially clear in photographs taken in ultraviolet light, Wood light and transparent light, and processed electronically. The fibrin had formed a firm border around the marks.

All the evidence that I have listed here has long since been published in the numerous scientific publications on the Turin Shroud. I have merely drawn new conclusions from research that has gone on for more than eighty years. The result might seem somewhat alienating at first. But it has nonetheless been arrived at logically, and it raises some puzzling questions, particularly that of the resurrection. To establish clinical death presents difficulties to doctors even today. The use of drugs for example can induce such a deep coma that false diagnoses may easily be made. A well-known method for establishing death used to be to make a small incision in the heel or the wrist. If arterial blood flows, the circulatory system is still operating. Corpses just do not bleed! In Jesus' case, there were a total of twenty-eight wounds that continued to bleed even after his removal from the cross. It can be regarded as a fact that Jesus could not possibly have been dead when his body was laid in the sepulchre.

The Resurrection in Historical Perspective

During Jesus' crucifixion and interment, people who had not yet been made members of the New Covenant became involved. The centurion who had given Jesus the potion that was to be of such great consequence, the soldier who grazed him with the lance with the intent of confirming Jesus' death, and the centurion who uttered the words, "Truly, this was the Son of God" (Matthew 27,54; Mark 15,39; Luke 23,47), all seem to have been one and the same man. In the apocryphal Acts of Pilate, he is referred to as Longinus, a captain responsible for supervising the crucifixions. The Greek legend, the "Martyrdom of Longinus", depicts him as the captain of Golgotha who came from Sandrales (or Sandiale) in Cappadocia, who also supervised the soldiers on watch at the grave. After the resurrection, Longinus received the precious shroud as a reward (cf. page 134) and was even later consecrated as a bishop in Cappadocia, according to a text by Gregory of Nyssa. The wonderful turnabout in his outlook,from Jesus' presumed mortal enemy to a Christian bishop, suggests that the centurion had had some kind of contact with Jesus and his followers even before the crucifixion.

If one accepts that the crucifixion took place under the supervision of a Roman officer who harboured benevolent feelings towards Jesus though he was in charge of all the soldiers present, then one can explain the mysterious events surrounding the crucifixion. The events can no longer be dismissed as the product of an over-active imagination.

The cross was removed and the interment took place under the auspices of the distinguished, very prosperous and influential merchant, Joseph of Arimathea. As a counsellor and member of the Sanhedrin, he had voted in vain against Jesus' conviction (cf. page 129). He had not, then, been able to assert himself in the face of such immense political power, but now at last he was able to use his wealth and influence effectively. It was he who managed to obtain Jesus' "corpse" from Pilate, probably through persuasive arguments. Joseph also paid for the linen shroud, certainly an expensive purchase, and had Jesus transported in a comatose state to the new stone sepulchre near Golgotha (= skull mountain, because of the hillock's shape!). Later Joseph of Arimathea was even canonised as a saint. The Roman Catholic Church celebrates his deeds on the seventeenth of March. The apocryphal gospel of Nicodemus relates that Joseph was later freed from a Jewish prison by Jesus himself (Nic. Gosp. 12,15). This Nicodemus was a friend of Joseph who helped at the interment and obtained the mixture of 100 pounds of myrrh and aloe. The same Nicodemus, mentioned only in the Gospel of Saint John, was also a Jewish counsellor and Pharisaic scribe (John 3,1–10), and was instructed by Jesus one night (John 3,2–12). Nicodemus also declared the Nazarene's innocence in front of the High Council (John 7,50).

It seems odd that the two counsellors should have taken so much trouble to recover the body of Jesus, which was actually the duty of the nearest relative. And why did the disciples never arrive on the scene? The "Gospel according to Saint Peter", preserved only in part, offers an answer: "I (Peter) was full of sorrow with my companions; and we went into hiding with wounded hearts, for we were being sought as misdoers and because we allegedly wanted to burn down the temple. We fasted the whole time, sitting in mourning and weeping day and night until the sabbath."[18] The other "sympathisers" of Jesus also did not come close to the cross, choosing instead to watch from a distance.

If one assumes that Joseph of Arimathea and Nicodemus were secret lay members of the Essene Order, it is logical that they would have been well suited for the task of treating Jesus' wounds and helping the healing process. As experienced healers, the Essenes were familiar with exotic drugs and remarkable methods of treatment.

Aloe and myrrh are still regarded as very effective medication for treating open wounds. The Gospel of Saint John expressly refers to medicinal aloe which is obtained from the broad-leaved, liliaceous plant, and not the so-called aloe wood, which is finely grated for use as a scented powder, called *ahalim* in the Old Testament. Medicinal aloe resin was used in India from as early as the third and second millennia B.C.. According to Dioskurides and Pliny the Elder, most of the aloe used in Palestine was imported from India. During the Middle Ages, aloe was then introduced into Europe as a vulnerary ointment, and it continues to be used in homeopathic medicine of today.

Myrrh is also resinous and contains up to 10 % etheric oil. Myrrh continues to be administered as a tincture (with alcohol) for the treatment of inflammations. The most well-known form of myrrh is *bdellium,* which is obtained from the plant *commiphora roxburghi* in India.

In order to understand the properties of the substances better, I experimented with aloe and myrrh myself, and gained some Interesting information in the process. Aloin, which is found in aloe in proportions of up to 25 %, is sensitive to light, darkening in the presence of light and air. Aloe reacts strongly with other substances. I

171

discovered that even to dissolve about 5 g of aloe resin in 15 cc of water can be not easy. I left the tough resin in the water in a sturdy drinking glass. During the night, I was awakened by a loud bang. The glass had burst into a thousand pieces and spread within a perimeter of four metres! No one was able to explain this reaction.

The violent behaviour does, at least, suggest that the impression on the shroud can certainly be attributed to an oxidation process, following various biochemical reactions (see previous section). I could also convince myself of the way a piece of cloth dipped into aloe and myrrh tincture becomes thoroughly impregnated by the rubbery resin. Such impregnation prevents further absorption, which is why the impression of the body and most of the blood clots were clear and not absorbed by the shroud; the chemicals would have only reacted on the surface of the shroud. That is why the impressions are only surface phenomena. Because the fresh blood could not penetrate the tissue, it coagulated on the shroud forming rings of serum – which are not present around the blood clots that had been dry when the body was removed from the cross. Moreover, the resin had made the material stiff and almost like a board. It was only thanks to the stiffness of the material that such clear and undistorted impressions of the body were at all possible.

Heat has a therapeutic effect in the process of healing; heat could have been produced by the mixture of aloe and myrrh (less intense under the large surfaces of the shroud than under glass).

Jesus was of course considerably weakened by the torture that he had been forced to undergo. Nonetheless, the loss of blood had been relatively little: all indications on the shroud point to a loss of less than one litre of blood. Surgical experiments with corpses have shown that being nailed to the cross destroys neither major blood vessels nor any bones. The nail was driven between eight wrist bones, pushing them slightly apart. The perforation of the feet took place at the second metatarsal specium, only causing wounds to the flesh. After the larger wounds had been sewn up, the injured man would have needed absolute peace and quiet, and this could have been ensured by the narcotic drink.

Three days later, a few women dared to approach the tomb. The Gospel of Saint Mark mentioned Mary Magdalene, Mary the mother of Jacob, and Salome, bearing balsam for the body of Jesus. In the Gospel of Saint Matthew, only two women came to the tomb, and in

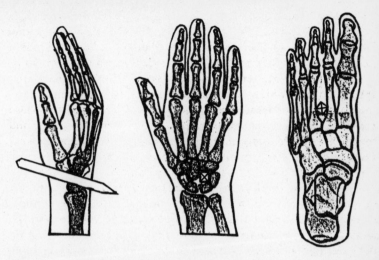

At these points the nails were driven through the wrists and the feet. No bones or main arteries were injured.

Saint John's Gospel it is only Mary Magdalene. But there is agreement in all four of the Gospels that the tomb was empty, save for one or more men in white robes. These "angels" could have simply been members of the Essene Order, who always wore white (cf. page 102). The Essenes were evidently the only people who had been let in on the entire mystery. Even the disciples seem to have been completely ignorant of the events when they later met their master.

Despite all contradictions and inexplicable claims in the Gospel accounts of the events following the Passion, several witnesses can be found in all the Gospels who are said to have seen Jesus in the flesh after the resurrection. Mary Magdalene at first thought he was the gardener (John 20,14); two disciples met him on the road to Emmaus (Mark 16,9; Luke 24,19). But they did not recognize the Nazarene until he ate with them in the evening, and from the manner in which he broke his bread, "And it came to pass, as he sat at meal with them, he took bread, and blessed it, and brake, and gave to them. And their eyes were opened, and they knew him . . ." (Luke 24,30–31).

173

This period of the events following the resurrection is frought with so many contradictions that it is impossible to ascertain its exact length. Three days were said to have elapsed between the crucifixion and Jesus' reappearance, but three is a mystical number which had played a role in earlier resurrection myths. Perhaps Jesus was treated longer, and only later began to show himself gradually to his followers. At any rate, the encounters seem to have been short and secret. Obviously Jesus could not appear in public, for he would have been immediately rearrested (although the injuries, or his miraculous recovery, or even his sheer divine normality, do seem to have altered his appearance; this made it difficult for his acquaintances to recognize him).

The disciples had dejectedly withdrawn from religious life and were again practising their former professions (Simon Peter, Thomas, Nathanael of Cana and the sons of Zebedee returned to fishing-John 21,2). Their old zeal did not return until Jesus communicated his desire to meet them in Galilee (Matthew 28,10). He then showed himself to his disciples, who at first thought he was a ghost and were afraid. "And he said unto them, Why are ye troubled? and why do thoughts arise in your hearts? Behold my hands and my feet, that it is I myself: handle me, and see; for a spirit hath not flesh and bones, as ye see me have. And when he had thus spoken, he shewed them his hands and his feet. And while they believed not for joy, and wondered, he said unto them, Have ye here any food? they gave him a piece of a broiled fish, and of an honeycomb. And he took it, and did eat before them" (Luke 24,38–43). Finally, Jesus even enjoined "Doubting Thomas" to touch the stigmata of his wounds, finally convincing the disciple of his master's actual physical existence.

In spite of all this, Jesus could no longer preach in public, for his persecutors would soon be on his tracks. His only chance was to escape forever the threats posed by his enemies. "Afterwards he appeared unto the eleven as they sat at meat , and upbraided them with their unbelief and hardness of heart, because they believed not them which had seen him after he was risen. And he said unto them, Go ye into all the world, and preach the gospel to every creature. He that believeth and is baptized shall be saved; but he that believeth not shall be damned. And these signs shall follow them that believe; In my name shall they cast out devils; they shall speak with new tongues; They shall take up serpents; and if they drink any deadly

174

thing, it shall not hurt them; they shall lay hands on the sick, and they shall recover" (Mark 16,14–18).

"And he led them out as far as to Bethany, and he lifted up his hands, and blessed them. And it came to pass, while he blessed them he was parted from them, and carried up into heaven. And they worshipped him, and returned to Jerusalem with great joy" (Luke 24,50–52).

It is easiest to reconstruct the farewell scene at the very place where it happened. From outside the town limits of Jerusalem, the path to Bethany, over the southernmost spur of the mountain range of the Mount of Olives, up to the Summit of the Ascension, climbs at a fairly steep incline. Whoever goes over the peak is quickly lost to sight and disappears from the view of those who remain near the top.

Jesus took great trouble to convince his followers that his body was earthly and real. He stressed the material nature of his body by allowing himself to be touched and by accepting food. He expressly declared that he was not just a spirit. His reappearance after his crucifixion was not the result of mistaken identity, deceit or visions, and his body was not unnaturally transformed or astral; he was neither a ghostly phenomenon nor an ethereal being.

One eye witness testifies that Jesus did not disappear beyond all reach, and he cannot be dismissed as untrustworthy. For it is Paul, the only one who provedly wrote the greater part of what is attributed to him in the New Testament, himself. Although he was not present at the events surrounding the crucifixion, he did meet Jesus some time after the ascension, an encounter which was to change his whole life.

Paul Meets Jesus in Damascus

Paul or Saul (see page 28) had been one of the most zealous and fanatical opponents of the "New Covenant". Probably he had heard rumours that Jesus had survived his execution by some trick and continued to intrigue against the orthodox Jews from some safe place. "And Saul, yet breathing out threatenings and slaughter against the disciples of the Lord, went unto the high priest, And desired of him letters to Damascus to the synagogues, that if he found any of this way, whether they were men or women, he might bring them bound unto Jerusalem" (Acts 9,1–2).

175

After intensive and extensive research, the psychiatrist Wilhelm Lange-Eichbaum was able to recreate a detailed portrait of Paul's character[19] in his well-known work *Genius, Madness and Fame*. Paul was frail, plain and small, yet at the same time harsh, rejecting, mpetuous and passionate. His zeal in the persecution of Christians was a compensation for his own feelings of inadequacy. The vast attraction of Paulinism is the idea of redemption and release from inner crises. Paul had boundless energy and matching ego. He suffered from severe attacks, which he blamed on demons. The latest sources have shown that there may have been a cause for what he ofted described as a "thorn in the flesh", his own personal cross. He might have suffered tragically from his own homosexuality. His problem caused him great antipathy towards sexuality altogether, and was decisive in his development of an ascetic doctrine of marriage, which has been of formative influence in the base image of sexuality and of woman that continued to dominate Christian thinking.

In the light of this psychology we can value the wonderful experience Paul had near Damascus even more highly: "And as he journeyed, he came near Damascus: and suddenly there shined round about him a light from heaven: And he fell to the earth, and heard a voice saying unto him, Saul, Saul, why persecutest thou me? And he said, Who art thou, Lord? And the Lord said, I am Jesus whom thou persecutest: it is hard for thee to kick against the pricks. And he trembling and astonished said, Lord, what wilt thou have me to do? And the Lord said unto him, Arise, and go into the city, and it shall be told thee what thou must do." (Acts 9,3–6).

Damascus was in the middle of Syria, where the Jews had been hated since the uprising of the Maccabees (165 B.C.), and where the Essene Order had their spiritual centre. Perhaps Jesus' brilliant white garments helped to dazzle Saul? It seems possible to me that Saul had taken part in an initiation ritual, and that his blindness over the following three days may be attributed to the effect of the soma drink (see Acts 9,8–9).

Sossianus Hierocles, one of the highest-placed Roman officers, the Governor of Phonecia, Lebanon, Bithynia and Egypt, who was considered one of the most brutal persecutors of the early Christian communities, has left us a work called "To the Christians", with this passage: "After fleeing (!) from the Jews, Christ collected as many as nine hundred men, given to robbery."[20] (compare our comments about groups characterized as 'robbers', page 124). It is quite possible that the Essene community in Damascus had nine hundred members.

Paul was baptized and introduced to the teaching by a disciple of Jesus in Damascus called Ananias. According to the sources, Ananias was commissioned by Jesus himself to visit Saul; but he at first refused, afraid of the persecutor. Jesus dismissed Ananias' objections with the words: "Go thy way: for he is a chosen vessel unto me, to bear my name before the Gentiles, and kings, and the children of Israel: For I will shew him how great things he must suffer for my name's sake" (Acts 9,15).

From this point on, Paul is considered the most zealous propagator of the new faith. He finally felt the fascination of Jesus' personality, and at once recognized the implications of the task that the Nazarene had given him. With even greater zeal than in his persecution of Jesus and his followers, Paul took on the task of spreading his own interpretation of the new teaching. The encounter between Jesus and Paul in Damascus took place around two years after the crucifixion.

Hardly 300 kilometres north of Jerusalem, Jesus would have felt relatively safe in the protection of the Essenes. Provided a religious community accepted the Roman state religion, the Roman government tolerated its practices. The Jews were even exempted from taking part in the Roman cult rituals of the state. The "New Covenant" at first benefited from this exemptory law, too. But when the Romans realized that Jesus' following had hardly anything in common with orthodox Jewry, and that the Brothers of the New Faith were even among the political incitors, the so-called Christians lost all special status and rights of toleration, and the conflict was waged in the open. Initially, the Christian communities were only persecuted by the Roman state on a local level as alleged disturbers of the peace. Broader state persecution was not to start until the second half of the third century. With the crucifixion still so recent, the added hostility of the Jews in Jerusalem forced the first Christians to direct their universal mission outwards, to more distant regions of the Roman Empire.

In Damascus, then, Jesus could enjoy the benefit of Essene protection. Around five kilometres outside Damascus, there is a place that is still called *Mayuam-i-isa,* "The place where Jesus lived". The Persian historian Mir Kawand has cited several sources that claim Jesus lived and taught here after the crucifixion.

The followers of the "New Teaching" evidently grew in number, not least because of Jesus' own personal efforts. But rumours of Jesus being in Damascus, which had spread to Paul's ears, would have spread even farther, so it must have gradually become too dangerous for the Nazarene to continue to reside in the Syrian part of the Roman Empire.

Chapter six

After the Crucifixion
Jesus goes East again

According to Persian sources, while Jesus was living in Damascus, he received a letter from the King of Nisibis, near Edessa (today Nusaybin, on the Turkish side of the border to Syria; see illustration). The king asked Jesus to come to Nisibis to cure him of an illness. Jesus allegedly sent his close disciple Thomas with the message that he would soon follow. Shortly after this, Jesus is indeed supposed to have travelled there with his mother. In *Jami-ut-Tawarik,* the Persian scholar Faquir Muhammed wrote that the king had already been healed by Thomas when Jesus arrived with his retinue in Nisibis. Imam Abu Jafar Muhammed wrote in his famous work *Tafsir-Ibn-i-Jarir at-Tabri* that Jesus' stay in Nisibis became dangerous; apparently the Nazarene even risked his life by appearing in public (Volume 3, page 197).

In Leh I met an ethnologist from Luxembourg who had spent several years among Kurdish tribes in eastern Anatolia. He told me that a number of stories continue to circulate among the Kurds about Jesus residing in what is now eastern Turkey after the resurrection. Until today, no one seems to have expressed much interest in such stories.

After leaving Nisibis, Jesus continued to move towards the north-west; and the apocryphal Acts of Thomas relate that Jesus suddenly appeared at the marriage festivities of the princess at the court of the King of Andrapa. Andrapolis was in Paphlagonia (today's Iskilip in the extreme north of Anatolia), and had belonged to the Roman province of Galatia since 7 B.C. The apostle Thomas and his master met once again at the wedding festivities, having arrived separately.

The apostle had been commissioned by Jesus to go to India. "But he did not want to go and said he could not travel because of weakness of the flesh, and moreover: How can I, a Hebrew, travel and preach the truth to the Indians? And when he considered and said this, the Messiah appeared to him in the night and spoke to him: Do not be afraid, Thomas, go to India and preach the word there, for

179

Ruins of the king's palace in Nisibis. Today Nusaybin, where the border between Turkey and Syria runs exactly across the historical site. (see map)

my Grace is with you. But he would not obey and said: Send me anywhere you want, but somewhere else! For I shall not go to India." (A. Th. I, p. 101).[1]

According to the Acts of Thomas, Jesus then sold the reluctant Thomas as a slave to the Indian merchant Abban who had been commissioned by his King Gundafor (Gondapharos) to find a carpenter. Old coins confirm that King Gundafor did indeed rule Parthia and India in the first century A.D. . Jesus signed a contract with Abban "parting with a sum of three pounds of unstamped silver". Jesus could only be sure that Thomas would arrive in India by resorting to such unusual means.

The Acts of Thomas, like the apocryphal gospel of Thomas, are of Syrian origin, and can be traced back to the missionary work of Thomas himself in Edessa (in the fourth century, after the apostle's

180

demise in southern India near Madras, his bones were conveyed back to Edessa). The Acts of Thomas and the gospel of Thomas are closely related. Both were gnostic scriptures of esoteric content, and used at the beginning of the third century by the Manichaeans (Mani was born in 217). A gospel of Thomas was first mentioned and quoted by Hippolyte (Ref. V 7,20) in his report on the "Naassenes" of c. 230 A.D. .

The name of the apostle, "Didymos Judas Thomas", means "Judas the Twin" (from the Aramaic word for twin, *toma*), and it suggests a particularly close relationship with Jesus. In coptic texts, the word "twin" is often replaced by "fellow companion". The Acts of Thomas are a testimony to Thomas' special relationship to Jesus. As his confidant, Thomas was priveleged to know Jesus' most profound secrets. In Chapter 39 of the Acts of Thomas, the apostle is addressed with his special title, "Twin brother of Christ, apostle of the Highest who shares in the knowledge of the hidden word of Christ, recipient of his secret pronouncements."[2] Another version addresses him as "you who have partaken of the secret word of the Giver of Life, and who have received the hidden Mysteries of the Son of God." Thomas is thus the keeper (= Nazarene, see page 94) of Jesus' most secret and esoteric words, revealed uniquely to him. In the gospel of Thomas (one of the finds of Nag Hammadi), one can read the following: "Jesus said to his disciples, 'Compare me to someone and tell Me whom I am like.' Simon Peter said to Him, 'You are like a righteous angel.' Matthew said to Him, 'You are like a wise philosopher.' Thomas said to Him, 'Master, my mouth is wholly incapable of saying whom You are like.' Jesus said, 'I am not your master. Because you have drunk, you have become intoxicated from the bubbling spring which I have measured out.' And He took him and withdrew and told him three things. When Thomas returned to his companions, they asked him, 'What did Jesus say to you?' Thomas said to them, 'If I tell you one of the things which he told me, you will pick up stones and throw them at me; a fire will come out of the stones and burn you up.'" (II,2, Logion 13)[3]. Thomas had evidently attained a profound state of consciousness and seemed to be almost an equal of Christ.

The conversion of the apostles plays a major role in the Acts of Thomas. One repeatedly comes across descriptions of initiations complete with sacred ritual. The conversion was finalized by anoint-

181

ing with oil, and the sacrament of the Eucharist. Only bread was taken at Holy Communion, and the chalice contained just water. In the second part of the Acts of Thomas, Misdai, an Indian king, noted that oil, water and bread were a part of the apostles' "magic". The initiate was called a servant or handmaid of God, was said to enjoy divine power, and was considered a member of the fold.

Thus one can reinterpret the Thomas story. Jesus "sold" Thomas as a "slave" to Abban (Abba = father). The initiate was elevated from common brother of the Essene Order to a Nazarene of higher status, by having consecrated oil poured over his head, and by having his naked body anointed with balm.

All the Nazarenes were easily mistaken for one another, because they all wore the same white robes , with their hair and beard in the same manner. Hence it is possible that the term "twin", when applied to Thomas, was simply an allusion to the similarity between the two men. Accounts of mistaken identity in the Acts of Thomas read like a comedy of errors, although Thomas was a good ten years younger than Jesus.

On the wedding night referred to above, the King of Andrapa showed the apostle Thomas into the bridal suite, so that he might convert the newly wedded couple. After Thomas had prayed with the couple, everyone present left the bridal suite. "But after everyone had left and the doors had been closed, the bridegroom raised the curtains in the bridal suite in order to join his bride. And he saw the Lord Jesus speaking with the bride, resembling Judas Thomas, who had just blessed them and left them. The groom said to Jesus: 'Did you not just leave? How did you get back in?' But the Lord replied: 'I am not Judas called Thomas, I am his brother.' And the Lord sat down upon the bed, ordering them to sit down on the chairs, and proceeded to tell them: 'Remember, my children, what my brother said to you and unto whom he recommended you . . ."' (A.Th. 8, 11). The anecdote is preceded by the account of an encounter between Thomas and a Hebraic woman who had played the flute at the wedding festivities.

Since the Israelites had first gone into exile (722 B.C., see page 58) scattered Israelite communities grew up throughout the Near East. One can assume that Jesus was always able to find refuge among the far-flung Children of Israel, or among sympathisers of the Israelites, on his flight eastwards. In Parthia (today Iraq and Iran) there were

Ruins of the king's palace in Andrapa. (Today Iskilip in Turkey; see map)

major Israelite settlements, according to the Book of Esther. The Israelite leagues were later to bitterly resist the invasion of Trajan (c. 115 A.D.). Numerous place names along the old Silk Road point to Jesus or Mary having stopped there. For instance, near Ephesos, on the west coast of what is now Turkey, there is a "House of Mary"; the travellers possibly sojourned there before continuing the voyage eastwards. Several sources indicate that Jesus was also sent further westwards in his mission to instruct related congregations which probably have existed in France and even in England.

There are various documents that refer to Jesus' stay in Persia. Jesus' name, title and occupation vary from country to country and from language to language according to local conditions and traditions. The names of those places where Jesus resided for a longer period were preserved over the years. After all, it seems that more than sixteen years elapsed from Jesus' crucifixion until his arrival in Kashmir with his entourage. By this time, Jesus was known by the

183

name "Yuz Asaf". The meaning of the name has been passed down to us in the *Farhang-Asafia* (Volume I), which relates that Jesus (Hazrat Isa) healed some lepers who were called "Asaf" – the purified – after being cured of their complaint. "Yuz" means leader, so Yuz Asaf means "leader of the healed", and it became a common appellation for Jesus. In a figurative sense, the name probably alluded to Jesus' mission to purify the world of "impure spirits", and lead all back to the true Faith. Jesus would be able to move with greater safety and escape his persecutors more easily using this new name. After all, the Persian priests probably had not forgotten his earlier debut in their land (see page 18). According to tradition, the prophet entered the land from the west; and the contents of the sermons that Yuz Asaf delivered were no different from those of Jesus Christ. Jesus is said to have resided in Mashag, where he visited the grave of Shem, Noah's son (*Jami-uf-Tawarik*, Volume II). According to numerous accounts, Yuz Asaf preached all over Persia (Iran), converting a vast number of people to his creed. Details in various accounts (such as Agha Mustafai's *Ahwali Ahaliau-i-Paras*) confirm that Yuz Asaf and Jesus were one and the same man.

The court poet of Emperor Akbar of India called Jesus *Ai Ki Nam-i to: Yus o Kristo,* or "Thou, whose name is Yuz or Christ". Although the Greek name *Chrestos* was altered in its forms in the various languages of the West, the name Yuz Asaf was preserved in its original form over the centuries. Place names connected with Jesus' presence and influence point on towards Afghanistan and Pakistan. In eastern Afghanistan, near Ghazni and Jalalabad, two plains bear the name of the prophet Yuz Asaf. According to tradition, Jesus had actually been here.

The Acts of Thomas describe the sojourn of Jesus and Thomas in Taxila (now in Pakistan) at the court of King Gundafor in the twenty-sixth year of his rule (= 47 A.D.). Thomas is commissioned by the king to build a magnificent palace; but the apostle uses the money for distribution among the needy.

Thomas thanks Jesus for the opportunity to do such good deeds with the following words: "'I thank thee, O Lord, in every respect, for dying for a short while (!) in order that I might live in you eternally; and for selling me, in order to emancipate many others through me.' And he did not cease to teach and give peace to the troubled, saying, 'The Lord gives you this and assures everyone of nourish-

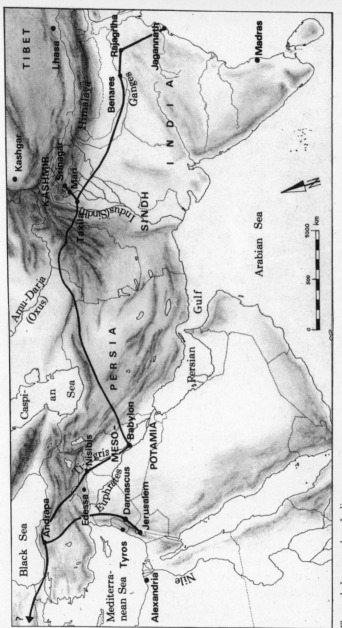

The path Jesus took to India.

185

ment. For he is the nourisher of the orphans and the provider of the widows, and offers the troubled recovery and peace.'" (A. Th. 19)[4]

The king was finally converted and did in the end receive a "Palace in the heavens"! Gundafor and his brother Gad were initiated by Thomas. They were "marked" by the baptism in water, the anointing with oil and the Eucharist, and were taken as sheep into the fold of the Lord. "For we have heard that the God that you worship recognizes his sheep by their mark." Following the initiation rite, Jesus himself appeared, saying, "Peace be with you, Brothers!"[5]

The text continues, "And after he (Thomas) blessed them, he took bread, oil, vegetables and salt, blessed it, and gave it to them. He himself continued his fast, for the Day of the Lord was approaching with dawn."

Apparently, Jesus did not reside continuously at the court of the king; though he returned there regularly. At any rate, he came the following night to Thomas who was expecting him, and said: "Thomas, rise early, bless everyone, and after prayer and service, go two miles along the path eastward, and there I shall show you my glory. For many will seek refuge in me, for the sake of the work for which you are setting off, and you are to expose the nature and power of the enemy."[6] At the place described by Jesus, the apostle found a lad who appeared to be dead, whom he awakened in the presence of a number of spectators. The comely youth tells Thomas of having seen Jesus. "For I saw that man, as he stood next to you and said to you, 'I have many miracles that I shall demonstrate through you, and have great works that I shall execute through you . . .'"[7]

The next clue on the road eastward is seventy kilometres east of Taxila, in a small town called Mari. In this idyllically situated mountain resort (called Murree in English), on the border to Kashmir, a grave has been maintained and honoured from as far back as anyone can remember, called Mai Mari da Asthan, *The Final Resting Place of Mother Mary*.

When Jesus reached this region with his group, his mother must have been over seventy years old, and strained by the long journey. Because there are no traces of Mary's tomb anywhere else in the world (Christian tradition insists that the mother of Jesus reached paradise by the Ascension, paradise also signifying Kashmir, heaven on Earth), it is conceivable that Mary was entombed here. Even if Jesus did not have a particularly intimate relationship with his physi-

The tomb of Mary, mother of Jesus, in Mari/Pakistan.

cal mother outwardly, he would certainly not have left her behind at
the mercy of his enemies without any protection. One of the notable
features of the grave is its orientation: in contrast to Islamic graves,
which point from north to south, Mary's grave points from east to
west (in Jewish fashion). It is located on the mountain Pindi Point
outside the small town, and is now sealed off by the military because
of its proximity to the Kashmirian border. The area around Mari was
under Hindu rule at the time of Christ. The Hindus cremated their
dead, and scattered the ashes, thus having no need of graves. Therefore the grave can have been neither Hindu nor Islamic. Nonetheless,
the monument continues to be honoured as the final resting-place of
Jesus' mother by members of the Islamic faith, because Jesus (Issa) is
also considered one of the most exalted prophets in the Islamic faith.

When northern India was converted to Islam in the seventh
century A.D., the fanatical conquerors destroyed all the monuments
of the "infidels". Because of the special position of Mary's grave,
however, the Moslems were able to recognize that the memorial was
a relic of a "People of the Book", either Christians or Israelites, and
thus spared it and treated it with respect.

In 1898, the British colonial army built a defence tower immediately next to the monument. This, of course, did not deter many pilgrims from visiting the place of worship. In 1917, the building surrounding the grave was partly torn down at the order of a certain Captain Richardson, so that pilgrims would remain at a distance from the military zone. Loud cries of protest from the population caused the local officials to intervene, and the complete destruction of the memorial was thus prevented. The events concerning the matter of Mary's monument are to be found in the archives of the local administration, dated July 30, 1917. In 1950, the monument was restored. After official recognition of the border to Pakistan, the defence tower was removed; in its stead, a network of antennae for a television station flanks the tombstone.

Today a 170 km road runs from Mari to Srinagar, the capital of Kashmir, through wooded mountain scenery. About 40 km south of Srinagar, between the villages of Naugam and Nilmag, the *Yus-Marg, the meadow of Jesus,* is to be found on a vast plain. Here it is the *Bani-Israel, the children of Israel,* who settled in the area after 722 B.C. and continue to live there as shepherds who have passed down the reports that Jesus preached there.

The Acts of Thomas relate how the apostle Thomas lived as a missionary at the court of the Indian King Misdai in southern India, where he gained many followers and converted a great number of people. Later he fell into disfavour and met the fate of a martyr. When Marco Polo returned to Europe from his twenty-five year stay in the Far East, in 1295, he was able to tell the West of the existence of numerous Christians who worshipped the grave of the apostle Thomas, on the eastern coast of south India (as we have already mentioned, the grave of the apostle Thomas continues to be honoured in Milapore, near Madras in southern India, although his bones had been transported back to Edessa at the beginning of the fourth century). According to Marco Polo, the "Thomas Christians" used a red earth tinted by the martyr's blood for healing the ill. There had also been Christians on the western coast of south India (now the Malabar Coast of Kerala); according to the great traveller, Christianity had been in existence there for a very long time.

There are even earlier records to bear witness to Christianity in India.[8] Tertullian listed India among those lands "ruled" by Christianity. Ephraem (c. 306–373 A.D.) wrote of Thomas' missions in

India, and Anorbius (c. 305 A.D.) also listed India among the countries under Christian influence. A person bearing the title "Bishop John of all Persia and Greater India" took part in the ominous Council of Nicaea.

In 1900, a short article appeared in an English journal which demanded the attention of the entire theological profession. It was reported that in the ruined Indian city of Fatehpur Sikri (175 km south of Delhi and c. 25 km from Agra), a saying of Jesus, completely unknown in the Occident, had been found engraved on an ancient wall. Fatehpur Sikri owed its short period of prosperity to the Indian Mogul emperor, Akbar the Great (1542–1605), who created the town from the ground up; the town was deserted a few decades later. In May 1601, the emperor made a triumphal entry into the city, and had the maxim inscribed on the southern main gate (Buland Darwaza) of the mosque. In 1582 Akbar had proclaimed a rational monotheism, in which he attempted to create a syncretic and unitarian harmony (din ilahi) among the various Indian religions. He had made sincere attempts to come to grips with the principles of Hinduism, Parsism and Jainism, and he was taught about the Gospels by Portuguese Jesuits who lived at his court. His plan was to unite India, then split into religious factions, in a single Religion that would contain the quintessence of all the various faiths as its one Truth. Akbar must have selected this particular saying of Jesus because it seemed to him to be the best representation of his ideas; otherwise he was hardly likely to have placed it in such an important place.

When leaving the precincts of the mosque via the main gate, one can read the inscription on the left side of the enormous archway, underneath a description of the occasion it celebrated and the date:

> *Jesus (Peace be with him) has said: 'The world is a bridge. Pass over it, but do not settle down on it!'*

A second inscription, this one above the archway of the northern wing (Liwan) of the mosque, gives the maxim in a slightly different form, "Jesus (Peace be with him) has said: 'The world is a proud house, take this as a warning and do not build on it!'"

The Portugese missionaries could not possibly have told the *agrapha (Gk. = sayings attributed to Jesus but not found written in the Bible)* to Akbar, for they are not to be found in any Christian source. The

189

The so-called Agraphon, engraved into the wall of the palace of Akbar in Fatehpur Sikri.

very extensive *Life of Jesus* which the Jesuit Jerome Xavier wrote for Akbar contains neither of the quotes. It is thus possible that the agrapha came from the early Thomas Christians. The form of introduction in the sayings, which is always the same, can be found in the later Islamic accounts about Jesus, so that most Orientalists have inferred that the saying can only have arrived in India via Islam. But this need not be the case, for there is a conspicuous agreement between this saying and the far earlier maxims of Jesus in the apocryphal Gospel of Thomas; this in both form and content. The Gospel according to Thomas is now accessible in its entirety thanks to the sensational finds at Nag Hammadi in 1945. The "Gospel" is not a coherent narrative like the synoptic Gospels, but a collection of 114 sayings of Jesus, in an arbitrary order. Most of the maxims are introduced with the same formula, "Jesus has said".

The anthology is introduced in the following way: "These are the secret sayings which the living Jesus spoke and which Didymos Judas Thomas wrote down. And he said, 'Whoever finds the interpretation of these sayings will not experience death.'"[9]

Even if it were not possible to prove that the apostle Thomas actually lived in India, there is much evidence of missionary activity throughout India long before the Mohammedans stormed the land. The Aramaic Gospel according to Matthew, which must have originated in c. 180 A.D., tells of a missionary voyage to the Indians undertaken by one Pantaenus of Alexandria.

The *Chronicle of Séert* (I 8, 25) relates that Bishop David of Basra (a contemporary of the Metropolite Papa who died in A.D. 316), went to India and preached there with great success.

In about the year 335, Emperor Constantine sent Bishop Theophilos to India to reform the ecclesiastical system there, according to accounts by Philostorgius from before A.D. 433.

In an account from the end of the fourth century, Symeon of Mesopotamia mentions the martyrdom of Indian "barbarians" for Christ.

The *Chronicle of Séert* II 9 also reports that in about A.D. 490, the Persian bishop Ma'an sent his writings to India.

In the accounts of Cosmas Indicopleusta, one can find precise geographical references about the voyage to India which he undertook in around A.D. 525. He found Christians on the island of Sri Lanka, and on the Indian west coast, "in Male, where pepper grows (= Malabar), and in the place called Kalliana (= Kalyan, near Bombay)", and he mentions that Kalliana was the seat of a bishop who had once lived in Persia[10].

This brief enumeration should suffice to disprove the theory generally held by Indologists that Jesus did not become known in India until he was introduced through Islam. Yet one must add that the Koran has a great deal to offer on the topic of Jesus' life in India. According to the Koran, Jesus did not die on the cross, but survived the crucifixion, and lived thereafter in a "Happy Valley".

191

The "True" Jesus of Islam

Issa (*Isa*), the name commonly applied to Jesus in Islam, derives from the Syrian form Yeshu, being altered to conform to *Musa* (= Moses). The reason for the extensive and thorough accounts about the prophet Issa in the Koran, was probably to correct the "distorted image in the writings of his followers". Jesus is considered to be Israel's last great prophet and the precursor of Mohammed. He is even said to have presaged the coming of the "Greatest of all prophets": "I have yet many things to say unto you, but ye cannot bear them now. Howbeit when he, the Spirit of truth, is come, he will guide you into the truth: for he shall not speak of himself; but whatsoever he shall hear, that shall he speak: and he will shew you things to come. He shall glorify me: for he shall receive of mine, and shall shew it unto you." (John 16, 12–14).

Because Mohammed considered himself to be the promised "Spirit of Truth", he felt that he was called upon to interpret the teaching of Jesus according to his lights, and to restore the honour of the man in the face of the Church's talk about the death on the cross. After being freed of the ignominy of crucifixion, Jesus was welcomed into the Islamic fold as a great precursor of Mohammed. Still, "The Messiah, the son of Mary, was a Messenger; certainly, he was preceded by other Messengers." (Koran V 79).

In the Koran, again, one can read the following about Jesus' mission: "To Moses We(= Allah) gave the Scriptures and after him We sent other apostles. We gave Jesus the son of Mary veritable signs and strengthened him with the Holy Spirit" (Koran II, 81).

There is a certain reserve in all this praise, for Islam clearly rejects the idea of Jesus as a human incarnation of what is purely divine: "People of the Book, do not transgress the bounds of your religion. Speak nothing but the truth about Allah. The Messiah, Jesus the son of Mary, was no more than Allah's apostle and His Word which He cast to Mary: a spirit from Him. So believe in Allah and His apostles and do not say: 'Three'. Forbear and it shall be better for you. Allah is but one God. Allah forbids that He should have a son! His is all that the heavens and the earth contain. Allah is the all-sufficient Protector. The Messiah does not disdain to be a servant of Allah, nor do the

192

angels who are nearest to him." (IV, 169). Another explicit passage reads: ". . . they imitate the infidels of old . . . They worship their rabbis and their monks, and the Messiah the son of Mary, as gods besides Allah; though they were ordered to serve one God only. There is no god but Him. Exalted be He above those whom they deify beside Him!" (IX, 30–31).

The Koran clearly states that Jesus did not die on the cross, and the Jews were deceived: "And because they were non-believers and slandered Mary severely; and because they said, 'We have killed the Messiah, Jesus, the son of Mary, the Messenger of God, although they neither struck him dead nor crucified him, but just made him appear so . . . thus we curse them, and behold, those who are not of the same mind in this matter are in true doubt; they have no proof, but just follow a suspicion; for in reality, they did not kill him. God raised him to himself, and God is mighty, wise.". The Arabian word for crucifixion means "death on the cross" in this context. Thus merely being nailed to the cross without dying is definitely not meant. In fact, during the period in which the Koran was written, the Jews themselves seem to have been unsure as to whether Jesus really died on the cross. The Koran also gives an answer to the question of where Jesus went after the crucifixion: "We (= God) made the son of Mary and his mother a sign to mankind and gave them a shelter on a peaceful hill-side watered by a fresh spring." (XXIII, 52). The similarities between this description and Kashmir are striking. In another translation, the place in the mountains is even called "a green valley".

Hazrat Mirza Ghulam Ahmad, born in India in 1835, was the Moslem founder of the Ahmadiyya sect, which held the conviction that the Koran confirms the truth that Jesus had been saved from death on the cross, an accursed death unworthy of him. The texts of the Gospels would also confirm Jesus' survival of the crucifixion by recounting the comparison Jesus drew between himself and Jona, who did not die in the belly of the whale before reappearing. If Jesus had been lying dead in his sepulchre, what sense would the analogy have? "For as Jona was three days and three nights in the whale's belly; so shall the Son of man be three days and three nights in the heart of the earth." (Matthew 12,40).

For the Ahmadiyyas (still a popular form of Islam today), Jesus' survival of the torment of crucifixion fulfils prophecies from the Old Testament. In the book of the prophet Isaiah, one reads: "When thou

193

shalt make his soul an offering for sin, he shall see his seed, he shall prolong his days, and the pleasure of the Lord shall prosper in his hand" (Isaiah 53,10). The book of the prophet Isaiah does not in fact claim that the promised servant of the Lord is to die. Even the prophecies in Psalm 34 do not indicate that the Messiah is to be killed: "Many are the afflictions of the righteous: but the Lord delivereth him out of them all" (Psalms 34,19). One can conclude that God had not planned that Jesus die the accursed death by crucifixion. According to Arabian tradition, a man can only be accursed if he turns away from God, becomes "black", lacks God's love, is in want of God's mercy for all time, and is void of all perception of God; if he, like Satan, is full of the poison of deception and is no longer reached by a single ray from the light of love; and if he rejects all relations with God, and is full of resentment, hate and enmity towards God, so that God becomes his enemy and turns from him in disgust! Mirza Ghulam felt that Christians could not possibly have been conscious of the significance of the expression, "accursed on the wooden cross"; otherwise they could never have adopted this feature in their teachings on the virtuous Jesus.

Jesus in Kashmir

If Jesus did indeed live in Kashmir for a long period of time, one should be able to find some traces of this fact in ancient Indian literature. Because one presumes that the Messiah did not die until he was more than eighty years old in Srinagar, it seems natural to suppose that there is evidence of how he spent the last thirty to forty years. But the Indian authors of antiquity resisted all alienation of their culture through foreign influence. For instance, not even Alexander the Great's conquest of India is mentioned in any writings, however significant the event may have been. Indologists are in agreement that there was no systematic history in India before it was invaded by Islam.

The ancient narratives of the Hindus are the Puranas (= old), and were continuously supplemented by further religious texts from the fifth century B.C. or before up until the seventeenth century.' The entire anthology currently comprises eighteen volumes, and the ninth volume, called *Bhavishyat Maha-Purana,* contains an account from the fifth century of how Jesus came to India. The description is so detailed that no doubt can exist as to the identity of the man in question. The Purana relates that Israelites settled in India, and in verses 17–32, describes Jesus' appearance on the scene:

"Shalivahan, who was a grandson of Bikrama Jit, took over the government. He vanquished the attacking hordes of Chinese, Parthians, Scythians and Bactrians. He drew a border between the Arians and the Mleacha (= non-Hindus), and ordered the latter to withdraw to the other side of India. One day, Shalivahan, the chief of the Sakyas, went into the Himalayas. There, in the Land of the Hun (= Ladakh, a part of the Kushan empire), the powerful king saw a man sitting on a mountain, who seemed to promise auspiciousness. His skin was fair and he wore white garments. The king asked the holy man who he was. The other replied: 'I am called a son of God, born of a virgin, minister of the non-believers, relentlessly in search of the truth.' The king then asked him: 'What is your religion?' The other replied, 'O great king, I come from a foreign country, where there is no longer truth and where evil knows no bounds. In the land of the non-believers, I appeared as the Messiah. But the demon Ihamasi of the barbarians (dasyu) manifested herself in a terrible form; I was delivered unto her in the manner of the non-believers and ended in Ihamasi's realm.

O king, lend your ear to the religion that I brought unto the non-believers: after the purification of the essence and the impure body and after seeking refuge in the prayers of the Naigama, man will pray to the Eternal. Through justice, truth, meditation and unity of spirit, man will find his way to Isa in the centre of light. God, as firm as the sun, will finally unite the spirit of all wandering beings in himself. Thus, O king, Ihamasi will be destroyed; and the blissful image of Isa, the giver of happiness, will remain forever in the heart; and I was called *Isa-Masih.*' After the king heard these words, he took the teacher of the non-believers and sent him to their pitiless land."

In this story (parts of which are translated literally here) it is very significant that the "teacher of the non-believers" called himself *Isa-*

Masih, which means quite simply "Jesus the Messiah". The "demon Ihamasi", appears to have represented everything evil and wicked in a general sense, though the name cannot be found anywhere else in the literature. The word *Naigama* evidently means some holy scripture(s), but here too, we find no indication as to what particular scripture is meant. According to Professor Hassnain, King Shalivahan ruled in the Kushan era from 39 to 50 A.D.

Text from the Bahavishyat Maha Purana (here a new edition) where the stay of Jesus in Kashmir is mentioned.

Further evidence of Jesus' stay in the Himalayas is a grave mentioned by Professor Nicholas Roerich in *The Heart of Asia,* published in 1930. The grave lies to the north of Ladakh in the neighboring Tibetan province of Sinkiang (= Xinjian in modern China), approximately six miles from the fair-size town of Kashgar, and is thought to belong to a certain Mary who was among Jesus' entourage. The apocryphal gospel of Philip mentions three women who did not leave Jesus' side after the crucifixion. All three were called Mary: his mother, her sister (the wife of Cleopas?), and Mary Magdalene "who was called his companion". Thus the grave of Mary near Kashgar could very well be connected with Jesus.

Jesus is hardly likely to have remained in one place during the remainder of his life in India. He probably moved from place to place as an itinerant minister, without a home and without rest, for as long as his health permitted such a life. There are numerous indications that he repeatedly returned to Kashmir.

About 60 km southeast of Srinagar and only 12 km from Bijbihara (the place of the 'stone of Moses'), a cave some twelve metres long opens into the mountain. In the entrance to the cave stands a magnificent building called *Aish-muquam*. The sacred building contains the reliquary of Zainuddin Wali, an Islamic saint, who lived in the cave during the rule of Sultan Zainul Aabidin Budshah (1408–1461). The saint was in possession of a precious rod, which he had been given by Shaikh Noor Din Wali. This rod is considered to be a valuable relic, is closely watched over by the tomb attendants, and is always covered with a green cloth. When the faithful of the region are burdened with great troubles or suffer contagious diseases, they make a pilgrimage to Aish-muquam in the hope of being helped by the miraculous power of the staff. The staff is 2.5 metres long and approximately 2.5 cm in diameter. It is dark brown, made of olive wood, and is called Moses' rod or Jesus' rod. Worshippers of this relic tell of the legend that the staff first belonged to Moses when he made his way to Kashmir and was later used by Jesus, a symbol of his Mosaic heritage. The staff was first preserved in Khangahi Moulla (Srinagar) before it found an honourable resting-place in Aish-muquam. The name *Aish-muquam* is said to bear a direct relation to Jesus. *Aish* derives from Isha/Isa, and *Muquam* means place of rest or repose. One might conclude that Jesus withdrew to this place for a time, where he devoted himself to inner meditation. This cannot, of course, be proved.

There is more concrete evidence for Jesus' presence in Kashmir, that offered by stone carvings which have survived the flow and eddies of the centuries. One such piece of evidence is an inscription on the Throne of Solomon which alludes to Jesus. In 1413, Mullah Nadiri, a historian who lived during the rule of Sultan Zainul Aabidin, recounted part of the history of the Throne. In his book on the history of Kashmir (Tarikh-i-Kashmir), he wrote that Gopananda,

197

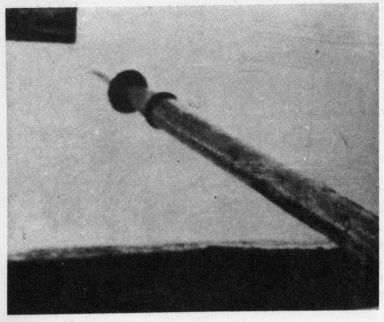

The so-called 'Rod of Jesus'

the son of Rajah Akh, ruled in Kashmir under the name of Gopadatta; and he had this Temple of Solomon (which was already a millenium old at the dawn of the Christian era) restored by a Persian architect. The Hindus noticed that the Persian was a non-believer and belonged to a different religion. On the occasion of the renovation, four sayings in ancient Persian were inscribed on the side of the steps at the threshold:

1. *Maimar een satoon raj bihishti zargar, sal panja wa chahar.* "The constuctor of these columns is the most humble Bihishti Zagar; in the year fifty and four."
2. *Een satoon bardast khwaja rukun bin murjan.* "Khwaja Rukun, son of Murjan, had these columns built."

198

3. *Dar een wagat yuz asaf dawa-i-paighambar-i mikunad. Sal panja wa chahar.* "At this time, Yuz Asaf announced his prophetic calling. In the year fifty and four."
4. *Aishan yuzu paighambar-i-bani israil ast.* "He is Jesus, prophet of the sons of Israel."

The ancient Persian inscription at the 'Throne of Solomon' above the town of Srinagar.

The historian Mullah Nadiri continues : "At the time of the rule of Gopadatta, Yuz Asaf came from the Holy Land up into this valley and announced that he was a prophet. He exemplified the heights of piety and virtue, and proclaimed that he was himself his own message, that he was in God day and night, and that he had made God accessible to the people of Kashmir. He called the people unto him, and the people of the valley believed in him. When the Hindus came to Gopadatta in indignation, exhorting him to deal with the man, he turned them away.

I read in a book of the Hindus that the prophet was really Hazrat Isa, the Spirit of God (God's peace and good will be with him), and he adopted the name Yuz Asaf. True knowledge is with God. He spent his life in this valley.

After his demise, he was buried in Mohalla Anzimarah. It is said that the light of prophecy emanates from the tomb of this prophet. King Gopadatta ruled sixty years and two months before he died. After his death, his son Gokaran mounted the throne and ruled for the span of fifty-eight years." (Takht-i-Kashmir, p. 69).

A page from the history of Mullah Nadiri from the year 1413.

King Gopadatta ruled in Kashmir from the year 53 onwards. The year given in the text as year 54 of the rule of Rajah Gopadatta was 107 A.D. by our reckoning. The Rajah's rule thus fell within the reign of the great King Kanishka of the Kushan dynasty. One cannot gather from the text whether or not Jesus was still alive at the time.

All in all, there are at least twenty-one historical documents bearing witness to Jesus' stay in Kashmir. Furthermore, a great number of place names in Kashmir offer geographical proof (cf. chapter 2), for instance:

Arya-Issa; Issa-Brari; Yuzu-dha; Yuzu-dhara; Yuzu-gam; Yuzu-hatpura; I-yes-Issa; Kal-Issa; Yuzu-kun; Issa-kush; Yus-mangala; Yuzu-maidan; Yus-marg; Aish-muquam; Issa-mati; Issa-eil; Yus-nag; Ram-Issa; Yuzu-para; Yuzu-raja; Issa-Ta; Yuzu-varman; I-yes-th-Issa-vara; Yusu.

At the time when Jesus lived in Kashmir, the "Happy Valley" was the centre of an enormous religious, cultural, intellectual and political ferment. The kingdom of Kashmir was the centre of the enormous Indo-Scythian empire and was ruled by the great Kushan king

Kanishka I (78–103 A.D.). An excellent statesman, a kind and wise ruler, Kanishka attempted to unite the motley mixture of races in his country by a policy of tolerance and generosity. In the culture of Gandhara, the harmony of Indian and Greek philosophy reached its height. The academic centre of such intercultural unity was the old University of Taxila, which was already famed far and wide.

Kanishka (like the great Ashoka before him) found the right setting for the realisation of his ideas in Buddhism and sought advice and instruction from Buddhist monks. He was, however, disturbed by the chaos of various schools and sects that had developed or fragmented in the course of the five centuries following the Buddha's departure. Following the advice of the philosopher Parshwa, he summoned the grand Council of Haran (Harwan), which was attended by 1500 Buddhist scholars. The Council of Haran (in Kashmir) was the fourth council that proved necessary in the course of three hundred years to establish the Mahayana as a religion of the people. The established priests of the old Hinayana Buddhism were reluctant to share their privileges with the masses, and made one last stand in opposition to the Council. But these orthodox monks were not to succeed in hindering the reforms of the Council of Haran, which turned Buddhism into a religion of the people. Haran's location just 12 km from Srinagar makes it feasible that Jesus himself was present at this important meeting.

At any rate, King Kanishka was so impressed with the results of the Council that he paid high tribute to the participants, converted to Buddhism himself, and employed his secular influence in its propagation. He turned the administration of his kingdom over to the community of Buddhist monks, whose spiritual leader was the wise philosopher Nagarjuna.

The *Rajatarangini* text provides a further clue about the residence of Jesus in ancient Kashmir. The work is a history of Kashmir, written in Sanskrit verses by Pandit Kalhana in the twelfth century. This Sanskrit record is actually the earliest known history book in existence. It is a summary of numerous legendary stories which had been passed down by oral tradition. The historical facts were partly altered during the passage of the generations so that the true kernel of the stories has been "embroidered" to some extent. In Rajatarangini there is an account of a God-man who performed miracles very

201

This file (found in Haran) shows the meeting between King Kanishka (on the left with assyrian hair-style) and a monk with mongolian appearance. The Buddhist lama presents a lotus flower (symbol of buddhism) to the king.

similar to those of Jesus. The saint's name was "Isana". Isana is said to have saved the influential statesman "Vazir" from crucifixion, and to have brought him back to life. Vazir subsequently became the ruler of India and governed for 47 years. Kalhana writes that the God-man Isana was Kashmir's last reformer and was influential in the first century A.D. It seems likely that Saint Isana was none other than Isa/Jesus.

Jesus' Tomb in Srinagar

During the Middle Ages, the story of "Barlaam and Josaphat" was an essential work of world literature with which every educated person was familiar. There were a great variety of translations and numerous versions of the story throughout Europe and the Near East, though the original was attributed to John Damaskenos, a distinguished Arabian Christian who lived at about A.D. 700 in Jerusalem. The story, also known in some countries as "The Prince and the Dervish", runs as follows: Abaner, a powerful king of India, is told by an astrologer that his virtuous and wise son, Josaphat (or Joasaph) will convert from Islam to Christianity. In order to avoid the fulfilment of the prophecy, the king has a magnificent palace built so that the prince might grow up and be educated in complete isolation. Despite all the security measures, Josaphat happens to see a blind man, an old man, and finally a dead man on separate occasions. Because the young man is only surrounded by young and beautiful people in the palace, the encounters are completely new experiences and open his eyes to the realities of life.

The prince then meets the ascetic Barlaam who converts him to Christianity. Although the King tries to dissuade his son from joining the new faith, and even offers him half his kingdom, Josaphat declines all offers, withdraws into isolation, and spends the rest of his life as a pious ascetic.

This charming tale is so moving and so full of profound truth that both Barlaam and Joasaph were canonised by the Roman Catholic Church in 1583, and placed in the calendar of martyrs. Under November 27, one can read: "In India, near the borders of Persia, Saints Barlaam and Joasaph. Their wonderful deeds have been portrayed by St. John of Damascus". Until the sixteenth century, it probably did not occur to anyone that the story was precisely the same as the legend of Prince Siddhartha, who left his family and lived without shelter in order to become Buddha. The name Josafat or Josephat sounds so Jewish that no doubt ever arose as to its origin. But in fact the name can be traced back without difficulty to the Greek name, Joasaph; further to the Arabic name, Judasaph; and finally to the Kashmirian name Yusasaph. If one knows that the letters "J" and "B" are nearly identical in Syrian, Arabic and Persian, one can recognize the name Budasaf in the word Judasaf. And Budasaf means nothing other than *Bodhi sattva,* or a Buddha in the making (Skt.root *budh* = know, *sattva* = Truth, purity; *buddha* = enlightened).

The exotic sounding name Barlaam can also be traced back to its original meaning via the bridge of languages. In Arabic, Balauhar means the same as the Sanskrit word *Bhagavan,* "The Exalted Divine One". The etymology of J(B)udasaf is a clear indication that the Islamic prophet Yuz Asaf was really a Buddhist Bodhisattva who had been generously incorporated into the Islamic faith by a rigorous conformation to its principles (and if the Bodhisattva, Yuz Asaf, was identical with Jesus, then the Magi from the East had indeed found the correct incarnation).

The description of the attributes of a Bodhisattva sound very much like a portrayal of Jesus. A principal quality of a Bodhisattva is such a degree of compassion that he is prepared to take on the burdens of others and help sinners attain salvation. Even if a Bodhisattva seems to become guilty while performing his duty or doing some deed out of compassion, his first duty remains to secure the salvation of others. Jesus pursued this ideal with absolute earnestness by accepting the responsibility for all the sins of the world, and allowing himself to be nailed to the cross as a sacrificial lamb. All the characteristics of a Bodhisattva can also be ascribed to Jesus.

In Buddhism, the transcendental figure of the Bodhisattva, *Avalokitéshvara,* is the embodiment of limitless compassion. Avalokite-shvara derives from the joining of *Íshvara* (= Lord, ruler) and *ava-lokita* (= he who looks down in compassion on the world). Avalokitésvara is nearly as consummate as Buddha himself, and possesses miracu-lous powers with which he surmounts all dangers and difficulties. From the beginning of the second century, Avalokitesvara has been portrayed with marks on the surfaces of his hands and feet, symboliz-ing the Wheel of the Teaching. Many Western authors have recog-nized the stigmata of Jesus in the wheel symbol and see this as proof that Avalokiteshvara and Jesus are one and the same.

During the important fourth Council of Kashmir in Haran near Srinagar under the auspices of Kanishka the Great, to which we have referred, Jesus must have been more than eighty years old, if he was still on earth. We have suggested that he may even have taken part in this event which was to have such great significance for the Buddhist world, as a revered holy man. Although such a supposition cannot be proved, all the known facts do allow scope for such speculation. At any rate, the reforms introduced by the Council are in complete accord with the teaching of Jesus.

Hadrad Fatimah Al-Zahra, a relative of Mohammed, passed on a pronouncement of the prophet to the effect that Jesus reached the advanced age of 120 years[2]. There is no archaeological proof for such a claim, but such an advanced age does not seem to be uncommon among those genuine ascetics who succeed in keeping their body under the complete control of their mind. Tibetan holy men have often attained ages of 130, 150 and even more. Shaik Al-Sa'id-us-Sadiq, a great Oriental historian who died in A.D. 962 in Khurasan, wrote of Jesus' two journeys to India and his demise as Yuz Asaf in Kashmir in his famous work *Ikmal-ud-Din*. The book was republished in Iran in 1882 and translated into German by the famous Orientalist Max Müller. The book contains a sample of the teachings of Yuz Asaf which could have been a parable straight out of the Gospels:

"People, hear my words: a farmer goes to sow his fields. The birds come and eat the seed. Other seed falls on the path. And behold, some seed falls on the rock where there is no earth, and withers away. Some falls under the thorns and cannot grow. The seed that falls on the good earth, however, sprouts and brings forth fruit. The farmer is the sage and the seeds are his words of wisdom. The seeds which are eaten by the birds means the people who do not understand the words. The seeds that fall onto the rocks are the words of wisdom that go in one ear and come out the other. The seeds that land under the thorns means those who hear and see, but do not act accordingly. The seeds which land on the good earth means those that hear the words of wisdom and act accordingly." (Ikmal-ud-Din, p. 327; cf. Matthew 13,1–23; Mark 4,1–20; Luke 8,4–15).

In an Arabic version of the story of Barlaam and Josaphat, *The Book of Balauhar and Budasaf* (pp. 285–286), which was published in Bombay, the story of the death of Yuz Asaf is given thus: "And he reached Kashmir, which was the farthest region at which he ministered, and there his life ended. He left the world and bequeathed his inheritance to a certain disciple called Ababid who had served him. Everything that he did was perfect. And he admonished him and said to him, 'I have found a worthy shrine and decorated it and brought in lamps for the dying. I have collected the flock with the true face, which had been dispersed and to whom I was sent. And now I shall draw breath through my ascent from the world, by the separation of my soul from my body. Obey the commandments that were given to you, and do not deviate from the path of truth but keep firmly to it in gratitude. And may Ababid be the leader.' He then commanded Ababid to level off the place for him; he stretched his legs out and lay down. Then, turning his head northwards and his face eastwards, he passed away.''³

The tomb of the prophet Yuz Asaf is in the middle of what is today Srinagar's old town, in Anzimar in the Khanjar quarter. The building that was later built around the grave-stone is called "Rozabal", an abbreviation of "Rauza Bal". *Rauza* means "the tomb of a prophet". The building is rectangular and can be entered by a small portico which has been added to it. Above the passage to the actual burial chamber, one can read an inscription explaining that Yuz Asaf entered the valley of Kashmir many centuries before, and that his life was dedicated to the search for the truth. There are two long grave-stones on the floor of the inner burial chamber, both surrounded by wooden railings covered in heavy cloth. The railing is surrounded in turn by a stable wooden shrine. The larger grave-stone is for Yuz Asaf, the smaller one for the Islamic saint Syed Nasir-ud-Din, who was not buried here until the fifteenth century. Both grave-stones point from north to south, in accordance with Moslem custom. But these grave-stones are in fact mere covers, and the actual graves are in a crypt under the floor of the building. A tiny opening allows one to look into the true burial chamber below. The sarcophagus containing the earthly remains of Yuz Asaf points from east to west, in accordance with Jewish custom! This is clear proof that Yuz Asaf was neither an Islamic saint nor a Hindu.

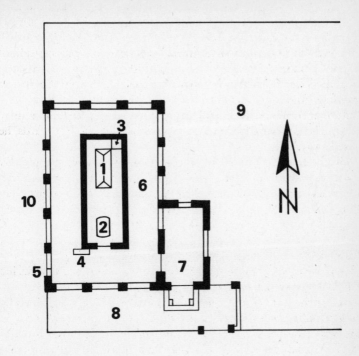

1 Gravestone of Jesus/Yuz Asaf

2 Gravestone of Syed Nasir-ud-Din

3 Chiselled footprints

4 Signboard

5 Walled-up entrance to crypt

6 Surrounding corridor

7 Entrance

8 Terrace

9 Moslem cemetery

10 Roadway

Ever since the days of the burial, worshippers have placed candles around the grave-stones. When Professor Hassnain removed the thick old layers of wax, he made a sensational discovery. The archaeologist found "footprints" carved into the stone and beside them a crucifix and a rosary. The "footprints" were meant to prove the identity of the deceased rather like fingerprints. As with the swastikas of Buddha's footprints, characteristics can be seen in Yuz Asaf's footprints which are a unique and unmistakeable proof of identity. The sculptor clearly illustrated the scars of the crucifixion wounds in the relief. The position of the wounds even indicates that the left foot had been nailed over the right, a fact that was confirmed by analysis of the blood marks on the Turin Shroud. Because crucifixion was unknown as a punitive measure in Asia, one could conclude this is the place of burial of Jesus. There are numerous historical sources in

The original footprints illuminated by candles.

Kashmir that confirm that Yuz Asaf and Jesus were one and the same. An old manuscript describes the memorial as the grave of *Isa Rooh-u-Ilah*.[4] Each year thousands of pious believers make pilgrimages to the tomb, not just Moslems, but also Hindus, Buddhists and Christians. The descendants of the old Israelites have remembered the true significance of the modest monument: they call the shrine "The tomb of Hazrat Isa Sahib", i.e. the tomb of the Lord (master) Jesus. Ancient documents state that a protective building was constructed around the grave as long ago as 112 A.D. The grave has been tended by a succession of guardians without interruption, since its construction. In 1766, the keepers of the tomb received a document of official confirmation about the significance of the sacred site. In the official document of the grand Mufti (or Moslem cleric) Rahman Mir one can read: "Here lies Yuz Asaf, who reestablished the temple of Solomon at the time of King Gopadatta, and who came as a prophet to Kashmir. He ministered to the people, declared his unity with God, and was a lawgiver to the people. Since then, his tomb has been honoured by kings, state officials, high dignitaries and the common people."

Inside the Rozabal building there is a wooden shrine.

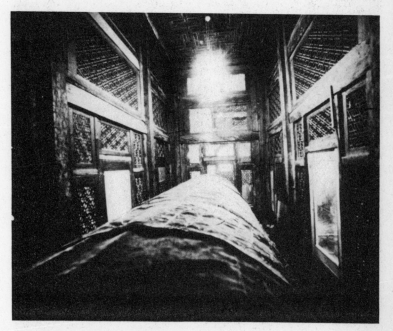

The gravestone is covered by a cloth.

The grayestone (sample, so-called cenotaph). Below it is the tomb of Yuz Asaph situated.

Final Remarks

The survival of Western humanity
depends on the re-introduction
of the concept of Karma
to the thinking of the people at large.

Paul Brunton

Our story has now ended, without anything having been said about how the reader can apply the newly acquired knowledge. Many letters came to me (after the German edition) with the criticism that I was pulling away the Christians' final source of solace, namely the belief in *redemption from the sins of the tortured world by the vicarious death of Jesus Christ*, for all those who resort to him. But it is precisely this salvation doctrine of traditional Christianity which rests almost exclusively on Paul, and was never promulgated by Jesus in this form.

Paul taught that the whole function of Jesus centred on his death which released the faithful from the burden of their sins, their misery and the power of Satan. In fact not a single word Paul wrote in the Epistles gives the actual teaching of Jesus, nor does he mention even one of his parables; instead he just spreads his own philosophy and his own ideas.

Paul tends to characterise all people as children of anger, i.e. as subject to the wrath of God (see Eph. 2,3). All are (without exception) quite lost (e.g. Romans 5,18; Cor. 15,18), without hope and without God (Eph.2,12), for Satan has power over everyone (without exception) (e.g. Rom. 3,9; Gal. 3,22; Col. 2,14). A sentence of damnation hangs like a sword of Damocles over all people (e.g. Rom. 5,16).

Thus Paul as a human teacher made out of the *joyous tidings* his *threatening tidings* and implied that *only he* could show the path to salvation. Of course with such an attitude one can hardly arrive at a natural view of death, for it makes death a solution to sin.

In no other religion we do find such cultivation of the fear of death as in the Pauline Christianity. With Paul Christinity became a religion in which Christians, beset by fears, would bow docilely under the yoke of threats. The religion was already veering away from the concept of the kind and loving, all-forgiving God of Jesus, and reverting to the crudities of the wrathful Old Testament God, as borne out by Paul's words.

The point comes home best when one considers Paul's explicit statement that the human individual can do nothing himself to secure salvation, " . . (cf. Rom. 3,24; 3,28; 9,11; 9,16; 1.Cor. 1,29; Gal. 2,16). For according to Paul salvation depends solely on the Grace of God . . .". (Eph. 2,8-9).

Thus the Pauline doctrine makes salvation a one-sided matter for God; people on earth have their hands bound (cf. Rom. 3,24; 4,16; Eph. 2,5; 2,8-9; 2. Tim. 1,9; Tit. 3,5-7). What Paul says here is of course quite attractive, because it is comfortable. By joining the fold, salvation ensues "automatically". No effort on one's own part is then necessary to arrive at the goal of life, for every *Christian* is saved once and for all by the sacrificial death of Jesus on the cross on Golgotha.

It means that one has only to sign up with this "institution", pay the "membership fee", and (lo and behold!) everything is settled for securing a seat in paradise for all eternity. Naturally such a teaching attracted many supporters and spread rapidly. After all it is easier to believe in something that can be had safely and comfortably.

Simply by the single act of conversion a person is then redeemed, saved, made a child of God, and becomes a completely new person. According to this teaching, every attempt on one's own part to work towards salvation plays down Jesus' role, is even a *deadly sin*. And conversely, every person, however exemplary and good his or her life may have been, is declared by this teaching to be lost if he or she does not gratefully acknowledge the sacrifice on the cross as constituting their entire personal salvation.

Most Christians think the greatness and uniqueness of Christianity stands and falls with the truth of this teaching. On closer inspection, however, it is found to be a fabrication far removed from the real ideas of Jesus. There is no hint of the so-called Christian doctrine of salvation in the gospels, either in the *Sermon on the Mount* – the quintessence of Jesus' Message – or in the *Our Father*, or the traditional parables of Jesus! Were it really so important, Jesus would of course have given at least some indication that his "sacrificial death" meant the salvation of mankind. Any intentional withholding of the facts would have been quite incompatible with his living ethics.

Jesus did not supply theories to be ground in the mills of academia, about his path and message - he just lived his teaching! Tolerance, unprejudiced acceptance of others, giving and sharing, the capacity to take upon oneself the burdens of others, in other words unlimited love in action and service for one's fellow human beings - this is the path which Jesus showed to salvation!

I personally find in Jesus an ideal example of the Bodhisattva, that is a Buddha in the making, a person striving wholeheartedly for absolute Enlightenment and fully at home in the Divine Reality. Jesus walked free of all personal attachments and all egoistic ambition. He saw the "real world" as the cause of all suffering, and preached renunciation of this worldly life to his disciples.

According to this Buddhist ideal in the endless cycles of reincarnations, what is vital is to constantly improve one's Karma by appropri-

214

ate actions in order to finally arrive on the plane of the Divine. I have already tried in the section "Reincarnation in the New Testament" (page 112) to make clear that Jesus – and after him all the early Christian communities – took for granted the idea of many successive lives, as expounded in the eastern doctrine of rebirth. It may be of interest here to relate how it came about that the principle of reincarnation became the victim of a tremendous historical error somewhere in the sixth century.

Up till now almost all Church historians have believed that the doctrine of rebirth was officially dropped at the Council of Constantinople in the year 553 and thus declared heretical. In fact however, the damning of the rebirth doctrine is traceable to a personal attack by the Emperor Justinian, which never entered the protocols of the Council. Justinian's ambitious wife, who actually held the reins of power, was (according to Procopius) the daughter of a bear-keeper at the Byzantine amphitheatre. She began her swift rise to power as a courtesan. In order to free herself of her shameful past, she later ordered the abuse and death of 500 of her earlier "colleagues". Because she would have had to suffer the full consequences of these cruel deeds in a subsequent life according to the Karma doctrine, she set about having the whole magnificent teaching of rebirth simply abolished. Undoubtedly she was confident of her success in this annulment by "divine order"!

Emperor Justinian then proceeded to declare war on the teachings of Origen as early as 543 A.D., without considering the views of the Pope, and had them damned by a special Synod. In his works *De Principiis* and *Contra Celsum* the great Church Father, Origen (185 – 253 A.D.), had quite clearly acknowledged the prenatal existence of the soul and its dependence on earlier actions. He thought that only in the light of reincarnation certain scriptural passages of the New Testament could be explained.

The Council summoned by Justinian was attended only by Eastern (Orthodox) bishops and none from Rome, and the Pope himself kept clear of it, although he was staying in Constantinople at the time.

The Council of Constantinople, the fifth of the Councils, was more or less a private meeting organised by Justinian, at which he (together with the vassals subject to him) imposed a ban and curse on the teaching of the pre-existence of the soul, despite the protest of Pope Vigilius, with the publication of his *Anathemata*.

The official reports of the eight Council sessions, which lasted for a total of four weeks, did have to be presented to the Pope for ratification. The fact is, however, that these documents (the so-called "Three Chapters") dealt only with the dispute about three scholars whom Justinian had declared heretical in an edict four years before. They contained no mention of Origen. The following Popes Pelagius I (556 – 561), Pelagius II (579 – 590) and Gregory (590 - 604) speak of the fifth Council without using the name Origen even in passing.

The Church has clung to the conviction that the ban by Justinian - "Whoever teaches the fantastic pre-existence of the soul and its monstrous restoration shall be damned." – is part of the conclusions of the Council. The prohibition of the rebirth doctrine is therefore simply an error of history and lacking all ecclesiastical validity.

If one manages to acquaint oneself (again) with the doctrine of reincarnation, then relinquishung the belief in the ascension of the physical body of the crucified Jesus will lessen one's faith in the truth of Jesus' own, unalloyed teaching, even for those brought up as traditional Christians.

Holger Kersten
Freiburg, September 1986

Letters to the author (in German or English): please include two international reply coupons.

Postal address: Holger Kersten
                    GPO Box 961
                    D-7800 Freiburg
                    W. Germany

Chronology (Indian Area)

Before the Christian Era

before 6000	Development of Brahmanic System
c. 4500	Origins of the Vedas (acc. H. Jacobi)
around 2500	Indus Culture (Harappa)
6th c.	The "Lost Tribes of Israel" settle in North India
5th c.	Sutras written down
563 - 483	Buddha
4th c.	First Buddhist Scriptures
around 250	The Indian Emperor Ashoka sends buddhist missionaries to as far as the Mediterranean
1st c.	Origins of Mahayana Buddhism with the idea of the Saviour (Bodhisattva)

In the Christian Era

before 50	Jesus stays in the university town Taxila and appears at the court of the Indo-Parthian king Gondophares
after 50	Jesus travels with the name Yus Asaf in Kashmir and neighbouring regions
after 70	Jesus meets the local king Shalivahan
c. 49 - 109	Reign of local king Gopadatta (Gopananda)
78	Inscription on the Temple of Solomon in Srinagar
78 - 103	Reign of King Kanishka
around 80	4th Buddhist Council at Haran (Harvan) in Kashmir
after 80	Jesus interred in Srinagar

Chronology (Near East Area)

Footnotes

Chapter 1 (p. 13 – p. 42)

[1] Nicolas Notovitch, The Unknown Life of Jesus Christ
[2] Issa is one of the many Arabian names of Jesus
[3] Sanskrit: pancha, Greek: pente = five
[4] Royal palace of the Dalai Lama in the capital of Tibet, Lhasa
[5] Levi, The Aquarian Gospel of Jesus Christ
[6] Akasha = primal matter (Skt)
[7] in Notovitch, Orsis (town in India)
[8] in Notovitch, Djagguernat (town in India, see map)
[9] Tacitus, Annals 15, 44
[10] Sueton, Nero 16 and Claudius 25,4
[11] Pliny the Younger, Letters 10, 96f.
[12] Josephus Flavius, Jewish Antiquities 18; 3,3 and 20;9,1
[13] Origenes contra Celsum, 147
[14] Arthur Drews, Die Christusmythe, 1911; 3
[15] Extracts edited and tr. by Wilh. Reeb (German), Leipzig 1923
[16] Clement of Alexandria, Stromateis 7; 89,2f
[17] Origenes contra Celsum 3, 12
[18] Der Spiegel Nr. 14, l966
[19] J. Jeremias, 1951
[20] Der Spiegel Nr. 14, 1966
[21] Wilh. Nestle, Krisis des Christentums 1947, p.89
[22] F. Overbeck, Christentum und Kultur - aus dem Nachlaß 1919
[23] H. Ackermann, Entstellung und Klärung der Botschaft Jesu 1961
[24] A. Deissmann, Paulus, 2nd ed. 1925
[25] E. Grimm, Die Ethik Jesu; 1917
[26] A. Schweitzer, Geschichte der Leben-Jesu-Forschung, Tübingen 1913, p. 512
[27] Der Spiegel Nr. 14, 1966
[28] Der Stern Nr. 16, 1973
[29] Nirad C. Chaudhuri, Scholar Extraordinary, p. 32
[30] Anagarika Govinda, The Way of the White Clouds

Chapter 2 (p. 43 – p. 83)

[1] H.P. Blavatsky, The Secret Doctrine, Vol. II, p. 210
[2] Jens Juergens, Der biblische Moses, 1928
[3] W. F. Irland, Die Memoiren David Rizzios, Kollmann, Leipzig 1852
[4] Dummelow, Commentary on the Holy Bible, p. 115
[5] H.P. Blavatsky, Isis Unveiled, Vol. II, p. 135
[6] Travancore-Cochin belongs to the province of Kerala in South India
[7] Blavatsky, Isis Unveiled, p. 136

[8] Bernier, Francois, Travels in the Moghul Empire, London 1891, p. 432
[9] G. Konzelmann, Aufbruch der Hebraer, Berlin 1976, p. 37
[10] Joseph Wolff (John W. Parker, London 1845)
[11] G.T. Vigne, Whittaker & Co., London 1840, p. 166
[12] Publ. by William Collins, London and Glasgow, 1880
[13] G. Moore, The Lost Tribes (Longman and Green, London 1861
[14] Abdul Ahad Azad, Kashmiri Zaban Aur Shairi, Vol. I, p. 10 (Jammu and Kashmir Cultural Academy)

Chapter 3 (p. 84 – p. 109)

[1] G. Kroll, Auf den Spuren Jesu, Leipzig 1964, p. 63
[2] P. Schnabel, Der jüngste Keilschrifttext, in Zeitschrift f. Assyrologie, NF 2 (36) p. 66
[3] see paragraph "Reincarnation in the New Testament"
[4] Origenes, Gen. hom. XIV 3
[5] Hennecke-Schneemelcher, Neutestamentliche Apokryphen Vol. I, 4th ed. Tübingen 1968, p. 98
[6] Dalai Lama, My Country and My People
[7] Heinrich Harrer, Seven Years in Tibet
[8] Ernst J. Eitel, Handbook of Chin. Buddhism, Tokyo 1904
[9] Robertson, John M., Die Evangelienmythen, Jena 1910, p. 51
[10] Jewish Antiquities XVIII,5,2
[12] H.P.Blavatsky, op. cit. p. 142
[13] J. Klausner, Jesus von Nazareth, 1952, p. 144
[14] In the jewish calendar one year has twelve months with 29 or 30 days; therefore 354 days or 50,33 weeks, each with 7 days. To compensate for the actual length of one year it is necessary to intercalate in a period of 19 years a 13th month every 3rd, 8th, 11th and 18th year. This 13th month is called the 'second Adar'. The jewish calendar begins with the 'Creation of the World' on the 20th of September, 3760 B. C.
[15] A. Hilgenfeld (Zeitschrift f. wissenschaftliche Theologie 1860-1882) or W. Bauer (Essener, in Pauly-Wissowa, Supplementband IV, Sp. 426)

Chapter 4 (p. 110 – p. 123)

[1] Friedrich Weinreb, Das Buch Jonah (Zürich 1970), p. 90
[2] J. M. Pryse, Reinkarnation im NT (Ansata 1980)
[3] Bhagvan Dass, Krishna and the Theory of Avatars
[4] Sri Yukteswar, The Holy Science (Self-Realization Fellowship, Los Angeles)
[5] F. Hitching, Die letzten Rätsel unserer Welt, (Umschau-Verlag,1982) p. 118

Chapter 5 (p. 124 – p. 178)

[1] Willi Marxsen, Die Auferstehung Jesu, Gütersloh 1960
[2] Ian Wilson, Eine Spur von Jesus, Freiburg 1980
[3] Hennecke-Schneemelcher, op. cit. p.104
[4] Doctrina Addai, 4th c., former nat.lib. of St. Petersburg (Leningrad)
[5] Euagrus, Historia Ecclesiastica, Migne, Patroligia graeca, LXXX, VI/2, Sp. 2748-49
[6] W.Bulst, Das Grabtuch von Turin, Karlsruhe 1978, p.111
[7] Ian Wilson, op.cit. p. 191
[8] H.Thurston, The Holy Shroud..., in The Month, 101, p.19
[9] John Reban, Christus wurde lebendig begraben, Inter-Found Zürich, 1982
[10] W.Bulst op.cit. p.123
[11] Applied Optics, Vol. 19, No. 12, 1980; X-ray Spectrometry, Vol. 9, No. 2, 1980
[12] R.Seydel, Das Evangelium von Jesus, Leipzig 1882, p. 273
[13] Ian Wilson, op. cit. p. 279
[14] J. Blinzler, Das Turiner Grablinnen und die Wissenschaft, Ettal 1952, p.31
[15] H. Bardtke, Die Handschriftenfunde am Toten Meer, Berlin 1958, p.42
[16] Giulio Ricci, Kreuzweg nach dem Leichentuch von Turin, Rom 1971, p. 68
[17] cf. John Reban, op. cit.
[18] Hennecke-Scheemelcher, op. cit., p. 27
[19] Wilh. Lange-Eichbaum, Genie, Irrsinn, Ruhm, (6th ed., Munich 1967) p. 496
[20] Lactantius, Institutiones, 5,3

Chapter 6 (p. 179 – p. 211)

[1] Hennecke-Schneemelcher, op. cit, vol. II, p. 299ff
[2] ibid, vol. I, p. 199
[3] ibid, vol. I, p.206f
[4] ibid, vol. II, p.316
[5] ibid, vol. II, p.319
[6] ibid, vol. II, p.320
[7] ibid, vol. II, p. 322
[8] Joachim Jeremias, essay in Nachrichten aus der Akad. d. Wiss. Göttingen, I.Phil.-Hist. Kl. 1953, p. 95
[9] Hennecke-Schneemelcher, op. cit. vol.I, p. 199
[10] cf. Joachim Jeremias, ibid, p. 99
[11] cf. H.v.Glasenapp, Die Literatur Indiens, Stuttgart 1961, pp. 129-135
[12] source: Kans-ul Ammal, vol. II, p.34
[13] D.W.Lang, The wisdom of Balahar, New York 1957, p. 37
[14] M.Yasin, Mysteries of Kashmir, Srinagar 1972

Bibiliography

Aron, R., Jesus of Nazareth: The hidden years, New York, 1962

Abbot, S., The Fourfold Gospels, C.U.P., Cambridge 1917.

Abdul Hag Vidyarthi, M., Rohi Islam, Lahore 1966.

Abdul Qadir bin Qazi-ul Qazzat Wasil Ali Khan, Hashmat-i-Kashmir, MS. No. 42, Asiatic Society of Bengal, Calcutta.

Ackermann, H., Entstellung und Klärung der Botschaft Jesu, Göttingen 1961.

Albright, W.F., The Archeology of Palestine, London 1951.

Allegro, J.M., The Dead Sea Scrolls and the Christian Myth, Newton Abbey 1979.

-, The Treasure of the Copper Scroll. The opening and deciperment of the most mysterious of the Dead Sea Scrolls. A unique inventory of buried Treasure, London 1960.

Allen, Bernard M., The Story behind the Gospels, Methuen, London 1919.

Ansault, Abate, La Croix avant Jesus-Christ, Paris 1894.

Apuleius, L., The Transformations of Lucius, otherwise known as the Golden Ass, tr. by R. Graves, 1958.

Augstein, R., Jesus, Son of Man, New York, 1972

At-Tabri, Iman Abu Ja'far Muhammad, Tafsir Ibn-i-Jarir at-Tabri, Kubr-ul-Mar'a Press, Cairo.

Bardtke, H., Die Handschriftenfunde am Toten Meer, Berlin 1952.

-, Die Handschriftenfunde am Toten Meer: Die Sekte von Qumran, Berlin 1958.

-, Die Handschriftenfunde in der Wüste Juda, Berlin 1962.

Barth, M., Israel und die Kirche im Brief an die Epheser (= Theologische Existenz heute, N.F., Nr. 75), Munich 1959.

-, Jesus, Paulus und die Juden, Zürich 1967.

Barth, F., Die Hauptprobleme des Lebens Jesu, Gütersloh 1918.

Bartsch, G., ed. De tribus impostoribus, new ed.: Berlin 1962

Basharat Ahmad, Dr., Birth of Jesus, Dar-ul-Kutab-i-Islamia, Lahore 1929.

Bauer, F.C., Kritische Untersuchungen über die Kanonischen Evangelien, Tübingen 1847.

Baus, K., Von der Urgemeinde zur frühchristlichen Großkirche, Freiburg 1973.

Bell, Major A.W., Tribes of Afghanistan, Bell, London 1897.

Bellew, H.W., The New Afghan Question, or Are the Afghans Israelites?, Croddock, Simla 1880

-, The Races of Afghanistan, Thacker, Spink and Co., Calcutta.

Ben-Chorin, Sch., Bruder Jesus, der Nazarener in jüd. Sicht, Munich 1967.

Bengalee, Sufi Matiur Rahman, The Tomb of Jesus, Muslim Sunrise Press, Chicago 1946.

Bergh van Eysinga, G.A. van den, Indische Einflüsse auf evangelische Erzählungen, Göttingen 1904.

Berna, Kurt, Jesus ist nicht am Kreuz gestorben, Hans Naber, Stuttgart 1957.

-, John Reban's Facts: Christus wurde lebendig begraben, Inter-Found, Zurich 1982.

Bernier, Francois, Travels in the Moghul Empire, tr. by Archibald Constable, London 1891.

Betz, Otto, Offenbarung und Schriftforschung der Qumran-Texte, Mohr, Tübingen.

Bhavishya, Mahapurana, see Sutta, Pandit.

Blank, J., Der Christus des Glaubens und der historische Jesus, in Der Mann aus Galiläa, ed. by E. Lessing, Freiburg 1977.

-, Paulus und Jesus. Eine theologische Grundlegung, Munich 1968.

Blavatsky, H.P., Isis Unveiled, Vols. I & II, New York 1891.

-, The Secret Doctrine, London 1908.

Blinzler, J., Das Turiner Grablinnen und die Wissenschaft, Ettal 1952.

-, Der Prozess Jesu. Das jüdische und das römische Gerichtsverfahren gegen Jesus Christus auf Grund der ältesten Zeugnisse dargestellt und beurteilt, Regensburg 1955.

Bock, E., Kindheit u. Jugend Jesu, Stuttgart 1940.

Bock, J., The Jesus Mystery, Aura Books, Los Angeles 1980.

Bomann, Th., Die Jesusüberlieferung im Lichte der neueren Volkskunde, 1967-69.

Bornkamm, G., Die Bibel. Das Neue Testament. Eine Einführung in seine Schriften im Rahmen der Geschichte des Urchristentums. Stuttgart/Berlin 1971.

-, Das Ende des Gesetzes, Paulus-Studien, Munich 1952.

-, Geschichte und Glaube, I & II, Munich 1969-1971.

-, Jesus von Nazareth, Stuttgart 1968.

-, Paul, London 1971.

-, The New Testament, Philadelphia 1973.

Braun, H., Qumran und das Neue Testament, I & II, Tübingen 1966.

-, Spätjüdischer-häretischer und frühchristlicher Radikalismus. Jesus von Nazareth und die essenische Qumran-Sekte. 1969.

Bruhl, Rev. J.H., The Lost Ten Tribes, Where are They?, Operative Jewish Converts Institution Press, London 1893.

Bryce, J. and Johnson K., Umfassende Beschreibung der Erdkunde, London 1880.

-, The Library Gazetteer, London 1859.

Bultmann, R., History and Eschatology, Edinborough 1957.

-, Jesus and the Word, New York 1958.

-, Jesus Christ and Mythology, New York 1958.

-, Primitive Christianity, London 1956.

-, Theology of the New Testament, SCM Press, 1958.

-, This World and the Beyond, London 1960.

Bulst,W., The Shroud of Turin, Milwaukee 1957.

Burdach, K., Der Gral, Darmstadt 1974.

Burrows, M., The Dead Sea Scrolls, with translations by the author, London 1956.

-, More Light on the Dead Sea Scrolls and new interpretations with translations of important recent discoveries, London 1958.

Campenhausen, H. von, Der Ablauf der Osterereignisse und das leere Grab, Heidelberg 1958.

-, Aus der Frühzeit des Christentums, Studien zur Kirchengeschichte des ersten und zweiten Jahrhunderts, Tübingen 1963.

-, Die Entstehung der Christlichen Bibel (Beiträge zur Historischen Theologie, Nr. 39), Tübingen 1968.

Carmichael, J., The Death of Jesus, London 1963.

-, Steh auf und rufe Seinen Namen. Paulus, Erwecker der Christen und Prophet der Heiden, Munich 1980.

Chadurah, Khwaja Haidar Malik, Waqiat-i-Kashmir or Tarikh-i-Kashmir, Muhammadi Press, Lahore.

Chandra Kak, Ram, Ancient Monuments of Kashmir, Sagar, New Delhi 1971.

Clemens Alexandrinus, ed. Loeb, Cambridge (Mass.) 1968.

Cohn, H., The Trial and Death of Jesus, London 1972.

Cole, Major H.H., Illustrations of Ancient Buildings in Kashmir, W. H. Allen, London 1869.

Danielov, Jean, Qumran und der Ursprung des Christentums, Mainz 1959.

Deissmann, A., Paul, London 1926.

Deschner, K., Abermals krähte der Hahn, Reinbek 1978.

Dautzenberg, Gerhard, Der Jesus-Report und die neutestamentliche Forschung, Müller, Würzburg 1970.

Dibelius, M., A fresh approach to the NT and early Christian Literature, New York 1936.

-, Botschaft und Geschichte. Gesammelte Aufsätze, I & II, Tübingen 1953-1956.

Dietz,M., Die Zeugnisse heidnischer Schriftsteller des zweiten Jahrhunderts über Christus, Sigmaringen 1874.

Docker, M.A., If Jesus did not Die on the Cross, A Study in Evidence, Roland Scott, London 1920.

Doughty, Marion, Through the Kashmir Valley, Sands, London 1902.

Drews, A., The Christ myth, The open court publ. 1911.

Drower, E.S., The Mandaeans of Iraq and Iran. Their cults, customs, magic legends and folklore, Leiden 1962.

-, The secret Adam. A study of Nasoraean Gnosis, Oxford 1960.

-, Water into Wine. A study of Ritual Idiom in the Middle East, London 1956.

Dummelow, Rev. J.R., Commentary on the Holy Bible, Macmillan, London 1917.

Dutt, Jagdish Chandra, The Kings of Kashmir, Bose, Calcutta 1879.

Eckert, W.P., et al., Antijudaismus im Neuen Testament? Exegetische und systematische Beiträge, ed. by W. P. Eckert, N. P. Levinson und Martin Stohr, Munich 1967.

Edmunds, A.J., Buddhist and Christian Gospels, Innes, Philadelphia 1908-1909.

-, Gospel Parallels from Pali Texts, Open Court Publishing, Chicago 1900-1901.

Eifel, E.J., Three Lectures on Buddhism, Trubner, London 1873.

-, Handbook of Chinese Buddhism, Tokyo 1904.

Eliot, Sir H.N., History of India as Told by its Own Historians, 8 vols, Thakker, Spink and Co., Calcutta 1849.

Epiktet, Discourses I & II, ed. Loeb, Cambridge (Mass.) 1967.

Epiphanius, Adversus Haereses, Basel 1545 (British Museum).

Epstein, L.M., Sex Laws and Customs in Judaism, New York 1948.

Faber-Kaiser, A., Jesus died in Kashmir, London 1978.

Farquhar, Dr. J.N., The Apostle Thomas in South India, Manchester University Press, Manchester 1927.

Ferrari, K., Der Stern der Weisen, Vienna 1977.

Ferrier, J.E., History of the Afghans, John Murray, London 1858.

Fiebig, P., Die Umwelt des NT, Göttingen 1926.

Finkel, A., The Pharisees and the Teacher of Nazareth. A study of their background, their halachic and midrashi Teachings. The similarities and differences, London 1964.

Flusser, D., The Last Supper and the Essenes, in: Immanuel, Jerusalem 1973.

-, Jesus und die Synagoge, in: Der Mann aus Galiläa, ed. by E. Lessing, Freiburg 1977.

-, Jesus, tr. by Ronald Walls, New York 1969.

Ghulam Ahmad, Hazrat Mirza, Jesus in India, Ahmadiyya Muslim Foreign Missions Department, Rabwah, Pakistan, 1962.

-, Masih Hindustan mein (Urdu), Qadian, Pakistan 1908.

Gillabert, Emile, Rôles de Jesus et pensée orientale, Edition Metanoia,

Marsanne, Montelimar 1974.

v. Glasenapp, H., Die nichtchristlichen Religionen, Frankfurt 1957.

Goddard, Dwight, Was Jesus Influenced by Buddhism? Thetford, Vermont 1927.

Goldstein, M., Jesus in the Jewish tradition, New York 1959.

Govinda, A., The Way of the White Clouds, London 1966.

Graetz, H. Geschichte der Juden von den ältesten Zeiten bis auf die Gegenwart. Aus den Quellen neubearbeitet, III & IV, Leipzig 1888ff.

Grant, M., Jesus, London 1977.

-, The Jews in the Roman world, London 1973.

-, Saint Paul, London 1976.

Graves, R., and Podro, J., The Nazarene Gospel Restored, London 1953.

Grimm, E., Die Ethik Jesu, Leipzig 1917.

Grönbold, G., Jesus in Indien, Munich 1985.

Haig, Sir T.W., The Kingdom of Kashmir, Cambridge University Press, Cambridge 1928.

Handbuch der Kirchengeschichte, Freiburg 1962.

Harnack, A. von, Das Wesen des Christentums, Munich 1964.

-, Die Mission und die Ausbreitung des Christentums in den ersten drei Jahrhunderten, Leipzig 1924.

Harrer, H., Seven Years in Tibet, London 1957.

Headland, A.C., The Miracles of the New Testament, Longman Green, London 1914.

Heiler, F., Christlicher Glaube und indisches Geistesleben, Munich 1926.

Hennecke, E., New Testament Apocrypha, Philadelphia 1963-1966.

Hennecke, E. and Schneemelcher, W., Neutestamentliche Apokryphen, I & II, Tübingen 1959/64.

Herford, R.T., Christianity in Talmud and Midrash, London 1903.

Herodot, The Histories, tr. by A. de Selincourt, London 1959.

Hitching, F., The World Atlas of Mysteries, London, 1978.

Holl, A., Jesus in bad company, London 1972.

Hollis, Chr. and Brownrigg, R., Heilige Stätten im Heiligen Land, Hamburg 1969.

Hugh, Rev. James, History of Christians in India from the Commencement for the Christian Era, Seeley and Burnside, London 1839.

Instinsky, H.U., Das Jahr der Geburt Jesu, Munich 1957.

Irland, W.F., Die Memoiren David Rizzios, Leipzig 1852.

Jacolliot, L., Le spiritisme dans le monde, repr. New York 1966.

James, E.O., Myth and Ritual in the Ancient Near East. An Archeological and Documentary Study, London 1958.

Jeremias, J., Unknown sayings of Jesus, London 1957.

-, The eucharistic words of Jesus, New York 1955.

-, Studien zur neutestamentlichen Theologie und Zeitgeschichte, Göttingen 1966.

-, The parables of Jesus, London 1957.

-, Jerusalem zur Zeit Jesu, Eine Untersuchung der wirtschaftlichen und sozialen Verhältnisse zur neutestamentlichen Zeit, Göttingen 1958.

-, Jerusalem und seine grosse Zeit . . . z.Z. Christi, Würzburg 1977.

John, Sir William, "Journey to Kashmir", in Asiatic Researches, Baptist Mission Press, Calcutta 1895.

Josephus, Fl., Antiquities of the Jews, ed. W. Whiston, London 1872.

-, Jewish War, ed. W.Whiston, London 1872.

-, Against Apion, ed. W.Whiston, London 1872.

-, Biography, ed. W.Whiston, London 1872.

-, Antiquities of the Jews, ed. Loeb, London/Cambridge (Mass.) 1924ff.

Juergens, J., Der biblische Moses als Pulver-und Dynamitfabrikant, Munich 1928.

Jung, E., Die Herkunft Jesu, Munich 1920.

Kähler, Martin, Der sogenannte historische Jesus und der geschichtliche, biblische Christus, Wolf, Munich 1969.

Kak, R.B. Pandit Ram Chand, Ancient Monuments of Kashmir, India Society, London 1933.

Kamal-ud-Din, Al-Haj Hazrat Khwaja, A Running Commentary on the Holy Qur'an, MM and L Trust, Woking, Surrey 1932.

-, Islam and Christianity, MM and L Trust,, Woking, Surrey 1921.

-, The Sources of Christianity, MM and L Trust, Woking, Surrey 1922.

Käsemann, E., Exegetische Versuche und Besinnung, Göttingen 1964.

-, A Testament of Jesus, Philadelphia Fortress Press 1968.

Kaul, Pandit Ghawasha, A Short History of Kashmir, Srinagar 1929.

Kaul, Pandit Anand, The Geography of Jammu and Kashmir, Thacker, Spink & Co., Calcutta 1913.

Kappstein, Th., Buddha u. Christus, Berlin 1906.

Kautzsch, E., Die Apokryphen und Pseudoepigraphen des Alten Testaments, I & II, Tübingen 1900.

Kehimkar, H.S., Bani Israel of India, Dayag Press, Tel Aviv 1937.

Keller, W., Und wurden zerstreut unter alle Völker. Die nachbiblische Geschichte des jüdischen Volkes, Munich 1966.

Kenyon, Sir Frederick, Our Bible and the Ancient Manuscripts, being a History of the Texts and Translations, Eyre and Spottiswoode, London 1939.

Khaniyari, Mufti Ghulam Mohammed Nabi, Wajeez-ut-Tawarikh, Research Library, Srinagar.

Klausner, J., Jesus of Nazareth, New York 1935.
Klijn, A.F.J., The Acts of Thomas, Brill, Leiden 1962.
Kissener, Hermann (ed.), Der Essäerbrief, Munich 1968.
Konzelmann, G., Aufbruch der Hebräer, Munich 1976.
Koran, Reclam edition, Stuttgart 1960.
Kosmala, H., Hebraer, Essener, Christen, Leiden 1959.
Kroll, G., Auf den Spuren Jesu, Leipzig 1974.
Küng, Hans, On being a christian, New York 1976.

Lang, D.W., The Wisdom of Balahar, New York 1957.
Lange-Eichbaum, Wilh. and Kurth, Wolfram, Genie, Irrsinn und Ruhm, Munich 1967.
Lawrence, Sir Walter, The Valley of Kashmir, Froude, London 1895.
Lehmann, Johannes, The Jesus Report, London 1972.
-, The Jesus establishment, New York 1974.
-, Buddha, Munich 1980.
Levi, The Aquarian Gospel of Jesus Christ, London 1908.
Lewis, Spencer, H., Mystical Life of Jesus, Supreme Grand Lodge AMORC, San Jose, California 1929.
Lexikon der Symbole, Fourier Verlag, Wiesbaden 1972.
Loewenthal, Rev.I., Some Persian Inscriptions Found in Kashmir, Asiatic Society of Bengal, Calcutta 1895.
Lohse, E., Die Texte aus Qumran, Kösel 1964.
Lord, Rev. James Henry, The Jews in India and the Far East, SPCK, Bombay 1907.

Maier, J., Die Texte vom Toten Meer, I & II, Munich 1960.
-, Jesus von Nazareth in der talmudischen Überlieferung, Darmstadt 1978.
Marxsen, Willi, Einleitung in das NT, Gütersloh, Munich 1964.
-, Die Auferstehung Jesu also historisches und theologisches Problem, Gütersloh, Munich 1965.
Marzell, Wörterbuch der deutschen Pflanzennamen, Stuttgart 1979.
Mensching, G., Leben und Legende der grossen Religionsstifter, Darmstadt 1955.
-, Buddha and Christus, Stuttgart 1978.
Merrick, Lady Henrietta S., In the World's Attic, Putnam, London 1931.
Mir Khwand, Rauzat-us-Safa, tr. E. Rehatsek, Arbuthnot, MRAS, London 1891.
Moore, George, The Lost Tribes, Longman Green, London 1861.
Mozundar, A.K., Hindu History (3000 BC to 1200 AD), Dacca 1917.
Mumtaz Ahmad Faruqui, Al-Haj, The Crumbling of the Cross, Ahmadiyya Anjuman Isha'at-i-Islam, Lahore 1973.
Murphet, H., Sai Baba: man of miracles, Muller, London 1971.

Naber, Hans see Berna, Kurt
Narain, A.K., The Indo-Greeks, Oxford 1962.
Nazir Ahmad, Al-Haj Khwaja, Jesus in Heaven on Earth, Azeez Manzil, Lahore 1973.
Nestle, Wilh., Krisis des Christentums, Stuttgart 1947.
Noelinger, Henry S., Moses und Ägypten, Heidelberg 1957.
Notovitch,N., Die Lücke im Leben Jesu, Stuttgart 1894.
-, The Unknown Life of Jesus Christ, tr. from French ed. by Heyina Loranger, Rand McNally, Chicago 1894.
Nyawang, Lobsang Yishey Tenzing Gyatso (XIV Dalai Lama) My Land and My People, New York 1962.

Origen, Origen against Celsus, tr. by James Bellamy, London 1660.
-, Origen on first principles, London 1936.
Overbeck, F., Christentum und Kultur, Basel 1919.

Pagels, E., The Gnostic Gospels, London 1979.
Pannenberg, Wolfhart, Grundzüge der Christologie, Gütersloh, Munich 1964.
Pesch., R., Jesu ureigene Taten? Freiburg 1970.
Philon, The Contemplative Life, ed. Loeb, London/Cambridge (Mass.) 1962.
-, The Embassy to Gaius, ed. Loeb, London/Cambridge (Mass.) 1962.
-, Every Good Man is Free, ed. Loeb, London/Cambridge (Mass.) 1962.
-, Flaccus, ed. Loeb, London/Cambridge (Mass.) 1962.
-, Special Laws, ed. Loeb, London/Cambridge (Mass.) 1962.
Philostratus, The Life of Apollonius, tr. by C.P. Jones, ed. G.W. Bowersock, London 1970.
Plange, Th.J., Christus - ein Inder? Stuttgart 1907.
Plinius, S.G., The Letters of the Younger Pliny, tr. by Bettey Radice, London 1977.
-, Epistulae, ed. Loeb, London/Cambridge(Mass.) 1969.
Potter, Ch. F., The Lost Years of Jesus Revealed, Greenwich, Conn. 1958.
Prause, G., Herodes der Grosse, König der Juden, Hamburg 1977.
Prophet, E. C., The Lost Years of Jesus, Malibu 1984.
Pryse, J.M., Reincarnation in the New Testament, Theosophical Society, New York 1904.

Rahn, O., Kreuzzug gegen den Gral, Stuttgart 1974.
Ramsay, Sir William, Was Christ Born in Bethlehem? Hodder and Stoughton, London 1905.
Rangacharya, V., History of Pre-Musulman India, Indian Publishing House, Madras 1937.
Rapson, Prof. E.J., Ancient India, C.U.P. Cambridge 1911.

Rau, Wilh, Indiens Beitrag zur Kultur, Wiesbaden 1975.

Ray, Dr. Sunil Chandra, Early History and Culture of Kashmir, Munshiram Manoharlal, New Delhi 1969.

Ray, H.C., The Dynastic History of Northern India, 2 vols, Thacker, Spink and Co., Calcutta 1931.

Reban, John, see Berna, Kurt.

Reilson, Col.W., History of Afghanistan, J. Ryland's Library Bulletin, 1927.

Ricci, G., Kreuzweg nach dem Leichentuch von Turin, Rome 1971.

Rihbani, A., Morgenländische Sitten im Leben Jesu, Basel 1962.

Ristow, H., and Matthiae, K., Der geschichtliche Jesus und der kerygmatische Christus, Berlin 1961.

Robertson, J.M., Die Evangelienmythen, Jena 1910.

Rockhill, W.W., The Life of Buddha, Trubner, London.

Rodgers, Robert William, A History of Ancient India, Scribner, London 1929.

Rose, Rt. Hon. Sir George H., The Afghans: The Ten Tribes and the Kings of the East, Operative Jewish Converts Institution Press, London 1852.

Schelkle, K.H., Die Gemeinde von Qumran und die Kirche des NT, in: Die Welt der Bibel, Düsseldorf 1960.

-, Die Passion Jesu in der Verkündigung des NT, Heidelberg 1949.

Scheuermann, O., Das Tuch, Regensburg 1982.

Schoeps, H.J., Aus frühchristlicher Zeit, religionsgeschichtliche Untersuchungen, Tübingen 1950.

Schrage, W., Das Verhältnis des Thomas-Evangeliums zur synoptischen Tradition und zu den koptischen Evangelien-Übersetzungen. Zugleich ein Beitrag zur gnostischen Synoptikerdeutung, Berlin 1964.

Schröder, H., Jesus und das Geld, Karlsruhe 1979.

Schubert, K., Die Gemeinde vom Toten Meer, Munich 1958.

-, Der historische Jesus und der Christus unseres Glaubens, Vienna and Freiburg 1962.

-, Vom Messias zum Christus, Vienna and Freiburg 1964.

-, Jesus im Lichte der Religionsgeschichte des Judentums, Vienna 1973.

Schulz, P., Ist Gott eine mathematische Formel? Reinbek bei Hamburg 1977.

-, Weltliche Predigten, Reinbek bei Hamburg 1978.

Schure, E., Die grossen Eingeweihten, Paris 1927.

Schweitzer, A., The quest of the historical Jesus, London 1945.

Schweizer, E., Jesus Christus im vielfältigen Zeugnis des Neuen Testaments, Munich and Hamburg 1968.

Seydel, R., Das Evangelium von Jesus in seinem Verhältnis zu Buddha-Sage und Buddha-Lehre, Leipzig 1882.

Shams, J.D., Where did Jesus Die? Baker and Witt, London 1945.

Smith, R.G., Early Relations between India and Iran, London 1937.

Smith, V.A., The Early History of India, Clarendon Press, Oxford 1904.

Speicher, G., Doch sie können ihn nicht töten, Düsseldorf 1966.

Sri Yukteswar, The Holy Science, Self-Realization Fellowship, Los Angeles 1949.

Stauffer, Ethelbert, Jesus, Gestalt und Geschichte, Bern 1957.

Stein, M.A., (tr.) Kalhana's Chronicle of the Kings of Kashmir, 2 vols, London 1900.

Strack, H.L. and Billerbeck, P., Kommentar zum NT aus Talmud und Midrasch, I-V, Munich 1956.

Strauss, D. F., The life of Jesus, London 1906.

Stroud, William, On the Physical Cause of Death of Christ, Hamilton and Adams, London 1905.

Suetonius, G.T., The Twelve Caesars, tr. by R.Graves, Harmondsworth 1957.

-, The Twelve Caesars, ed. Loeb, London/Cambridge (Mass.) 1970.

Sutta, Pandit, Bhavishya Mahapurana (MS in State Library, Srinagar), Venkateshvaria Press, Bombay 1917.

Tacitus, P.C., The Annals of Imperial Rome, tr. by M. Grant, Harmondsworth 1956.

-, The Histories, r. by Kenneth Wellesley, Harmondsworth 1964.

-, Annales, ed. Loeb, London 1968-1970.

-, Historiae, ed. Loeb, London 1968-1970.

Thomas,P., Epics, Myths and Legends of India, 13th ed. Taraporevala, Bombay 1973.

Vigne, G.T., A personal narrative of a visit to Ghuzni,Kabul and Afghanistan, London 1843.

Vielhauer, P., Geschichte der urchristliche Literatur. Einleitung in das NT, die Apokryphen und die Apostolischen Väter, Berlin 1975.

Vögtle, A., Exegetische Erwägungen über das Wissen und Selbstbewußtsein Jesu, Freiburg im Breisgau 1964.

Waddell, L.A., Lhasa and its Mysteries, Sanskaran Prakashak, New Delhi 1975.

Walsh, J., The Shroud, New York 1963.

Warechaner, J., The Historical Life of Christ, London 1927.

Watzinger C., Denkmäler Palästinas, Eine Einführung in die Archäologie des Heiligen Landes. I & II, Berlin 1911.

Weinreb, F., Das Buch Jonah, Zurich 1970.

Wheeler, M., Alt-Indien, Köln 1959.

Widengren, G., Die Religionen Irans, Stuttgart 1965.

Wilcox, R.K., Shroud, New York 1977.

Williams, Sir Monier, Buddhism, Macmillan, New York 1889.

236

Wilson, H.H., History of Kashmir, in Asiatic Researches, Baptist Mission Press, Calcutta 1841.

Wilson, I., The Shroud of Turin, 1978.

Wilson, W.R., The Execution of Jesus, New York 1970.

Wolff, J., Erzählung einer Mission nach Bokhara, London 1845.

Wright, Dudley, Studies in Islam and Christianity, MM and L Trust, Woking, Surrey 1943.

Wuenshel, Edward, Self Portrait of Christ, New York 1954.

Yadin, Y., Bar Kokhba, the rediscovery of the legendary hero of the last Jewish revolt against Imp. Rome, London 1971.

-, Masada. Der letzte Kampf um die Festung des Herodes, Hamburg 1972.

Yasin, Mohammed, Mysteries of Kashmir, Kesar Srinagar 1972.

Younghusband, Sir Francis, Kashmir, Black, London 1909.

Zahrnt, H., Es begann mit Jesus von Nazareth. Zur Frage des historischen Jesus, Stuttgart 1960.

Zimmermann, H., Jesus Christus: Geschichte und Verkündigung, Stuttgart 1973.

Zimmern, H., Zum Streit um die "Christus Mythe", Berlin 1910.

Zöckler, Otto(ed.), Die Apokryphen des Alten Testaments, Munich 1891.

237

INDEX OF NAMES

Names in the Notes appear in the Bibliography

238

239

Sakyamuni 70, 38, 120
Salomé 172
Samson 95
Samuel 56
Sang Bibi 54
Saul 56, 66
Schelling, F. W. 29
Schnabel 85
Schweitzer, A. 22, 31, 102
Schuré 50
Shem 184
Seneca 151
Seydel 153
Shaikh Al-Sa'id-us-Sadiq 197
Shalivahan 195
Shargon II. 58
Shiva 61, 120
Simon 87
Solomon 56, 64
Sossianus Hierocles 124, 197, 209
Sri Sathya Sai Baba 176
Sri Yuktesewar 120
Stephen 119
Sueton 45
Sultan Zainul Aabidin Budshah 23, 117
Syed Nasir-ud 'Din 197
Symeon of Mesopotamia 206

Tacitusn 23, 117
Tarah 44
Tertullian 23, 96, 188
Thackeray, W.M. 119
Thaddaeus 135, 133

Theophilos 190
Thomas the Apostle 174, 179, 184, 190
Thurston, H. 144
Tiberius 23
Timothy 28, 99
Titus 28
Togarmah 69
Trajan 183
Tsong Kapa 88

Umberto II. of Savoy 144
Utnapishtim 60

Vaivasvati 60
Vazir 202
Vespasian 117
Vigne, G.T. 65
Vignon, P. 149
Vishnu 60, 117, 120

Wali Rishi 90
Weinreb, F. 112
Wilson, I. 134, 137, 155
Wolff, J. 64

Xavier, J. 190

Yuz Asaf = Yus Asaph = Jesus 184, 188, 199, 203, 205, 207

Zainuddin Wali 197
Zarathustra = Zoroaster 50, 76, 123, 153
Zechariah 113

Plates

Coloured photographs:
p. 165 (Buddha with lamb) Ars Mundi, all others by Holger Kersten.

Black and white photographs:(Author, p. 2) S. Lettow. (Notovitch, p. 16) from his book. (Diary, p. 36) F.M. Hassnain. (Egypt. paint, p. 44) archives. (Sculpture Michelangelo, Julius monument in Rome, p. 51) photo archives. (Stone, p. 65), F.M. Hassnain. (Qumran, p. 101), archives. (Shroud, p. 136), G. Enrie. (Shroud, p. 140), G. Enrie. (Sculpture, p. 138). Lateran Museum, Rome. (Bahavishya Maha Purana, p. 196) and (Inscription, p. 199) and (Rod of Jesus, p. 198) all F.M. Hassnain. (Photos inside the Tomb, p. 208-212) all E. Mörck, BUNTE Illustrierte.

All others by Holger Kersten.

All maps drawn by Klaus Dümmen.

Graphics: (Blood-stains, p. 160 and 168) by The National Geographic Society. (Temptation, p. 105) 1947 by A.D. Thomas. (Asclepias acida, p. 154) H. Kersten. (Lying fig., p. 157) drawn by Alexander Schönfeld. (Figure, p. 159) H. Kersten. (Lances, p. 162) H. Kersten (Bones, p. 173) H. Kersten. (Tomb, p. 207) K. Dümmen.

245